WHAT SPIR...

I seem to have found myse... ...one hand (or should I say horn?) ... ...n the other side of the world for an article which might help ... ...nbers who wish, apparently, to confine Spiritualism within certain proscribed limits both in concept, teaching and application, and appear to be dissatisfied that too wide a field is being embraced at their Centre.

On the other hand, I receive letters from readers in Britain who are just as dissatisfied, *but for the very opposite reason*. They deplore the narrow limits within which Spiritualism seems to be constricted and complain that unless the field is widened considerably to embrace the more far-reaching ramifications of its universal philosophy, including what is called New Age Teaching, they will no longer feel able to call themselves Spiritualists!

So once again we are faced with the vexed question: what is the definition of Spiritualism? Quite obviously there are widely divergent opinions, and my Concise Oxford Dictionary is so concise as to be ludicrous — as well as patently uninformed. It merely states:

"Belief that departed spirits communicate with and show themselves to men, especially at seances by means of spirit-rapping, spirit-handwriting, etc. (!) Philosophy: doctrine that spirit exists as distinct from matter, or that spirit is the only reality."

What sort of *philosophy* is this, I wonder, for men and women to relate to their daily living, thinking and doing? Could not the compilers of this dictionary have given, at least, the Seven Principles of Spiritualism, as its philosophy?

The glossary of the latest *Dictionary of Mysticism* is better, as far as it goes. It states that "Spiritualism is based on conviction that individual survival after death is demonstrable and has religious, scientific and philosophical implications." Fair enough for one sentence, I suppose. But *what* implications?

Far too many people, it seems to me, having proved to their own satisfaction that survival and communication are facts, thereupon call themselves Spiritualists, and give little or no thought to the "religious, scientific and philosophical implications" hinted at in the above description.

Surely this is analogous to a thirsty and hungry traveller who has been lost for a long time in a dark, impenetrable forest from which there appears to be no way out. He has fallen into bogs and stumbled round in circles in an endeavour to find a path which leads somewhere, till he is well-nigh exhausted.

Suddenly he sees a light through the trees. He can hardly believe it. He makes his way towards it, and the light grows brighter. At last he sees an open portal through which light streams, inviting him to enter. He has found sanctuary, and conviction in his extremity that he will not now die in that dark, forsaken forest. In his relief at no longer feeling utterly lost, he even forgets for the time being that here, surely, will be food and drink without which he can go no further towards his journey's end.

He almost runs through the open doorway and into the hall of the Castle. It seems homely, as if he had always known it existed somewhere, and now here he is! At the end of the hall is a huge door, on the jar. A delicious aroma fills his nostrils. He pushes it open little by little, for it seems too heavy for his weak strength. But he is able to glimpse what lies beyond.

There before him, on a great round table, is a prodigious feast of succulent dishes, flagons of many kinds of wine, and crystal jugs of pure, sparkling water. But what does this strange man do? *He closes the door,* saying to himself: "No, no! It's too much! I wouldn't know what to start with . . . I might get indigestion . . . I'd rather stay in the hall, and if someone comes I'll just ask for a corn-beef sandwich and a cup of tea."

This is the Spiritualist who has placed his foot on the first rung of the ladder, unaware that it reaches to infinity. Or one who is content to remain in the hall of what is in truth a vast castle containing a multitude of wonderful and varied rooms. A castle with towers and turrets rising so high that from their windows can be apprehended innumerable living universes within the Being of limitless Spirit, and from which it is possible to look down and perceive the nature of our own living planet of which we are at once the temporary children and custodians.

And most important of all, we find a room within which we see our true selves in a mirror, not as we imagined ourselves to be, but as we really are. Above are the words: *Man know thyself,* and not until we have sojourned in this room of mirrors can we mount higher.

Now I do not deny or decry that first rung of the ladder, for it is always a most important step which all have to take sooner or later, here or hereafter. The child has to learn its A B C if it is to learn the lessons to come in more advanced classes. And for this reason definitions of Spiritualism will always vary according to which rung the person defining it happens to be standing on at that moment in time.

But it is regrettable indeed when those in the Kindergarten (metaphorically playing with plastacene and learning the alphabet) wish to confine the rest of the school to their level of awareness by denying the existence of a Sixth Form, let alone a University, and insist that nursery rhymes are the thing, when there is Shakespeare . . . .

The "religious, scientific and philosophical implications" of Spiritualism *embrace all that there is,* visible and invisible. Unity in diversity.

NEW AGE COMPANION

by

PEGGY MASON

Come give me your hand
If you're going my way
Let us travel this road
For a night and a day

The journey is long
My sister my brother
Companions we'll be
And learn from each other

For nothing that's shared
With the heart and the mind
Can ever be wasted
Or left behind.

Blessings

Peggy Mason

First impression 1975
Second impression 1977
Third impression 1978
Fourth impression 1982

ISBN 0 905512 00 6

Printed in Great Britain by
Brown Knight & Truscott Ltd.
London and Tonbridge

DEDICATED TO

Geoff and Sandra

in gratitude for so much

CONTENTS

INTRODUCTION

This little volume is really a continuation of my previous book *Tales of Two Worlds* which appeared in 1972 and is now in its fifth impression. The publication of this companion volume has been prompted by the wonderful and most heart-warming response I have received from readers in so many parts of the world — readers who have become my "absent friends" — and who have requested me to produce a further collection of my writings in the monthly magazine *Two Worlds*. I am therefore indebted to Mr Maurice Barbanell, the Editor of *Two Worlds* and the weekly newspaper *Psychic News*★ for permission to do so.

One senses a great feeling of urgency as the world enters the last quarter of the Twentieth Century and approaches the year 2000. The transition from the Piscean Age into the Age of Aquarius is indeed a period of stress, anxiety, change, and challenge, in which the Powers of Darkness and Materialism appear to be gathering for a final, despairing onslaught against the Forces of Light and the spiritual resurrection of Humanity.

Yet there are encouraging signs on every hand that, whilst the orthodox religions are losing, or have lost, their grip, a new awareness of the spiritual nature of Man and the Cosmos is gathering momentum. What, for lack of a better word, is called Spiritualism is no longer a suspect subject. Psychic research and psychic science have become "respectable" and also respected.

The experience of living for a period of six years with "Catherine," who developed into a gifted psychic and dedicated medium, was a rare one indeed, much of which I have described in *Tales of Two Worlds*. To live, as it were, on both sides of the veil, in daily contact with friends and teachers in the next phase of life, was a great privilege. But I have studied the subject of metaphysics for the best part of fifty years. In fact I do not remember a time when, even as a child, I did not *know* that life is continuous, and our appearance in the flesh on this (or any other) planet merely an interlude.

If any of the thoughts, information or experiences (both grave and gay) contained in the following chapters prove an aid to other seekers, and serve to stimulate their own research or widen their mental and emotional horizons I shall be amply rewarded — never forgetting that knowledge of itself is meaningless without love, for Love is God and God is All.

Peggy Mason.

July 1975

★23 Great Queen Street, London, WC2B 5BB.

From the energy within the atom, and the sleeping life within the stone, to perfected consummation in All-Being, All is One.

> "A firemist and a planet,
> A crystal and a cell,
> A jelly-fish and a saurian,
> And caves where the cavemen dwell;
> Then a sense of law and beauty
> And a face turned from the clod —
> Some call it Evolution
> And others call it God."*

Even now Physics has become Metaphysics, beyond the physical. In Psychics the phenomena called "physical mediumship" are being superseded by higher forms: an upsurge of healing for bodies and minds in a mentally sick world; a vast increase in meditation groups to achieve self-awareness, mental and emotional control, a higher level of consciousness and intuition, the capacity for the individual to "tune in", and having received, to send forth.

Little by little Psychiatry is being compelled to include exorcism. Medical science must soon recognise the existence of the etheric body through Kirlian photography. Already it is recognised that nearly three-quarters of dis-ease and illness is psychosomatic, of the mind, often the result of faulty attitudes and emotions, faulty values, faulty character. Many more doctors than is generally supposed call in or recommend spiritual healers.

Astronomers will perforce become Astrologers in this New Age when the sun is passing from Pisces into Aquarius — symbolised by the Water-Carrier with an overflowing pitcher on his shoulder — for they will recognise that entirely new vibrations, rays and influences will be brought to bear, stimulating the mental rather than the emotional (often fanatical) aspects of the Piscean Age. (The sun takes approximately 2,230 years to pass through each of the twelve constellations.)

They will know, very soon now, that "empty space" is teeming with evolving consciousness in many forms — the forms matter not, since material diversity ultimately becomes spiritual unity. The knowledge that we have companions in the universes is now widespread. In the United States, in the last 3 years alone, 15,000,000 responsible people have witnessed or had some contact with "Flying Saucers," including the astronauts, and polls show that two out of three people "believe" in our visitors from other worlds. There is now, too, a generation of children in incarnation who can bend metal and mend broken watches, among other feats, *by the power of thought,* as demonstrated by Uri Geller.

All the arts and sciences, whether all-important education, art, music,

---

From the poem "Each in his own tongue" by William Carruth.

3

chemistry, physics, geology, ecology, agriculture, conservation (one could enumerate indefinitely) play their role in the discovery and understanding of the laws of the Great Spirit, for all is one, interdependant, and the penalties of flouting those laws through gross materialism, and exploiting Nature, the lower kingdoms and our Mother Earth for greed and temporary expediency are dire indeed. In so many fields of activity, too, man has made it impossible for the elementals and nature spirits to fulfil their proper function, and the devic kingdom must be acknowledged, understood and co-operated with.

One can truthfully say that there are *no* subjects which do *not* come under the "religious, scientific and philosophical implications" of Spiritualism, from animal welfare to psychology, from gardening to cosmology, from learning how to live harmlessly to the enlightened mental and spiritual status of the Adept.

In fact all these things enter into the teachings we receive from the higher planes of the world of spirit through the great teachers of the White Brotherhood such as Silver Birch, White Eagle, and a host of other dedicated souls who sacrifice the bliss of their attained spheres in order to communicate what they know to be truth to their brothers and sisters on the earth plane who are, for the moment, lower down the ladder.

Books of their teachings are available to all who care to read and digest them — *and live by them!* Why, then, do so many who call themselves Spiritualists fail to apply themselves to these teachings (or these teachings to themselves), or, as is often the case, reject them? A World Religion is promised and prophesied in this New Age, and this can only be Spiritualism, or based on Spiritualism, whether it is called Spiritual Science, Psychic Science, or New Age Teaching, or whatever, by those who may prefer to call it so. For Spiritualism embraces all the facets of *truth* which have been revealed in *all* religions throughout the ages, the shining jewels hidden beneath layers of accumulated rubbish and top-soil. Some, indeed, shine brightly through, for if one reads the books on Yogi Philosophy by Ramacharaka, for example, (especially *Gnani Yoga,*) one could be reading Silver Birch or White Eagle in every particular.

For truth is truth, wherever it is found, and the more jewels of truth we can find, the better. The leaven of enlightenment is working slowly but surely; the yeast cells multiplying, for they cannot do otherwise. The forms they take under the microscope vary in pattern. Every snowflake, too, has a different design — but with two important constants: all are hexagonal, and all are *snow*.

In Spiritualism we also have two constants: the proof of continued life after so-called "death," and proof of communication with those who have shed the physical body. The implications and ramifications of these two facts are cosmic in scope. So whatever level of understanding we have reached, or whatever rung of the spiritual ladder we are on, let us always remember this.

4

But let us remember, too, the most important of all teaching from Spirit: the message of Love. *Without this our erudition avails us nothing.* A reader told me recently that when she needed practical and urgent help, it was not those who called themselves Spiritualists or any other "ists" who came to her aid. It was those who did not call themselves anything, but who had love in their hearts!

With our discussions and arguments about this or that facet of the same jewel, we often resemble a lot of bickering, babbling little brooks, each so full of bustle and hustle that we are apt to forget that the multiplicity of streams will later form one of a multiplicity of rivers, and these in turn will ultimately be unified and purified in the great ocean of Love.

SPIRITUALISM VERSUS WITCHCRAFT

Several readers are kind enough to send me, from time to time, newspapers and magazines from different parts of the English-speaking world, especially if they contain subject matter which they know will interest me.

I am frequently horrified, and much saddened, by the ignorance displayed by journalists and others, including ministers of varied denominations, who insist on bracketing Spiritualism with witchcraft, black magic and satanism.

As an example typical of many a minister in South Africa, while quite rightly warning youth against witchcraft, says: "Some are bored, young, sophisticated people, victims of an affluent, materialistic society, without faith in anything very much. Others look for the meaning in life, start with mysticism, dabble in Eastern philosophy, and end up *hooked on spiritualism and witchcraft.*"

The use of the word "and" makes the sentence as meaningless and illogical as if, when instructing a person how to drive a car, one told them: "If you put the gear into reverse, the car will go forward." For Spiritualism is the exact *reverse* of witchcraft, black magic and satanism, as the day is the reverse of the night, the light of the darkness, the Christ to the anti-Christ.

We all know that the Forces of Evil are indeed making a great and desperate onslaught against the Powers of Light — desperate because the time is not far off when the darkness will be swallowed up and cast out by the Light of the Christ Spirit which is very close to us even now.

It is the individual who has to choose, for everyone has free will and free choice. Here, as well as hereafter, *like attracts like.* Listen to what the one known as St. Francis of Assisi has to say on this, through his chosen and trusted instrument:**

** *The Shining Brother* and *Francis Speaks Again* by Laurence Temple. Psychic Press Ltd.

"Man groweth in knowledge and in his power of choice. Therefore to him is the world of spirit opening out, and *according to the desire of his heart doth he choose, and draweth to him that which is attuned to his inmost being* .... *The capacity, both for good and evil, will be greater than heretofore;* for man eateth again of the tree of knowledge, and receiveth fuller illumination; therefore is his sin greater if he turneth from the light .... And now that man is conscious of the world as a unit in space, now that the human voice can be heard across the oceans, and man can traverse the skies and gaze like a kite into the secret places of earth, now is the choice once again before man, to use his knowledge in accordance with divine laws, or be destroyed by the powers he hath created.

"The time is at hand when the holy ones will use their forces upon the outer plane, and from the chaos shall ye see the birth of a new order, and a race of man who understands the hidden way .... Now is a time of testing and of training the instruments of the new era of man's emergence from the swaddling clothes of infancy to the free movements of the growing child. Already doth he show his restlessness, and casteth from him the supports of the past, which now do but enhance the sufferings of his expanding consciousness .... He seeketh for new garments which shall express the quality of his soul ...."

When one considers that at the dawn of this new Aquarian Age — with the Seventh Ray already stimulating the psychic centres and causing an upsurge of interest in and awareness of the spiritual nature of man and the cosmos there is also an influx into incarnation of those very egos who brought about the downfall of Atlantis by their evil and obscene practices, and who are now being given the opportunity to make a better choice, one can understand the situation more clearly.

At the same time there is also an influx into incarnation of highly evolved souls and sons of light who have chosen to incarnate at this critical time to spread the light and combat the powers of darkness by forming "power stations," by creating networks of light through innumerable groups and centres, by becoming true instruments for the Christ Spirit in whatever fields of endeavour their gifts lie, and above all, by living and demonstrating the Law of Love in all its ramifications.

It can be seen, therefore, why the powers of darkness in general, and in particular those men and women who deliberately *choose* darkness and the Left Hand Path are marshalling their forces and continually endeavouring to find new recruits. They even have international conferences on this subject!

Lest I be accused of exaggeration, let me quote Mrs Doreen Irvine, a former Black Witch who, despite threats to her life, escaped the net of evil, was converted, and testified against Satanism on British television. She also wrote an account of the subject called *From Witchcraft to Christ*.

She tells of a great ceremony on Dartmoor where witches from all parts of England, Germany and France arrived to choose the next queen of black witches. "They arrived in smart cars," she says. "They booked in at hotels looking for all the world like successful businessmen and women — which some were."

During the ceremony seven witches competed for the title by performing tests of power — needless to say, destructive. She says: "A bird was released from a cage. *I killed it in flight.*" Other "supernatural" feats of a similarly obnoxious nature were performed, which culminated in her being crowned queen. "Wild and frenzied celebrations" followed.

As Queen of the Black Witches Mrs Irvine visited Europe where foreign witches entertained her and her master, the chief Satanist, "in grand style." "We stayed only at the best hotels, or sometimes in large expensive houses in beautiful grounds — the homes of other witches. Many discussions were held about how to make witchcraft more attractive, to give it a new look."

Among the new guidelines laid down was this instruction: "Make it look like a natural, innocent adventure, and cover up evil with appealing wrappings." Then comes this significant item: "*New recruits were needed if evil was to conquer. Time was short. Now was the time to trap people.*" The note of urgency and desperation is evident here.

So the battle is on. Let us make no mistake about that, lest we be tempted to sink into a comfortable state of apathy and spiritual sloth. The enemy is at the gate, and we have to be on constant guard. The enemy is responsible, too, for much which passes as "entertainment," whether in unsavoury television plays, pornography, or revolting and obscene films like "The Exorcist," with which the makers hope to net £100,000,000 by giving susceptible people of all ages nightmares.

I think that all people who try to dedicate their lives to the spreading of truth, and in service to others with no thought of reward or self-seeking, find themselves targets of attack at some stage by those who are inspired by evil, in an attempt to divert them, stop them, or bring them down. It was ever so. Even in our very humble endeavours my husband and I have had ample experience of this, and I am sure others have found the same.

Perhaps these things also serve as tests, for however flabbergasted or even outraged one may be momentarily, the rule must be: never to retaliate, surround yourself with a circle of light, project a beam of light to the aggressor, and dismiss the whole thing from your mind. Thus the evil intention can find no entry. It boomerangs, and a potentially destructive "plot" simply fizzles out for lack of fuel or friction. In other words, turn the other cheek, in a positive way.

It is sheer stupidity to shut one's eyes to the fact that evil and destructive spirits do use and influence those people whose character failings, weaknesses or undesirable leanings open the door to such influence.

Hitler was a prime example on a world scale. I had a part in the translation of Eva Braun's diaries, and I shall never forget one entry she made. She wrote that Hitler had been cowering and trembling in his bedroom the previous night, pointing into the corner and mouthing the words: "My Master is there! My Master is there . . ." He appeared terrified. As everyone knows, the top Nazis were deeply involved in black magic.

It is those who, in their ignorance, laugh at such ideas (or, if they don't laugh, make-believe that everything in the next sphere of existence is wonderful) who are most at risk. For of *course* there are "evil spirits" — call them "demons" or "devils" if you like — for this is what they were when they lived their debased, cruel and sadistic lives on earth.

History, alas, is full of characters who delighted in deliberate and diabolic doings. They do not change just because they shed the physical body in death. Freedom of choice remains — to sink lower still by continuing to indulge their evil practices, or eventually to sicken of their ghastly state and face the awful prospect of purging themselves, little by little, by suffering in themselves what their victims have suffered, for they must become their *own* judges before they can rise. No one else judges us — only the spark of God within us. And this is perfect justice.

Only Spiritualists, or those who have some *knowledge* (not speculation) of after-like conditions, both good and bad, can understand the reality of what is involved in possession, obsession, evil spirits, earthbound spirits, and the like. For these spirits are *people* — not some weird species of "supernatural beings" or hobgoblins with horns, but people who have lived on earth and delighted in evil ways.

The Nazarene was only too well aware of them. How often he cast them out, and freed those who were possessed. But he also warned us that exorcism by itself was not enough. Unless the formerly possessed person *changed*, that is, rectified the flaws of character which usually *allowed* the possession in the first place, that person was not immune against further possession. (Math. 13. 45)

Anyone who includes the word Spiritualism in the same sentence as witchcraft, black magic, voodoo or satanism betrays abysmal ignorance, and should be encouraged to make an effort to acquire some knowledge of what they are talking about. And it is our task to help them to do so.

What person, not knowing how to do a simple equation, would presume to discredit a finding of Einstein's? It is therefore highly impertinent to discredit Spiritualism without researching the findings of the hosts of eminent men and women who have devoted their lives to the subject.

Spiritualism, one can tell them, means the opposite to Materialism. That is, a concept of a spiritual universe as opposed to a chemical "accident;" the concept that all is Spirit, or God, manifesting in manifold forms. The concept that man is spirit, a soul clad in a physical body while on earth, and in finer bodies of a higher vibrational frequency in other spheres after physical "death."

One can tell them that Spiritualism is based on proven communication with the so-called "dead" who are very much alive, and that the teachings of Spiritualism have been and are being given to us by highly evolved discarnate teachers, specially trained for this contact, generally referred to as The White Brotherhood, acting on behalf of the Christ Spirit which is universal.

One can tell them that the fundamental law of the universe is Love, Service, the overcoming of the lower self, and continuous spiritual progression up the spheres of light — the exact opposite to black magic or witchcraft which desecrates love, seeks only power over others, power over material gain, serves the worst instincts of the lower self to a bestial degree, and pushes people down into the spheres of darkness.

Tell them that Spiritualism is not a belief, nor does it rely on faith, because it is based on *knowledge*. To ask: "Do you believe in Spiritualism?" is like asking "Do you believe in motor cars, or trees?" It is not something you believe in, but something you seek to practice and live daily, as a way of life.

One can tell them that all great artists, composers, poets and inventors from Leonardo da Vinci to Beethoven, from Galileo to Sir Alexander Fleming, from Shakespeare to William Blake, were in fact Spiritualists because they were aware their inspiration came direct from the world of spirit.

Finally, one can tell them that Spiritualism *is* religion, *all* religion in its pristine form before it was corrupted by man-made theologies; and that in this sense the Buddha was a Spiritualist, that the Koran was written in trance, that the Nazarene was probably the greatest Spiritualist of all time; and that the origins of this cosmic philosophy trace back to the Ancient Mysteries.

Perhaps we can play our part in divorcing Spiritualism from the spurious and misleading associations it so often has in the minds of many by lifting its image from ouija boards and fortune-telling on the pier to the inspiration of the Christ, from the concept of just another sect, cult or "ism" to a realisation that its truths reveal the spiritual science on which the entire Cosmos is based and has its being.

We must educate those who are blindly searching for they know not what, fumbling in a cloud of unknowing, uncertainty and doubt. We must do it lovingly — not only by words but by example, for never was there a truer saying than "By their fruits ye shall know them." Let it be seen, therefore, that our fruit bears the bloom, colour and texture which only comes from ripening in the light of the spiritual sun.

BEYOND A SHADOW OF DOUBT

It seems to me that in recent years the demonstration of what is called physical mediumship has become in some measure demoded. It tends to be regarded, at least in some quarters, as rather "low," appealing to sensation-seekers who would be better engaged in improving themselves spiritually rather than looking for psychic phenomena.

With this view I do not agree. In fact I find it rather snobbish. To my mind there is room, and need, for *all* kinds of mediumship, to suit the widely differing levels of each person's development, and also to fulfil widely differing purposes.

A bone I have to pick with the Anthroposophists (founded by Dr. Rudolf Steiner after he parted company with the Theosophists) is that they appear to condemn "third party mediumship" out of hand, presumably on the grounds that everyone should seek higher knowledge through developing their *own* spiritual attunement and psychic resources.

This, admittedly, is the desired and desirable goal for humanity — in due time. Teachers from the world of spirit often tell us so. But, meanwhile, how do we receive these teachers' teachings? How have we acquired the great fund of knowledge now available about life after death and its implications? Why, *through mediums,* (including Dr. Steiner himself!)

Is it not vastly more beneficial to have the incomparable wisdom of Silver Birch, of White Eagle, and of a host of other great souls who have dedicated themselves to enlightening mankind through their chosen instruments? That each individual should endeavour to seek closer attunement, and thus progress spiritually (and within their limits, even psychically) is a right thing. But mediums are *born* with their gift, even though that gift may be ignored, or sometimes denied, or developed later in life.

I asked my own guide about this, and his reply (through Catherine, our home circle medium) was very down to earth as far as I was concerned! "*All* have *vibrations,*" he said, "but you have not the *make-up* for what is called mediumship." Spasmodic clairvoyance, the awareness of a spirit presence, or being impressed by or receptive to thoughts — these things he classed as "vibrations." The gift of mediumship is far beyond these limited sensitivities. So — to each his gifts, as described so well by Paul in his famous letter to the early Christians at Corinth.

And when I have asked numerous Anthroposophists how many among them have actually attained clairvoyance at will, through their devoted practice of Dr. Steiner's methods, they have all replied, "None that I know of." Which just goes to show!

Every kind of manifestation is but a means to an end, whether it be simple raps and taps or Direct Voice. The world is full of doubting Thomases who can only *begin* their search for truth through the demonstation of physical phenomena. They have first to *see* in order to believe.

Now for those who need to see to believe, what greater evidence could their possibly be than the full materialisation of "dead" persons, who can walk and talk, shake hands, embrace them, even sign their name, or stand on a weighing machine, before melting away? And not only persons, but sometimes fully materialised animal friends: dogs who can bark, jump up with delight and lap water, birds that can fly, and so on, before disappearing "in front of one's very eyes," as they say.

If Jesus had not materialised himself so conclusively to his disciples they would doubtless have remained sad, dejected, disappointed men after the brutal murder of their beloved Master. Whereas they were galvanised into magnificent, dedicated activity for the remainder of their earthly lives, till they themselves, and thousands who followed them, did not shrink from terrible deaths rather than deny the *truth*.

A good materialisation demonstration brings conviction without a shadow of doubt to those present, and we are indeed fortunate in having physical mediums still with us, like Gordon Higginson, who possess the necessary ectoplasmic make-up for this form of communication to be possible.

Very recently a woman materialised at a Gordon Higginson public seance and held a quiet conversation with her brother, who was among the sitters. The fact that her body had only been cremated two weeks earlier made this appearance unusually remarkable, I thought.

I am always interested in what has happened to people I know *personally,* and two friends have granted me permission to pass on something of their individual experiences in this field, and I quote from the notes they gave me. The first, a man, writes:

"It was the first materialisation circle my wife and I had attended, and for three weeks beforehand we did all we could to prepare ourselves, for we wanted it to be a real success." The seance was held in a small Christian Spiritualist church; the medium was Mrs Lilley, who sat alone behind the curtains of a cabinet. Several hymns were sung, and then a rich baritone voice was heard joining in, subsequently appealing for all present to forget their outside interests for many spirit friends had come, and if conditions were right, all would show themselves.

"Immediately the introductory talk ended," he goes on, "a tall, well-proportioned Arab emerged from the cabinet and, slowly going round the circle, gave a greeting to each sitter. That completed, he stood in the centre of us all, and melted away. But almost at once his voice was heard, high up, giving a beautiful and rhythmic invocation. The words we could not understand, but the sincerity and grandeur of their delivery was uplifting and inspiring.

"I felt sure great things must happen, and the first figure to come through the cabinet curtains and pick up the illuminated plaques, came direct to me without any hesitation in the darkened room. With a plaque in each hand, he held them for the light to fall on his face. And there in front of me stood my father, exactly as I knew him before the fatal illness struck him down.

"Instead of his being cool, calm and collected, as I said he would be should he materialise, *he pushed me on the chest* and said, " 'Lad, I *am* excited!' " (Oh, how natural and homely — how un-spooklike! If only more people could realise that our loved ones are just the same when they have shed the body, not unsubstantial ghosts!)

"After greeting my wife, whom he loved dearly, and giving me a personal message about changes to come, I asked if any friends were with him, and he said, 'Yes! Clara, (my sister who had been on the Other Side for 23 years), and Mother. We've brought her along, too.' This last reference puzzled me for a few seconds, as *my* mother was always 'Ma'! But I noted he had turned to my wife as he said this.

"Now my wife's mother passed over when my wife was only 3 years old, so when she came from the cabinet, after my father left, we did not know who this beautiful young woman could be. Although she wrote 'Mother' with her forefinger, it was hard to realise one so young and amazingly lovely could be the mother of a middle-aged woman.

"The guide, in the cabinet, spoke out to say she looked too young to be the mother of the little lady on my right, but she had been over a long time, which made it possible. I was completely captivated by her, and thrilled when she turned towards me and I became aware of love flowing from her to me in a steady stream.

"When my wife first saw the materialised form of her mother she felt great concern, for a moment, because she was so like her sister, who had emigrated to Sydney long years before, that she thought this sister must have passed over suddenly. Later on my wife's eldest sister, who mothered the young ones for some years, confirmed that their sister in Sydney was indeed the image of their mother.

"It was now the turn of other sitters to receive their visitors from the spirit world, and as time passed I began to think my sister Clara was not coming through. But suddenly a young feminine figure came out of the cabinet and straight to us, and there before us *was* my sister, dressed in full bridal attire — gown, train and veil. Before we could say anything the veil was being flung around us and on to us, and for softness and delicacy it was quite unique — like gossamer.

"You see, my sister passed over suddenly, only 6 weeks after her wedding day, which was the last occasion we saw her on earth. But 23 years in the spirit world had not wiped out the memory. Before fading out she turned around in the centre of the circle for everyone to see her, veil in her left hand, and throwing kisses with her right.

"A deep impression was made on all present. It was much more than evidence my wife and I received that Sunday afternoon — it was proof beyond any shadow of doubt. And during the terrible war years we feared no death, for we had seen three of our dear ones return to us after being 'dead' (so-called) for years." What a truly wonderful experience!

My other friend, a woman, gave me her abbreviated notes of a circle she attended in 1956 at the White Rose Sanctuary, London, so as space is limited I will copy them as written:

"I witnessed 12 full materialisations. The medium was Arthur Phillips, (asleep) in view of visitors (8) all the time whilst, singly, the Other World guests walked around the room, hugged us, kissed us, held our hands with their warm, pulsating materialised hands. Red light, but occasionally, as forms were built up in the curtained recess, the Guide asked 'No light.' Music playing quietly in the background.

"The first one to come was a John McMorland, 41 years old when he passed over a year previously. He stood in the room as he said to his wife: 'Don't get agitated, darling. I will see if I can come over to you.' He picked up two plaques with phosphorus light on them, and walked across the room to stand in front of his wife. He said, 'Look, I have the grey suit and brown shoes I bought before I went.' It was a wonderful reunion. From an unhappy woman dressed all in black, she was smiling happily when the seance finished.

"Many relatives spoke to those they had left on earth. The Sanctuary owner's wife, known as White Rose in the spirit world, spoke to all of us, and thanked me for helping her husband. She gave me three gorgeous pink roses tinged with gold — no thorns, no veins in the leaves. They did not open, but remained for 6 weeks before they finally shrivelled. John McMorland covered his wife's lap with beautiful Parma violets — exquisite flowers, nothing on earth like them.

"One visitor who came to speak with us was an Eastern visitor, beautifully garbed in Eastern robes and jewelled head-dress. A bearded face. Someone said, 'Oh! here is an Arab!' but he bowed, saying 'Lady, I am Persian. I was the one who took the myrrh to the newborn child . . .'"

On this fascinating note I must end this chapter, but in the next one I will tell you a great deal more about this remarkable Persian, Chief of the Magi, who became so intimately acquainted with the boy Jesus during his formative years.

HAFED, PRINCE OF PERSIA, CHIEF OF THE MAGI

At Eastertide, as well as at Christmas, our thoughts turn more than ever to the beloved Nazarene, and so I want to tell you about the Persian mentioned in the last chapter, and how his life, and his "death" became inextricably linked with the one he recognised as the Light of the World.

A reader, whom I have only once met, was impressed to pass on to me a most precious gift, on condition I never let it go but passed it on to my son. It is a book of nigh on 600 closely printed pages called *Hafed Prince of Persia*, first published in 1875, the seventh edition being issued in 1935. Why no publisher has made it available subsequently I cannot think.

Briefly, the book contains, among much other matter, verbatim records of 100 sittings which took place in Glasgow, Scotland a century ago, the remarkable medium being Mr David Duguid. The first 75 sittings give a most detailed account of Prince Hafed's life on earth, and then in the spirit world. The remaining sittings are devoted to his younger friend Hermes, an Egyptian, who also came to dedicate his life to the one he had known when still a laughing boy . . .

To any student of the history, cultures, customs and religions of the times, this book is a veritable mine of information. But it is of Hafed himself that I wish to tell. Though brought up a wealthy Prince, a leader of men, and widely travelled, he renounced the worldly life after his beloved wife and baby son were cruelly murdered by invading barbarians who left his home a smoking ruin.

He joined the Order of the Magi, who were not only priests and seers but the only educators of the people. Many of them were married, with families of their own, great attention being given to the crucial importance of pre-natal influence.

Prince Hafed soon became Chief of the Magi, as from early childhood he was most psychically gifted and able to hold converse with his guardian spirit on many subjects (to the joy of his mother). As Chief Magus, he and his colleagues thrice weekly entered the Sacred Grove (all worship being in the open air, never in a building) and held communion with a high spirit referred to as the Spirit of the Flame — for the symbolical flame on their altars never went out.

The Magi received their learning from the spirit world. Various bands of spirits instructed them not only in the duty of man to God and his neighbour, but in subjects such as physiology, biology, the secrets of the animal plant and mineral kingdoms, astronomy, and knowledge of other peopled worlds.

The teachings of the Prophet Zoroaster (from whom Hafed's house was directly descended) had made Persia the most enlightened country at that period. Both Egypt and India's greatness had for the most part degenerated long since, Greece and Rome indulged in a multiplicity of scarcely believed-in gods, while the Hebrews had once again fallen into a state of corruption, bigotry, and violence, and the country had become the prey, like so many others, of the Roman Empire.

Yet the sacred books of Persia (as well as of the Hebrews) prophesied that the Deliverer of Mankind, the Light of the World so long awaited, was to be born in that despised land. "Oh, that it could have been Persia!" cried Hafed in his youth, when learning of this from his guardian spirit.

Incidentally, the reply given by Hafed when questioned by the sitters on the doctrine taught by the Magi in regard to the spirit world, is of great interest: he says, "In their sacred books the Persians taught that Spirits existed before all worlds; that the Son was the First of the Immortal Spirits, and was placed over the Spirit world of our planetary system; that as mankind had fallen from their allegiance to him, it became him, who was their Great Lord, to take on himself a mortal body, and endeavour by his example and precept to draw them back to himself." (How simply and beautifully this great truth is expressed.)

Hafed was 43 years of age — about the same age as Joseph — when the momentous message from the spirit world was given to him and two chosen colleagues, called Parcorus and Cofdraes, commanding them to depart immediately for Judea, where the "great and glorious event" was about to take place. They were not to look for the Child in the courts and palaces of Jerusalem. He would be in a much more lowly place. "I shall be your guiding star by night," said the shining spirit, "and a felt presence by day. I myself will lead you to the sacred spot." Moreover they were told, to their amazement, that within the altar they would find costly treasures to take as gifts to the Child's parents, for they were poor, and would need such gifts.

Hafed adds: "On coming out from the Sacred Grove to the light of day, we were greatly astonished to see the assembled brethren fleeing from our presence. We knew not the cause, until we heard the voice of the Spirit bidding us veil our faces which had become so dazzlingly bright that our friends imagined we were spirits and not mortals."

The coming of the three Magi to Bethlehem is a wellknown story — and the awful consequences of Herod hearing of their presence in the land. Yet those slaughtered innocents were at once translated into the warmth and love of the spirit spheres, later to become ministering spirits to him on whose account they died; while the Spirit informed the Magi "We shall send the Child to Egypt, so that he may be educated for his high mission."

The Magi had planned to journey home to Persia by a certain route which meant taking ship down the Red Sea, but spirit planning was otherwise. Chased by pirates, they sought refuge on the western shores, and thus finding themselves in Egypt, decided to travel to Thebes. Though the Temple of the Nile had been ravaged, the inner temple still stood in all its interior beauty, in the care of a lovable and venerable priest known to Hafed, called Issha, and of the Head Priestess who was, as always, a medium.

Issha had long yearned for the advent of the looked-for Prince of Light, and was overwhelmed with joy at the Magi's tidings. Yet even more was to come, for that night he was told by the Spirit Messenger: "Thou has been kept alive for Heaven's purpose. The child shall be brought here, and he shall be guarded by thee . . ."

Thus it was that when Joseph and Mary, guided by spirit, in due course fled with the child to Egypt, this saintly old man, so closely in touch with the spirit world, made all arrangements for their welfare, and the growing child formed a great love for his aged tutor. Hafed gives the text of several long letters received by him from Issha over a period, brought by merchant caravans to Persia, and once by the young Hermes who shared these very early years with Jesus.

During the "exile" in Egypt, which lasted till the eventual death of Herod, Joseph carried on his skilful craft, and he and Mary remained in Egypt when the aged Issha, under spirit guidance, took the boy — now about 8 years old — to Hafed in Persia. The boy showed such gifts of the spirit that he was loved and revered by all the Magi.

It is impossible to tell of the many experiences he shared with Hafed, for whom he formed a lasting love, always calling him affectionately "My father." The boy's power to heal was demonstrated, and the inner knowledge he displayed made Hafed marvel at his young charge. When it was at last safe to enter Judea, the family sent for Jesus, and he arrived, with Hafed, not long before the Passover Feast when he so confounded the teachers in the Temple debates when only 12-years-old. Hafed was present on these occasions, before taking leave of him to return to Persia.

A few years passed (during which Jesus learnt Joseph's skills with wood, but also spent a short time with the Essene Brotherhood, and visited our Western Isles with Joseph of Arimathea, the merchant kinsman of Mary, who befriended the family after the ailing Joseph's death.) Hafed's old friend Issha, the Egyptian Priest, had meanwhile passed to spirit, but communicated with him frequently "in such tangible shape "— he says —" that I might have forgotten he was not in the body."

Hafed goes on: "In a letter I had received from Jesus he expressed a wish that I should travel with him to the East, and having received my promise to do so, he once more arrived in Persia. He would be about 18 years of age, a tall, fine-looking young man. He was complete in education. Indeed, I question if anyone in the whole civilised world at that time was at all able to compete with him. He could speak and teach in a number of languages and was conversant with many subjects of which very few knew anything . . .

16

"A company of the younger Magi went out to meet him; and I am certain no king ever received such a welcome as was accorded to this Hebrew youth. He was carried in triumph . . . to our holy hill . . ."

Later, alone with him in his cell, Hafed says: "Methinks I see him now, as he, with all the simplicity and humility that marked his every action, flung himself on the ground at my feet, and leaning his arm on my knees, looked up into my face with filial love and reverence. I besought him to rise. But no; that was his place, he said, adding, 'You are one of the few who understand why I am here, and who I am; for there are not many in this world to whom such mysteries have been revealed . . .'

"That night we were witness of many lovely visions . . . We saw our friend Issha, clothed in robes of celestial brightness. The form of my beloved wife also came before us, in angelic beauty; and we likewise beheld my Spirit Guide, and many others besides. Sweet was our intercourse with the spirits on that memorable night."

Yet in giving these very brief glimpses of Hafed's life, I feel I must jump many, many years to an *especially* memorable night — though there had been so many. He did not again see 'his Prince' in the flesh after their return from the journey into India. It was Hermes, the young Egyptian priest, who later went to Judea to join the followers of the Nazarene during his public ministry, for many nationalities joined the brethren, especially those with the gift of healing and other spiritual gifts with which Hermes was endowed. *His* life and contact with Jesus, both before *and* after the crucifixion, is another complete story.

It was not till Hafed was sent by the Persian Government on an embassy to Rome, years later, that the pattern of his life changed completely. For, returning via Greece, he came upon Paul in Athens . . . The meeting was decisive. With amazing endurance, this remarkable Prince of Persia, now over 80, devoted the rest of his long life to teaching the existing communities and founding new ones over an incredibly wide area. His arduous and dangerous journeys took him to Barcelona, Lyons (where he was put in prison, but freed by the spirit intervention of Jesus), Nice, Genoa, Venice, the Balkan and Dardanelles, Tunis, Sicily, Corinth, Egypt, and at last via Syria to Persia.

He went at once to the beloved City of the Grove, longing to set foot one last time in the grove of the Sacred Flame. But he was denied entrance. The Magi had long known of his "defection." Some understood. Others did not. His heart wept as he renounced his old and loved associations, and threw off his robes, (which he had always continued to wear.) The two aged Magi, Parcorus and Cofdraes, who had accompanied him to Bethlehem so long ago, likewise disrobed on hearing from him all that had taken place, declaring that for the truth's sake they would leave all and go with him to the ancient capital of Bushire. And here they gathered together the first Christian community in Persia. (Needless to say, spirit communication took place in all the early

17

Christian gatherings).

But now Persia had fallen under the cruel, licentious influence of Rome, and Rome had brought its circuses to debase the people. Nor were Christians to be tolerated, in Persia or elsewhere in the Empire under Nero. Even meeting at night, in secret, they could not escape.

And so we come to that other memorable night, when the glorified Prince of Light comes to the frail, 100-year-old Prince of Persia, ex-Chief of the Magi, in his cage — separated by only a few thin bars from the hungry, roaring beasts for which he could not but feel compassion.

Early one morning the old man who shared his cell suddenly awoke him. "Look, my brother! Our den has been transformed!" It was no dream. The dungeon was filled with the light of a shining throng, and "there walked forth One whose head bore a crown brighter far than mortal can describe. It was my Prince, the blessed Jesus, and I bent low . . . 'Do it not, my beloved father. Thou and thy fellow-servant will be here on the morrow. They think *this* day shall be thy last, but another night will pass before thou comest, and then we shall meet thee . . .'"

Thus with confidence the two old men faced the day's ordeal, for they had the word of Jesus. Calmly they stood with folded arms in the arena before the assembled thousands as the animals were let loose. But neither lion nor tiger would approach them — except two which finally sprang, but fell dead at their feet! They were led out to the disgusted jeers of the drunken spectators at such poor sport, for after the women and children were burnt, and the men despatched by the gladiators, the programme usually ended at dusk by the oldest and frailest facing the wild beasts, armed with short knives which they mostly threw down.

Yet Hafed says: "A work was done that night, however, for the cause of truth which could not have been accomplished by a hundred years' orations. Many who witnessed the scene rose and left (as I afterwards learned) and were so deeply impressed that they became earnest enquirers and afterwards converts to the faith.

"The second day came, which we knew to be our last. Both of us knelt in prayer to the Great Spirit and asked our Prince to receive us. We rose not. The beasts made a great spring. I saw one of the animals fix on my companion. That is the last I remember seeing in the body: I opened my eyes and found myself in the glorious home on high.

"I looked round: he that died with me, still lay by my side . . . First my own beloved wife embraced me, and then my child, now a stately man, hung on my neck . . . and my own dear father and mother . . . and then the whole region shook with a grand burst of harmonious music while heralds proclaimed the welcome to the martyrs. I enquired if such a welcome was accorded to them all. 'Yes,' I was told, 'but you seem to get a louder welcome.'

I can but give abbreviated excerpts of what followed. "My venerable friend, Issha, came towards me and invited me to go with him to the great

Temple . . . my whole soul was ravished by the scene . . . I think there must have been some earthliness clinging to me, for I felt dazzled as the bright ones looked at me. But such sensations soon wore off, and earthly weaknesses were no longer felt . . .

"As I gazed in awe and wonder a shout as if from ten thousand trumpets rent the air . . . I turned to my Egyptian friend and asked him what it meant. He at once replied, 'Look! He comes! The Prince!' He was clothed in garments of spotless purity, and following in his train were thousands of bright ones, all moving on towards the Temple . . . At first I felt impelled to rush towards him and throw myself at his feet; but a sense of unworthiness coming on me, I drew back. He saw me, however, and coming up to me he clasped me in his arms, exclaiming, 'Father, thou art welcome! All Heaven shouteth for joy that thou art come home. Come, my father, come, let us walk up to the Temple that we may worship the Great and Good, the Almighty Father.'"

And here we must leave Hafed, Prince of Persia, former Chief of the Magi, as he walked amid that company, side by side with Him whose mortal birth he had honoured, whose youth he had cherished, and for whose Truth he had willingly "died."

THE RESURRECTION

As the daffodils reach up their long stems from the earth's darkness, and turning their trumpets to the light, offer their golden radiance to the sun; as sensitive ears catch whispered melodies from multitudes of nature spirits, busy in every bud and bough; and as birds and creatures on every hand revel in the eternal miracle of Spring, let us pray that Mankind, too, will feel the stirring of resurrection in the heart.

Let us pray especially for our brothers on that little island beyond that little sea where misguided fanatics daily crucify the Prince of Love by hatred, violence and murder, and more vicious still, the poisoning and corruption of the souls of children. (Do mothers, I wonder, tell their little ones to leave their nail-bombs at home when they go to Mass? They need not bother: the nails are already driven deep into the wounds of the murdered Son of Light.)

At Eastertide in the spheres of spirit there are wonderful Festivals of light and joy, love and reunion, dedication and renewal. And there is also a strange stirring in the darker realms of unquiet souls, like the faint echo of a distant bell, or the fleeting glimpse of a radiance of light which some will flee, but a few will seek to follow. Even as in that other time, when the Master, leaving his body lifeless upon the cross, let the light of his glowing Spirit suffuse those same dark regions, and some there were who were stirred to seek the sunlight they had forgotten, as he passed by, leading the Good Thief at his right hand.

Let us, as Spiritualists, make no mistake about Whom we are referring when we speak, a little glibly, of the Master Jesus, or the Nazarene, or the Galilean. Many, it seems to me, having freed themselves from the shackles of unintelligible theological doctrines and dogmas, have tended to "throw out the baby with the bath-water" and become, on the rebound as it were, so rationalistic and "down to earth" that they appear veritably earthbound on occasions!

Their thinking becomes limited, or preoccupied, by such things as "proof of survival," the phenomena of the seance room, ESP, psychic researches, clairvoyants and mediums, receiving little messages from departed loved ones, and so on. All very well, even necessary, but there is nothing *spiritual* in any of these interests or activities, *by themselves.* Indeed many, having gained much experience of these subjects, show little or no interest in the *teachings* of Spiritualism as revealed through high spirit entities. Yet it is only by studying the teachings, taking them into our innermost beings, applying them to daily life and events, by personal commitment and *individual mystical experience* that our own lives and characters can be re-orientated, and the redemption of the world hastened.

Thus it is that so many Spiritualists, when it comes to the Festival of Easter, miss the point, or tend to overlook it. They have proved to their own satisfaction a) that we *all* survive the death of the physical body, b) that having done so, it is possible to communicate in given conditions with those still in the flesh, and c) that it is further possible (again given certain conditions) to fully materialise the spirit body so that it becomes tangible, active and visible to all present.

Having accepted this to be so (which indeed it is) they say something like this: "Of course, this is just what Jesus did when he manifested himself to the women in the garden of Joseph of Arimathea, and on all the other occasions when he met, walked and talked with his friends and followers over a certain number of weeks. Not only was he himself a great medium," they say, "but he was also aided by being able to draw on his psychically gifted circle of close disciples. So that explains the so-called Resurrection and the events which followed, doesn't it? I mean, in the modern light of psychic science there was nothing so very *unique* about it, surely?"

But that is where they are quite wrong. In their unthinking haste to demote Jesus of Nazareth to the rôle of a teacher and reformer *only,* (an attitude of thought much encouraged by "clever" Left-wing mass-media writers who like to portray him as some kind of Arch-Hippy who proclaimed love and brotherhood and got killed for his pains) they entirely overlook the fact that at this moment in time the Master Jesus was and is the *first* and *only* individual born of woman who was able to transmute and spiritualise the atoms and cells of his physical body to such an extent that they took on a vastly higher rate of vibration, thus making his "body of light" visible or invisible *at will*.

As White Eagle puts it: "The very atoms of his physical body were changed and spiritualised. His body became transmuted from pain and darkness to light and freedom."

In the Aquarian Gospel Jesus tells his friends and loved ones after his first appearance to them: "Behold! for human flesh can be transmuted into higher form, and then that higher form is master of things manifest, and can, at will, take any form. And so I come to you in form familiar to you." And again, when he appeared to the Eastern sages in India, where he had studied as a young man, we are told "He pressed the hand of every man and of the royal host, and said, 'Behold, I am not myth made of the fleeting winds, for I am flesh and bone and brawn: *but I can cross the borderland at will.*'"

And to the magi in Persia: ". . . this flesh in which I come to you was changed with speed of light from human flesh. To you I come, *the first of all the race to be transmuted . . . What I have done, all men will do;* and what I am, all men will be."

This is a far cry from the materialisations of the seance room, wonderful as they are — for the simple but vital reason that the *physical* bodies of those spirit friends who materialise their etheric forms, through drawing on the ectoplasm of a powerful medium, have long since disintegrated in the churchyard, or been cremated. In fact one can go so far as to say that it is something of a reverse process: our friends are *lowering* the vibrations of their *spirit* bodies, whereas the Master Jesus *spiritualised* the atoms of his *physical* body!

In doing so, he was indeed the Forerunner, the Demonstrator of the intended goal for every man, in time to come: the control of the lower by the higher, the mastership of Matter by Spirit. White Eagle explains: "The whole purpose of life here is the continued etherealisation of man, and of the fabric of this earth . . . This earth planet, very dark at present, is slowly quickening in vibration . . . Do you know that there are already planets in existence in your solar system which have become so etherealised that they are outside the range of the most powerful telescopes? Yes, these are planets of light . . ."

In the midst of the present turmoil and seeming chaos which are the birth pangs of the New Age of enlightenment and "break-through" on many fronts, White Eagle gives us this prophecy of mankind's eventual resurrection: "We are able to speak of what we ourselves have seen concerning the future of mankind — of a life dawning for man which can only be described as celestial, when the light of the Son of God will shine through man's faces, when they will live without sickness, pain, want or suffering, a life harmonious and beautiful in every respect, warm and human, and where the fullest expression of the spirit can be given.

"This is where all you people have a great work waiting," he goes on. "Try and put into practice the Christ-thought; try to live the Christ life; then you yourself will be aiding in the creation of a brighter world, and this dense matter, this darkness, will gradually be dissolved."

We have been given a Pattern to follow, an Example to do our best to emulate in the One we call the Nazarene, whom Silver Birch describes as "the greatest manifestation of the Great Spirit that your world has yet received."

Let us not despair because that Example was given by a Being whom the high spirit spheres refer to by many great names: the Greatest Adept — the greatest of the Sons of God — the Lord of the First Solar Plane — the Controller of the Silver (Radium) Cosmic Ray of Life and Love — the First of the Twelve Hierarchical Adepts of Solar Birth (of whom the one we know as the Archangel Michael is the Twelfth), and so on.

For in entering into our humanity he had to face, endure and overcome all human problems which constantly surrounded him on all sides in a most augmented degree and *still* maintain and show forth the Christ Light — becoming, for us, our Beloved Brother on the path, our Compassionate Friend when we have fallen low, the very Heart of Love, the Great Healer.

Let us, then, meditate on the Festival of Easter, and like the daffodils in their humble simplicity, reach up from the earth's darkness, opening our hearts to the Light of the Son, and offering ourselves anew in an act of resurrection and re-dedication.

White Eagle's quotations from *The Path of the Soul*. White Eagle Publishing Trust.

PICKING UP THE CHURCH'S CASUALTIES

I am sitting in our Sanctuary, for it is my turn to be "on duty" for 'phone calls from those in distress or despair. From one window I see the leafless weeping willows beside the pond. The view from the other window is more seasonal — a Holly Tree covered all over with red berries. Its companion, the Ivy, is keeping warm its tall trunk, and in amongst the bright branches is a busy flutter of blue-tits. It is not yet Twelfth Night. But the New Year has dawned, and with it, all our resolutions. Long may we keep them. We also make a Big Wish at this time. I wonder what yours is?

My Big Wish is for the continued dissolution and disarray of an Organisation which I have long felt to be the greatest enemy of the spirit and teaching of the Nazarene which man could possibly have devised, aided and abetted by the powers of darkness which ever seek to confound both the ignorant and the innocent, and to smother the Torch of Truth.

I make this statement with love and compassion for the numerous kindly, well-meaning souls whose desire to "serve God and their fellow men" has drawn them into the confined confines of this Organisation — this now withering tree with its many branches which serve not to give shelter in the storm but rather to obscure the light of the sun; branches not bright with berries, but with blood; twigs that have kindled the flames for its victims in the past, and even now fan the fires of hatred, murder and revenge on our island's doorstep.

I, for one, am heartily sick and tired of picking up the pieces: the pathetic, tragic casualties who turn to us for help. All too often that help is too late — twenty, thirty, even forty years too late! For do not the Jesuits allegedly boast: "Give us a child until it is seven, and we have it for life?"

How is it possible *really* to de-indoctrinate a woman of 50 who can say "Bless you" but who cannot say "*God* bless you" because she is totally unable to force her lips to utter the word "God?" She is far from being unique, for scores of those who come to us beg us not to mention the word "God," which to them is synonymous with wrath, vengeance, guilt, judgement, punishment, fear.

Terms such as "those who *fear* God," and "bringing up children in the *fear* of God," and similar phrases, have done untold damage to people's lives. The word "fear" means only one thing to a child: to be frightened. And however much that child may dismiss it or rebel against it in later life, the fear and the dread, and of course the guilt, remain in the subconscious.(Yet the Nazarene constantly reiterated:"*Fear* not!") This is what *Churchianity* has done for them. It has succeeded in making the very word "God" anathema. It is a reminder of Orwell's *1984* in which the legend "Big Brother is watching you!" is everywhere to be seen.

"God loves you" is written up in the infants' room in many Catholic schools. Yet these same infants have been shown pictures of eagles pecking out the insides of chained victims in hell. Infants in one school, to my knowledge, were told they would go to hell if they told a lie. (This in itself is even embroidering Catholic doctrine, for a lie is classed as a venial, not a mortal sin.) A scared little boy of 5 asked me, "If you go to hell, can't you ever, *ever* get out?" You can imagine my reply — but no wonder so many of them were having nightmares.

One mother had made some strawberry jam, and her small son clapped his hands and started running across the kitchen, shouting, "Oh, I *love* straw . . ." Suddenly he stopped in mid-run, shrank visibly, blushed scarlet, and said in a dead, monotone voice, "Sister says we mustn't love anything but God." This child naturally took this to mean that he shouldn't love Mum and Dad, the cat or the dog, or the sun or the flowers, let alone jam . . . (Yet God is ALL LOVE!)

When the irate parents protested to the Sister in authority, saying with some justification that they were murdering the souls of little children, and they were taking their child away, she only replied, whitefaced with repressed rage, "I shall pray for you." Doesn't this make you want to raze the Vatican to the ground? It does me. Hope rises within me, therefore, every time I read in some newspaper that x-thousand more priests have left the Church.

Yet the depressed and guilt-ridden souls who come to us, with broken wills, tormented by traumas, afraid to *live,* and still more afraid to die, will in most cases take to the philosophy and teaching of Spiritualism like a duck to water. For the first time in their lives (for they have been quite ignorant of it) they suddenly find something which makes sense! Something which appeals not only to their reason and sense of justice, but which touches a chord deep within them. "This is what I've always felt it *ought* to be like," they say. And "the Great Spirit," "the all-loving Father-Mother," and similar names become acceptable substitutes for, to them, the awful word "God."

"I try to pray," they will say, "and I visualise Christ on the cross." "Please *don't!*" we beg them. "Please don't keep in your mind the gruesome picture of his murder! But picture him as he *is now* — stretching out his arms to you with a tender smile of complete understanding and compassion; and radiant, vibrant with Life and with Love, the Great Healer."

Many will ask to be taken to a spiritual healer — on condition that the healer functions in a house and not in a building which in any way reminds them of a church. (And it is with good reason that the Samaritan organisation — though founded by the *Rev.* Chad Varah — has a rule which discourages clergymen from answering the telephone because it has been shown that more often than not a distressed client feels worse rather than better when interviewed by a minister of the Church.)

We are fortunate in possessing some 100 hours of teaching tapes spoken with deep love by a superb spirit teacher through a remarkable trance instrument. Even *one* hour's tape played to such a depressed person can have an overwhelmingly comforting and beneficial effect. Yet the pattern of fear, anxiety and negative thinking over many, many years will "take over" the lower mind the next day — inevitably, for alas it could scarcely be otherwise. There is no magic wand that can undo the damage of 20 or 30 years in a week.

Yet, taking the long view, seeds have been sown, even though they may lie dormant a long time, or possibly not germinate till that person has passed over and the memory revivified. Important as "rescue circles" are, to aid those in confusion or ready to rise out of lower astral conditions in the *next* state of existence, I feel it equally important to endeavour to rescue those who are *already* in these conditions on *this* plane, thus saving them from gravitating to those same conditions after transition.

How heart-warming it is when one comes across ministers here and there who have become enlightened! There is one splendid young

Methodist minister whose eyes have been opened — and are opening wider and wider every day. He is attending an excellent home circle, assisting a saintly medium and healer in his work, is reading voraciously, and told us (of course) that he is now reading the Bible in an entirely different light to when he was a theology student. He also said, with vehemence, "the Church is dead on its feet."

But what can these comparatively few enlightened clergy do when there is so much deep and bitter division of opinion within every sect of the so-called Christian churches? At the same time as one minister rings me up from Scotland to praise and eulogise my book *Tales of Two Worlds* and to express his appreciation during a half-hour trunk call, it seems that another minister (having found that same book by the bedside of someone we took in and helped when everyone else refused to do so), has burnt it!

How long, I wonder, can enlightened clergy remain within their churches *and* be true to their consciences, when they must perforce reel off a liturgy most of which they know to be false? A liturgy *not* based on the teaching of Jesus, but mainly on the reputed teachings of Paul who never met him in the flesh and was steeped in the Jewish laws and traditions. A liturgy concocted, centuries later, moreover, by men who had already thrown out the inspired and spiritual teaching of Origen, the greatest of the Early Church Fathers, pronouncing them "anathema," at the same time as they expurgated nearly all references (but not quite all!) to reincarnation in the Gospels, hid many other Gospels away in the secret vaults of the Vatican, and wrote into others whatever suited their purpose.

The pernicious doctrine of the Vicarious Atonement must surely have landed more millions of souls in the lower astral regions than any other. For in *direct contradiction* to the teaching of Jesus that "whatsoever a man sows, that shall he also reap," this doctrine in facts tells people that Jesus took on the sins of the world, and paid for them once and for all, by his sacrifice on the cross — "this sacrifice of himself once offered, as an oblation and *satisfaction* for our sins" — and paid for them in advance, as it were, so long as certain outward requirements of the Church are observed!

Every single spirit teacher condemns this barbaric and beastly notion that the all-loving Father required the sacrifice of his greatest son (or of any of his great messengers) as a scapegoat. Yet Paul dished this out to the Hebrews who (as he himself had formerly done) purified themselves not by shedding their *own* blood, which would have been uncomfortable, but by the blood of bulls and goats, and sprinkling themselves with the ashes of a poor slaughtered heifer.

He speaks of Jesus "annulling our sin by his sacrifice" (if we are to believe his reputed letters), and goes so far as to say "unless blood is shed, there can be no remission of sins." He speaks of "the blood of Christ, who offered himself as a victim unblemished in God's sight," referring to the

25

Jewish law that only an "unblemished" animal can be a sacrifice for sin — (which is why even the modern Jewish priest refuses to use a humane killer, because it causes a small hole or blemish in the forehead *before* the throat is gashed in ritual kosher killing.)

As one spirit teacher put it, in words that any child can understand: "*No one*, however much he might wish to do so, can pay for another's sin. If any amongst you, my children, decides to eat a quantity of very green apples, it is that one who suffers the ensuing stomach ache."

How long, I ask, can enlightened clergy compromise their consciences? How long can they kid themselves that "Spiritualism can be incorporated into the Church?" Will they not find themselves, sooner or later, in much the same position in which I was placed when, at 17, I was asked to add some "young blood" to the Sunday School? All appeared to be going well. I enjoyed it and so did the youngsters. Until one day the vicar invited me to tea. It had "come to his knowledge" that my beliefs were not strictly orthodox, and though he had no personal quarrel with them, it was obvious that I could not continue . . .

Fair enough! For I had indeed committed the heresy of denying the awful Day of Judgement, together with the Last Trump and the physical Resurrection. I had taught the children that "dying" was as simple as going through a door into a lovely garden, and that their grannies and grandads were *not* waiting for Gabriel's horn in the damp churchyard, but were in that lovely garden *now*, still loving them and caring for them. I even told them how Jesus had promised the thief beside him: "*This day* you shall be with me in paradise." Of *course* this would never do in a "Christian" Sunday School!

For what words of real comfort, based on the knowledge they are *supposed* to have of matters of life and death, does a bereaved person obtain from priest, parson or minister? Absolutely none. Only vague platitudes and pious hopes, at a time when the distressed person longs to *know*, and is beset by a hundred questions which need answers.

And how, too, can the clergy really help and prepare someone who knows he or she is dying, and who is afraid (if they believe there is "something" afterwards) of being lost in some fathomless limbo? How different, and how beautiful, is the passing of someone who *knows*, and is able to be aware of what is taking place!

I am greatly indebted to a reader who described to me the truly wonderful transition of her 49 year old daughter. She had been rushed to hospital and operated upon, but the malignancy was too widespread for her body to survive. She was an Outer Brother of the White Eagle Lodge, and a lovely soul.

On the 25th she was "very far away," but was heard to be whispering: "It's all *so* beautiful . . . *so* beautiful! The room is full of beautiful Blue Beings, and oh! the Joy . . . and the flowers! If only they would let me stay, but they keep bringing me back."

26

On the 26th her spirit body was loosening its hold, but she opened her eyes, looked at her mother, and whispered: "White Eagle! . ." And a little later she opened her eyes again, and in a strong voice almost of exultation, said: "*I am raised!*" (This was when she felt her spirit body separating and lifting up.) Then her breathing gradually became slower and slower, until it was no more. Her mother says: "My darling was received into those waiting arms, and I knew she was *safely Home*. I can never cease to thank God that she was allowed to slip Home so swiftly and peacefully." And I thank this mother for wanting to share this intimate experience for the benefit of others.

There are those who like to say that Spiritualism is not a religion. Well, it is not *a* religion — it *is* Religion. Through actual communication with those now in many differing spheres of life beyond "death" we are taught the fundermental laws of how to live, how to "die," what happens and can happen after that step is taken, and the purpose and goal of our existence and evolution in the universe. Is this not Religion, embracing *all* religions? *Beyond* all religions? As Silver Birch puts it: "Our allegiance is not to a Creed, not to a Book, not to a Church, but to the Great Spirit of life and His eternal, natural laws."

The whole can never be incorporated in the part. It is the separate parts which must coalesce into the whole. It will not happen yet. But it *will* happen, in due time. And I believe that the disintegration of the Churches is a step in the right direction — a step nearer to the Christ Spirit, whose messenger the Nazarene was, and is.

SEEING IS NOT ALWAYS BELIEVING

The other summer we made the acquaintance of a young man of about 30, and for some reason he started talking about dreams. It transpired that from time to time he had "flying" or "hovering" dreams in which he travelled about and in many of these dreams he found himself visiting his childhood home and district. He thought all this very queer.

I assured him there was nothing queer about it, and he should be pleased that he could remember what were, quite evidently, excursions in his astral body during sleep. At first he looked at me as if I were mad, but as in every other respect I don't give the impression of being in the least mad or even vaguely cranky he became genuinely interested when I mentioned my own experiences in this field.

He was also astonished when he learnt that this was a subject on which many books had been written; that Dr. Robert Crookall, for instance, had published several volumes in which many hundreds of people's out-of-the-body experiences were recorded in detail; and I showed him a copy of

Carrington and Muldoon's book *The Projection of the Astral body* which has become a classic. In showing him the illustrations in this book, where the astral or etheric body is shown rising up from the sleeping physical body, attached by the tenuous and elastic "silver cord" issuing from the top of the head, I explained that this was the *real* body which kept the physical "alive" and which, when the cord was broken, causing "death," persisted as the vehicle of consciousness.

This naturally led to talking about the continuation of life, and as I knew he would have run a mile at the slightest hint of the idea of "religion" or "God," (both of which he associated with the Church's unfortunate image of the one, and anthropomorphic interpretation of the other, which he had totally rejected) I kept the conversation on a purely scientific level. After all, it does not sound in the least "religious" to speak of the invisibility of infra-red or ultra-violet rays, invisible to our limited range of vision simply because their rates of vibration are either too slow or too high for human perception, though these and other-frequency rays are known scientifically and as constantly used as, say, radio waves, and so on.

Well, he went away with two copies of *"Two Worlds"* magazine and two books on astral projection — and now comes the main point of all this. During the past months he has come from time to time to play the guitar with our son. Each time he sees us he promises "to drop the books in tomorrow, or anyway next time." But he does not do so. Why? Because he still has not read them. And why does he put off reading them, while at the same time refusing to part with them? His own astonishing explanation was: *"I'm afraid that if I read them I might believe it!"*

To the question: "But would that matter, if it is the truth?" he could find no reply. Yet the very existence of those books haunts him and bothers him all the time. He is like a dog worrying a bone. It is tempting to have a good gnaw at it, but instead he decides to bury it in the garden! He reminds me of an elderly bachelor I knew who had kept his old Army uniform, complete with medals, locked away for several years in a wardrobe. And there it remained.

"I'm scared stiff of opening that cupboard," he once said to me, "because I suspect that clouds of moths will erupt from it!" So he continued to give the moth he feared (if indeed they existed) the opportunity to feed and multiply for another few years, until he was *forced* to open the cupboard because his landlord was about to demolish the building to make way for a new block of flats. The Great Reaper, so to speak, had pounced out of the blue. (I never did hear in what condition he eventually found his much-prized status symbol, but there is a moral to this story.)

Our guitar-playing friend is fond of saying: "As far as I'm concerned, *seeing is believing.*" Fair enough. So his brave words were put to the test. Catherine, our home circle medium, asked her twin-sister in spirit if she could manage an apport on some occasion, for his benefit. This event actually occured as I was with him, a little way up the drive. Catherine had come up, her walking-stick in one hand, offering him a drink with the other. At that moment a rose materialised a few feet directly above him and fell softly. I myself saw the exact point in space where it "appeared."

Now he knew for certain that no one was in the house we had just left, but after a moment of blank astonishment his material mind insisted that it must have been thrown from the nearest upstairs window. However, not only was the house empty, but *had* anyone even been able to throw it such a long distance it would have arrived at an acute angle, and certainly been damaged by the impact of such a forceful throw, instead of dropping gently in a perpendicular fashion. He acknowledged the logic of this, but still his mind could not really accept it. He departed (with the rose) full of conflicting thoughts, for in his case seeing was *not* believing.

This applies to so many people in like case, who go about asking for "signs" as they did in the days of the Master Jesus, not understanding that conviction and acceptance must first come from *within;* and unless there is an open-minded willingness to acknowledge an *unfamiliar* truth, then any amount of "proof" and "evidence" or signs and wonders will fail to convince. One is reminded of the man who remarked, when first face to face with a duck-billed platypus: "But there *ain't* no such animal!"

It is a human characteristic for people to hang on to what they know or think they know. They resist change, whether in habit or thought. In matters of belief, or non-belief, they hang on for grim death (an apt expression!) even to what they *don't* know: for to believe in *nothing* gives them the illusion of freedom. They prefer not to know, to remain uncommitted, with no strings attached, no responsibilities of conscience and, as they fondly imagine, unprejudiced and "open-minded."

But this so-called freedom is not only an illusion but usually stems from being bound by the chains of fear, as in the case of this young man. Far from being open-minded, he is afraid to open the door even an inch to have a peep through, for having opened it he suspects that he won't be able to shut it again and forget all about it, but will be drawn to go through it and be faced with still more doors to open; and because, in his personal experience, the Church has inculcated into him the negative ideas of restriction, repression, endogenous guilt and "not being able to do what you want to do," he is afraid of losing the illusory "freedom" of ignorance.

Yet it is the truth alone that makes one *free.* To be uncommitted is about as insecure and lonely as being adrift on the ocean in a rudderless boat and without a compass, not knowing which way to go nor having the proper equipment to get there even if one did know. Technically one would have "the freedom of the seven seas," but in reality be a completely static prisoner.

The pearl of great price has to be sought and worked for. It is not handed to anyone on a platter. If it were so, it would be valueless. Of course there is no telling where the search will lead or how it will affect or alter our lives, work, relationships, outlook or former beliefs. One has to have the courage to cast off the mooring ropes, metaphorically speaking. It simply won't do to cling on to the familiar post which made one feel "safe," refusing to let go until one is sure there is another post quite close by to hang on to, like a nervous swimmer afraid to take the plunge and just *swim*.

I am constantly reminded of this by the many Roman Catholics I know who cling rigidly to their religion and even go to confession if they so much as miss a Holiday of Obligation, but at the same time run round from one medium to another, year after year, seeking "proof" or "evidence" which will satisfy their sceptical minds and bolster up their very vague belief in "the life of the world to come." They are rarely satisfied.

One cannot serve two masters. Such people are neither faithful to the tenets of the religion they cling to, nor willing to learn anything about spiritual growth or spiritual laws — or about the complications of communication, which they seem to regard as an automatic tuppence-in-the-slot telephone mechanism. (Would it were so!) They fuss and fume when they don't get connected, and are quite frankly furious when anyone else does, resorting to suggestions that it must just be "wishful thinking" on their part. They become tense with frustration, more and more sceptical — and search for yet another sensitive to book a sitting with!

Their object, alas, is usually a selfish one. A Catholic woman I knew rushed off to mediums and clairvoyants over a period of 20 years whenever she wanted to know what her husband was up to! She hoped to use someone else's psychic gift as "a private eye," and certainly not to learn how to progress in spiritual understanding or to find out in what way she could best be of service. In refusing to investigate the wisdom of the great teachers from beyond the veil, she was wanting to have her cake and eat it, at the same time complaining that departed friends never seemed to "get through" to these mediums, or only in such a nebulous fashion that she was always left "unconvinced" and doubting whether communication was ever possible at all.

To all these dissatisfied and doubting Thomases I would repeat: *First seek the kingdom of God — the Christ within —* and these other things shall be added. As to the young man who finds it so difficult to envisage a spiritual universe or a "divinity which shapes our ends," and for whom seeing is not believing, is he not surrounded on all sides by "signs and wonders," not least by the fact of his very existence as a thinking, feeling human being?

"COME FLY WITH ME . . ."

Our spirit friends have such a nice way of doing things! There was I, dog-tired after a more than usually busy few weeks. In fact I was assailed by the hopeless conviction that however long I might remain on this earth I would never, ever catch up with what I have to do, not least my large mail. How I sympathised with the American lady who put a notice on her door, reading: "On strike — for one day off a year!"

Yet something told me there was one more letter which *must* go off promptly, so it was 3 a.m. when I turned out the light. "No wonder," I thought rather crossly, "I don't remember any out-of-the-body experiences during sleep just lately, if I go on like this. One should be peacefully relaxed. Ah well, I suppose first things come first . . ."

So, setting my alarm for 7 a.m. I fell asleep. And then I "awoke" — to find myself moving along a most enchanting woodland path in the company of a dear spirit friend, Brother Julian. (Before he passed over he was a most unorthodox Benedictine monk, and I had first known him when we were both six years old, his mother and mine being best friends in those days.) And, running back and forth in huge delight, ears back, tail wagging, was our much loved dog Tippy, who left this life in December 1966 after over 14 years of faithful friendship.

When, later on, I awoke in my bed, I could still see my friend's knowing, smugly triumphant smile, as much as to say, "What about *that*, then?" I felt completely refreshed, as one always does after such an out-of-the-body experience, or "astral projection." Many are the times that my spirit helpers have come to the rescue when I have felt very depleted, whisked me out of my body, and taken me to innumerable scenes of beauty in the spirit world, where I have not only met relatives and friends, but also our beloved animals of all descriptions that have passed into the loving care of the hosts of Keepers of the Animal Realms.

Our own particular Keeper is Brother Jo, for animals that have lived together and shared the same homes are usually kept together in the spirit till their human friends arrive — unless taken care of by other family members in spirit who know them.

We have been told that each Keeper has his own "Realm," assisted by many loving, dedicated souls — sometimes those who have longed to have animals during earth life but have not been in a position to do so. Others, (like the farming uncle of Catherine,) were intimate with animals on earth, and find joy in continuing to be so. Those readers who have read my book *Tales of Two Worlds,* will remember some of the stories I have recounted of the animal spheres.

31

As I keep a Psychic Diary, I can look back through many volumes, and in so doing, experience again the never-to-be-forgotten visits I have had the privilege of being given. Often I have been taken in company with Catherine, so we were able to compare the notes we had written down on waking. Sometimes my son Gavin has been taken along, for our spirit friends wanted to encourage his memory of these excursions. Usually, however, he has only remembered some particular aspect or event.

As an example, I will quote from my notebook for Tuesday, March 16, 1971: "Last night had a projection to the Children's Realm — and Gavin came with me. It was delightful. There were great tall rocks to climb, seeming to shelter large sandy pools and little rivers of crystal clear sea water, (or I took it to be sea). Beautiful sunny, amber light. Gavin was joining in with the children enjoying themselves in the water. There were also flowery meadows, and little buildings near by, and pretty, very friendly chestnut ponies trotting about quite freely.

"*Later*. When I asked Catherine about it, this morning, she said she would ask Gretcha (her twin sister in spirit) for she had not been well enough to accompany us herself. This afternoon, on her usual visit, Gretcha confirmed the following, clairaudiently: a) they *had* brought Gavin, too, b) that he saw his brother and sister (never born through miscarriages) and remarked, "Mum, they look rather like you!", c) he had swum in the "Play Pool," and I in the "Refresher Pool," and d) the ponies were for the children's enjoyment, playing among them. I do hope Gavin will remember, even partially."

Gavin was boarding at his school 10 miles away, at this time, and I did not see him till the Saturday, March 20. I wrote under that date: "Gavin *did* remember swimming among rocks in his 'dream' on Monday night, and tried hard to fix it all on waking, but unfortunately much had faded." Which is little wonder, considering the boys had to leap out of bed when the House Mother came to get them up in the mornings!

It was a joke with our spirit friends that young Gavin always made swimming movements with his arms when floating or gliding in his etheric body. I, too, used to do this, for the sensation of flying in a forward position is reminiscent of swimming, and though one can change direction at will, one is still apt to use the arms. On these journeys I have often felt the reassuring hand of one of our spirit friends placed gently between my shoulders. On other occasions I have felt quite independant; or, in most cases, just found myself at my destination.

When I was very much younger I used to have out-of-the-body experiences from time to time. In a particular memorable one I was hovering over an animated, colourful, happy scene of daily life in a city of ancient Egypt. How this came about I do not know, except that one can "time-travel," I suppose. Or perhaps I was shown this for some purpose. In others I would find myself skimming over gorgeous blue mountains, or exploring strange places. Others would just be of floating downstairs, or merely being conscious that "I" was wide awake in another part of my own room, while my body was asleep in the bed.

But for some years now these excursions have been planned by spirit friends and teachers for the purpose of instruction. Thus I have seen the wonders of the Halls of Learning, visited the Temple of Love with its translucent golden dome; and the gardens to suit every taste — lawns and banks of magnificent, shining flowers and shrubs bearing huge blooms, shady bowers and nooks with exquisitely carved seats; massive trees of all kinds, and woodland walks by crystal streams amid the most enchanting scenery one could imagine — and always the happy birds as friendly companions . . .

I have seen the Reception Centres for those who have just arrived and need to sleep for a while, tended by loving souls, and rejuvenated by wonderful colour-rays and music; Education Centres where kindly and expert help is given to those who were mentally disturbed; the Gardens of Rest; Initiation Centres for those under instruction for spiritual work in one form or another; the creation and construction of new buildings by the power of thought; and many other things.

I have also been shown the darker side — the indescribable conditions of filth and degradation created by those who have only fitted themselves during earth life for the lower regions, and exist in a state of appalling, almost mindless apathy, when not engaged in the most unpleasant pursuits. It may be a very long time before such as these begin to sicken, and a desire for escape from these conditions is born. Then, and only then, can the ever-watchful, ever-willing teams of rescue workers from higher spheres *start* to help them, and instil into these deadened souls enough will-power and courage to make the first step towards the light. And how much they have to learn, experience and, indeed, suffer on the way.

At other times I have been shown the most glorious things and places, too dazzlingly beautiful for any earth words to describe. And here I must apologise for being so personal and, of necessity, so full of "I." But these experiences are "first-hand," and although there has been an enormous amount of research done on the subject of astral projection, out-of-the-body experiences, or "ecsomatic experience" (as it is called by Celia Green, Director of the Institute of Psychophysical Research at Oxford), and although there have been a great many most erudite books written about it by "projectors" and researchers, the vast majority of them only deal with what I call the "earthbound projections" of the astral, or etheric body, or "double."

Rare indeed are those who have written about projections to the *spiritual* spheres, either high or low. So as it is this type of experience which I feel readers are most interested in, I can do no better than recommend two most wonderful, fascinating and instructive books by people whose "projecting" over the years make my own exploits in this field pale into insignificance. They are *The Ministry of Angels* by Mrs Joy Snell, and *Excursions to the Spirit World* by F. C. Sculthorpe, with a most interesting Appendix by Dr. Karl E. Muller.*

I must just mention that on one August 28, (my friend Julian's earth birthday) he took Catherine and I to visit one of the Bird Sanctuaries. It was beautiful. Birds of all kinds, many of them with gorgeous plumage, flew freely around us in a lovely setting of trees, and came to rest all over him as he held out his arms. Even during his life-time the wild birds were attracted to come to his outstretched hand, for there was some quality of St. Francis in him. So he takes great delight in visiting these wonderful sanctuaries in the spirit world, and wished us to share the experience.

This reminds me that a kind friend sent me the script of a communication from his wife, now in spirit, through the trance medium of a dedicated private circle, and he has allowed me to quote the following excerpt:

". . . On earth I know birds will feed at your back door, but here the birds will fly to your seat or chair, and they will come and sing to you — and more, they will know your thoughts, and so it is with all animal life. They are in the beautiful parks that we have — they will follow you and keep you company until you ask that they should wander away. The wonder of all this is beyond human conception . . ."

Yet sometimes the wonders of the spirit world are reflected here on earth, for some days ago, "out of the blue," a magpie suddenly came through the open kitchen window, hopped on to the table, and then jumped up to sit on my shoulder as I was cooking at the hot Aga stove! He seems to prefer human company, runs after us as we walk, calls to us when we appear (fluttering his wings in greeting), pokes his inquisitive beak into everything, and settles down to have forty winks on our knee or shoulder, over after-lunch coffee.

Has our friend Julian, the lover and protector of birds, guided him to us — as he once guided a little owl to seek sanctuary from a snow-storm in my bedroom? And who, more than once, has told Catherine clair-audiently when birds were in distress in our garden or wood?

It was the arrival of this cheerful, friendly bird, just after my "trip" to the spirit world during sleep, which lifted my thoughts away from the cares and troubles and tragedies of the world, and which prompted me to invite my readers to lift their thoughts up also, and to "come fly with me . . ."

* * * * * *

Note. It is two and a half years since I wrote the above, and Joey, as we call the magpie, is still with us, as devoted as ever! He roosts in the house at night, and every morning comes into my room and hops on the bed to see if I am getting up. He loves to be stroked, and kissed on

*Both obtainable from The Greater World, 3 Lansdowne Road, London, W.11.

34

the head. He often sits on my typewriter when I am working, riding backwards and forwards on the carriage as I type! He is always interested in visitors, too, though inclined to be jealous of women, for I fancy "he" is a female, for in the spring he bring in masses of sticks and lays them in a heap inside the window-sill of an upstairs room. But though other magpies have tried to entice him away, he remains ever faithful to his human friends, demonstrating the most touching affection and companionship. How "at home" he will be when, one day, he finds himself in the spirit world . . .

I VISIT A "DIRECT VOICE" CIRCLE

All those who have read my book *Tales of Two Worlds* will know who I mean when I mention *Captain Ben.*

He it was who first controlled Catherine, when her astonishing gifts were first developing. It was his great deep voice speaking through her which startled her as she was coming out of her first trance, even before her own guide and teacher spoke through her.

Perhaps it was the family relationship which facilitated this, for he was her great-grandfather on the Cornish side of her Dutch-Cornish family. A towering figure of a man, with reddish-auburn beard and curly hair, like many Celts, and a booming voice. "There were no loudspeakers in our day," he has told us, "we had to use our lungs!"

For he was a sea captain, like his father before him, and he sailed the seven seas. Many are the tales he has told us of those adventurous times — of wrecks, pirates, and even cannibals — while his devoted wife Phoebe waited and prayed for his safe home-coming.

No wonder that now, in her peaceful retreat amid the beauties of the spirit world, she says she still dislikes the sea. It claimed her Ben in the end, for he would never give up, and at the age of 82, when no longer sailing his own ships, he was captain of the Lizard Lifeboat! But on what was to be his last trip, when there was no more space in the crowded, tossing boat after rescuing survivors of a wreck, old Ben gracefully gave his place to a younger man, and the great waves swept him into the heavenly haven. Phoebe followed him very soon afterwards.

Yet he is still doing the same job in another sphere of activity. He leads a team of rescue workers who are always "on call" to help succour those in the lower astral regions and to lead them up into the light. Sometimes, too, *we* have asked him to enquire into the conditions of someone we have known — someone we suspected might be in need of assistance after passing to the spirit side of life. On these occasions he has gladly acceded to our request, located them, brought us news of them, and has been assigned to "tackle" them.

Always, during the years he communicated through Catherine in trance, he used seafaring language and metaphor which amused us greatly at times. "So-and-so is now ready for a hoist up. Can you man the boat?" and so on. Though he never minced his words they were spoken with the bluff, rough kindness of his noble and compassionate heart. As an example, here is an extract from our tapes, when he was assigned to help someone we had known — an eminent Roman Catholic, much *persona grata* with the Vatican, having received many Orders and decorations from the then Pope:

"*My*, what a cracker he is to be sure! But we'll get him. Nobody ever beat old Ben. He seems to think he's still in his mortal body, with everyone at his beck and call — bewildered because now he is alone, and all the pomp and show is nought. He never knew what truth was, even in himself . . . Your prayers will be appreciated concerning this, for he has got to know himself as he was, *and still is*. But yet he *can* be what the spirit of love could make him, when all the rotten old framework of the battered ship is built up and cleaned for sailing . . . He hasn't the courage of a decklouse, the old reprobate!"

Though the words he used were often strong and colourful, they were delivered with the vigour, vitality and joyousness of a great love. He was something of an orator, too. Apparently, when on earth, he used to preach on the beaches — for he did not hold with the churches. "Glory be to Jesus, I never belonged to any of 'em he told us. Here is one more extract from our early tapes:

"The Great Spirit be with you. He directs your efforts, inspiring you in all your ministrations. His the will to comfort the afflicted, the sick, and those in need, trying to enlighten the ignorant, and giving courage to the tired ones. We are here to help direct, and to prove to the unbelieving that there is another world when the mortal life is done. This one is much better — beauty beyond words. As I used to direct my boat, so does the Great Spirit guide and lead into the calm waters of peace. Through the storms and conflicts he brings safely through the willing ones . . . We from the spirit world have passed through the storms, but our labour goes on, guiding and directing the old battered vessels into safe harbour. Glory to the eternal Spirit of Life which enables us to do so. Keep on top of the wave of Truth, and your feet will find the Rock which will hold you safely . . ."

Dear Ben. How we miss his booming voice, and the voices of our many other friends and guides these last few years since Catherine's heart condition made trance impossible, and her age and health problems necessitated her entering a Home. We can always call on them, of course, knowing they hear us, but it is very one-sided after the daily contacts we became so used to in previous years.

It was with great anticipation, therefore, that my husband and I and our son Gavin, recently attended a Direct Voice seance with the famous medium Leslie Flint, for Captain Ben told Catherine that he would "have a go" if he could, and if conditions allowed. Conditions are not always favourable for a variety of reasons, including the variation in the health of the medium who, for the phenomenon of Direct or Independant Voice must have a lot of vital ectoplasm for the spirit "mechanics" to call upon.

Mr Flint, as is wellknown, has dedicated his life to this rare form of mediumship, and the first time I attended one of his amazing seances was some 35 years ago. On that occasion at least 20 different voices "came out of the air" and conversed naturally and happily with loved ones. It must be a difficult and strange experience for the communicators, especially if quite unused to it, for we are told they have to put their faces into an artificial larynx, or etheric "voice box" built up with the aid of the medium's ectoplasm. When they are trying this method for the first time they cannot tell if their voices are getting through or not, so it is important for the sitters to answer and converse, and reassure them that they can be heard.

There were ten of us in the group, and we waited about half an hour, keeping up a desultory conversation with Mr Flint (who no longer needs to be in trance) before we were interrupted by Micky's voice greeting us. Micky is the medium's "doorkeeper" and master of ceremonies, and speaks in a young, boyish voice, for though he is advanced and experienced in spirit he likes to retain his earth personality when communicating, and he passed over when quite a lad during the first Wold War.

Now he had something to say to all of us, often making us laugh with his quick wit and pertinent remarks. He said there was an enormous crowd gathered round, on the spirit side, including a beautiful black shaggy dog. He introduced one speaker after another, both men and women, who all wanted to converse with their friends or relatives who were present. It was so entirely natural. "Well! I never thought I'd ever speak to you like *this!*" said one. Sometimes the voices were strong and clear, while others were more like hoarse whispers, though plain enough to hear. We all had our tape-recorders switched on, and at one point, when Gavin was trying to turn the tape over in the dark he was very amused at Micky's remarks about his fiddle-faddling. "Are you having trouble over there, mate?"

I would not presume to describe the personal conversations which took place between the sitters and their loved ones in spirit, for these were intimate, private things. Though I will just mention happy news from a little girl who drowned, and equally happy news from a lad who was killed on his motor-bike and wished a message passed on to his mother by one of the sitters.

There was one communicator, however, who knew no one present and who amused us vastly, for he must have been a still-prejudiced, somewhat earthbound person who had slipped in. He told us his name was Pat Shaughnessy, from Donegal, and he said "this sort of thing" was all wrong and should never be allowed! In his village, he said, there had been those who had attended "spook meetings," and the priest had told them they would be damned in hell! (Yet here he was, apparently happily taking part in what he called a spook meeting!)

Another communicator also amused everyone by complaining in no uncertain terms about the method he had to use, saying querulously, "Can't they invent something better than this?" Well, they are always trying.

Then came the moment we had hoped for. Micky said to me: "There's someone called Ben. He's quite a character, this Ben. A rough diamond, I'd say. He's laughing all over his face. He says he knows you and your husband and your son, and he only comes to see you in your home. He says he's Ben. A big fellow . . . He was, I think, a captain on board ship. He's a real character. A seafaring type."

Then we heard Captain Ben's excited but hoarse voice, as if he were shouting for all he was worth down a bad telephone line: "Hallo, hallo, *hallo!* bless you all! And you, laddie! Hallo my boy, how are you? It's difficult to . . . Hallo, can you hear me? . . . Yes, everyone's well and happy. No need to worry about US. *We're* alright. How about YOURSELVES?"

I asked him if he could give us a helping hand with our work. "I'll do what I can, but I must say you've got your hands full one way and another. But you'll come out alright, given time. Gavin, Gavin, how are you, laddie? Growing up . . . Don't go to sea. I don't advise that . . . I'm afraid I'm not too good at this sort of thing, not this method. I got so used to coming through the other way. It's so much better the other way. If I get in the habit of talking to you in this way no doubt I'll be able to speak a lot better than I do now. It's very difficult . . . Yes, Geoff's here, and all my mates. Everyone's here . . ."

"And Gretcha?" I asked. (Gretcha is Catherine's twin sister who was killed during the invasion of Rotterdam in 1940. She was, of course, a constant visitor to Catherine and to us, and still is. She also adopted Gavin, calling herself his spiritual godmother.)

Then dear Gretcha made a valiant effort to talk to us, in her heavy Dutch accent. "I don't know if I can manage it . . . it's very complicated. Better later. I get more used to it. So happy, you know, to be here. Hallo, I am here — Gretcha. Yes, with Ben, with Ben. It's complicated . . . I just want you to know I am here, ya, I am *here* . . . Gut!"

A beautiful modulated and fluent woman's voice broke in here. It is said to be that of the actress Ellen Terry, who for many years has communicated at Mr Flint's seances. She told us: "Even though perhaps a person may have been so used to communicating in some other fashion, perhaps over a long period, through a certain instrument or medium, when they come for the first time they find great difficulty as the method is so different, transmitting as best one can one's voice and personality, and the message as well, trying to remember past events and circumstances, trying to convey so much in a strange method. Like so many things, practice makes perfect. And I think most of *your* friends have been coming for a long period in an entirely different way . . ."

For the sake of brevity I have had to omit and condense what took place and what was said. For us, as well as for Captain Ben and Gretcha, it was as tantalising as trying to have an important telephone conversation on a bad line. But yet how splendid and gratifying it was to hear their very own voices, and I do thank them for "having a go!" And as Micky seemed anxious for young Gavin to come back another time, our friends may put in some practice in the meantime.

I was not able to take the tape-recording for Catherine to hear for a couple of days, but of course Ben and Gretcha had told her all about it clairaudiently, and how all our friends were there in force, and apparently laughing their heads off at Ben's and Gretcha's efforts!

May their laughter and happiness be infectious in this rather grey world.

CONCLUSIVE EVIDENCE

It is often said by unconvinced psychic researchers that the fact that a clairvoyant can have a vision or picture of a person who has passed over is not proof of survival, because knowledge of that person is in either the conscious or subconscious mind of the sitter. It could therefore be a form of telepathy between sitter and medium, they say; and further argue that by this means a thought-form can be built up which the clairvoyant sees and mistakes for a "living" spirit person.

It is indeed true that a thought-form *can* be built up in the mind of a sitter, in the same way that a writer creates a character, and this has at times been used by unscrupulous and ignorant newspaper reporters to try and "catch out" a medium. They have created in their minds a purely fictitious "Aunt Sally," have told the clairvoyant that they hope to get a contact with this invented relative, and when the clairvoyant has "seen" the thought-form (as has occurred on one or two occasions) the reporters have immediately and gleefully dubbed the medium a fake.

This is extremely unfair. Although an experienced sensitive knows very well the difference between a thought-form and a real person in spirit, sensitives are not machines, and it is possible that through tiredness, pressure of work, or perhaps some emotional upset or worry which interferes with concentration and the required amount of discrimination, a mistake could be made. But this is *extremely rare*. Were it not so, we would not so often be disappointed, when visiting a clairvoyant medium, that the person we *so* hope will "put in an appearance" and of whom we hold a picture in our minds, in fact fails to do so!

39

The following case, however, would seem to give *100% proof of survival* to the most sceptical researcher — or, indeed, to any objective-minded person. The evidence is absolutely conclusive. This remarkable story is best told from the written account of it by H. Norman Hunt, who was a party to it. In deference to the wishes of some of those involved the proper names have been altered, except that of Edith, who is known to me personally. She was a member of Norman Hunt's circle, and was herself gifted with extra-sensory perception. I quote:

"On May 17, 1955, Edith remarked: "There is someone who is trying to give me her name. I hear her saying that she was Matron of a hospital in Norwich and that she has not been very long dead. She is trying to give me her name in full.""

The process of arriving at this name was interesting. Edith insists that she does not "hear" in the common, auditory sense, but that letters and sounds "come into her mind." The whole name was built up slowly and laboriously, but when it was complete, Edith had a strong sense of conviction that it was correct. The name received was *Eileen Mary Hewlett*.

Edith then relayed the following: "I was a Spiritualist, just as you are, and I would like some of my patients to know of this communication. I would especially like my brother to know; I had several sisters but it would be useless trying to tell them."

As Edith could not relay accurately the name of the hospital, I wrote to the Civic Centre at Norwich asking for a list of hospitals in that city. This was kindly supplied and we were confronted with the names of nine hospitals, three of which were identical but had different street addresses. At Edith's request, I read these names aloud and, as I came to one of them, she said: "That's the one; I heard the name of that street."

I then wrote a letter to the Matron of this hospital, asking whether at any time someone named Eileen Mary Hewlett had been Matron there. I received a reply saying: "Miss Eileen Mary Hewlett was Matron of this hospital for 10 years. She died last November" — i.e. six months earlier. Thereupon I wrote again, explaining fully the circumstances, and expressing the hope that this remarkable piece of psychic evidence should be passed on in whatever quarters it might be useful. To this letter I received no reply.

On June 10, Edith reported that Miss Hewlett was again making contact and was saying: "The letter has gone to the wrong person; she is keeping it to herself. You will not receive a reply, but do nothing for the present. There is another woman in the picture and I am working hard to get her to see your letter. Please concentrate your thoughts on its not being destroyed."

On July 26 Miss Hewlett added further pieces of information. "I did not die at my own hospital but at another. I had a very dear friend who is still alive; her name is Ruby. She is unmarried; at present she is ill but when she is better you will hear from her." After considerable effort it became clear to Edith that the full name of this friend was *Ruby Mottram-Shaw.*

On August 9. Edith remarked: "I have just seen a most vivid picture. It was as clear as if I had been present. I saw a man walking along and the lace of his right shoe was untied. He tripped over it and fell heavily in the street. I haven't the least idea why I saw this nor with whom it has any connection." (Please note the date of this "vision" — August 9.)

On August 16.Edith once more reported contact with Eileen Mary Hewlett. She said: "She wants you (Norman Hunt) to repeat your name and address slowly and distinctly. Please do so several times." I complied, but Edith could not feel sure if we had been successful. A week later I was asked to do the same thing again, and this time Edith was reasonably certain that it had "got through." *"Eileen says that you will receive a letter from her friend Ruby which will make everything clear."*

We had now two names supplied by Edith's clairaudience — Eileen Mary Hewlett (Matron) and Ruby Mottram-Shaw (her friend). The first of these had been verified, and we could but hope that the second would prove equally factual. Consider, however, the fantastic request that I should repeat my name and address aloud to an unseen listener entirely unknown to anyone present! Consider further that this unseen person proposed to make an effort to impress this name and address on the mind of someone who was asserted to be in a named Manchester nursing home!

The reality of telepathy, at any rate between living and "dead" persons, would seem about to be put to a crucial test. Our first thought had been to write a letter to Miss Ruby Mottram-Shaw, but Edith "heard" Eileen Hewlett's voice begging us not to do so but to wait for a letter from Ruby herself. We were indeed happy that we had not done so when, on October 4 — after seven long weeks of silence — I received a letter from the Manchester nursing home, signed *"Ruby Mottram-Shaw!"*

It is interesting to note that Ruby had received the impression that she was dealing with a woman (as in fact she was) for the letter was addressed to "Miss Hunt." My address therefore had got through correctly together with my surname, but it would appear that my Christian name had been "overlaid" by the sense that the origin of the message she received had been a female one. The letter was as follows:

"Dear Friend, I feel I may address you thus. I was a very close friend of Mary Hewlett. We 'indulged' in the philosophy of survival and promised to prove survival to each other. Seven weeks ago . . . (this brings us back to August 9, the date of Edith's 'vision') . . . I sat quietly, inviting Mary to speak to me. For no apparent reason I thought of Mary's brother whom I had not seen for years. I had in fact a vision of him — tripping over his shoelace. He crashed heavily to the ground and I heard Mary's voice, clearly and distinctly: 'Peter has arrived.' A few days later, Mary's sister informed me of their brother's death, due to a head injury caused by a fall. I accepted this as Mary's promised proof of survival. I told the Matron of this nursing home. She then told me in strict confidence of a letter which her sister-in-law (who was Matron of the . . . hospital in Norwich) had received from a stranger and then followed extracts from your letter.

"I knew that some misunderstanding had arisen — Mary would not wish to prove her survival to anyone at her hospital. My attempts to obtain name and address of the writer failed completely. Both Matrons have strict orthodox beliefs and are not prepared to 'give the Devil a helping hand.'

"I visited three mediums with no result. I then attempted my own communication in Mary's fashion — automatic writing — but I could also hear and feel. If this letter reaches the right person it will bring me proof of my own mediumship.

"You will be glad to hear from me and have this confirmation of your own outstanding mediumship. Mary wanted to prove her survival to me and has succeeded. Tremendous efforts must have been involved and I wish to thank you for your efforts. I am deeply grateful to you. I look upon you as a friend and not a stranger; I seem to know you so well; fairly young, vivacious, passionate, very sincere, unattached — am I right? (The description given of Edith is an accurate one.)

Yours sincerely, RUBY MOTTRAM-SHAW."

Edith thereupon wrote to Miss Mottram-Shaw and later spoke to her on the telephone. Various small points referred to by her friend Mary but not mentioned in the letter, were confirmed. It was true that Mary did not die at her own hospital but at another. She herself had had a serious illness (as we had been told) but was now recovering. As a direct result of this revelation of psychic activity she had lost her job, but had secured another which involved her going to Central Africa. This, from our point of view, was a most unfortunate circumstance and more especially so when it turned out that her depature was only a matter of a day or so.

The particular value of this case lies in the unshakeable fact that absolutely no knowledge of the existence of either Eileen Mary Hewlett or Ruby Mottram-Shaw, let alone the circumstances of their lives, could conceivably have been present in the mind of Edith or in the minds of any other person taking part.

Further, as if to establish once and for all the reality of telepathy, there is the strange experience of giving one's name and address to "the empty air" and of its being received by the one person for whom it had immediate significance. Finally, we have the striking fact of two persons — utterly unknown to each other — simultaneously "seeing" an accident which had actually taken place — and on the same day!"

It is a pity that the Matron of the hospital and the Matron of the nursing home, who were sisters-in-law, should be so averse to publicity (and this was made clear to Edith in her telephone conversation with

Ruby) that names and places should have to be given in disguised form. But the facts remain unshaken. This case, which will stand up to any kind of investigation or analysis, can only be ignored by the most wilful determination to stop one's ears to the truth — the wonderful truth of continuous life in whatever sphere of manifestation.

FOR THOSE IN THE VALLEY OF THE SHADOW

I seem to have received a lot of letters lately from people who have "lost" someone very dear to them, many due to accidents. Every time I read such a letter, and my heart goes out to identify with them in loving sympathy and compassion, I send forth two heartfelt prayers. One asks for strength and comfort to be directed to the person who is suffering. The other is on behalf of the one who has passed over.

This, of course, is no more and no less than what any Spiritualist would do. Little enough, you might say. But for the benefit of those who ask, "How can I best help my loved one?" I would like to quote from a communication from someone else's loved one on the Other Side:

"I never knew what prayer was until I came here. It is *the* force that operates in my world, as electricity does in yours. *Prayer materially alters our conditions. When you pray for those who have passed on it is like giving them presents: you alter conditions that can be changed only by the force of prayer.*"

Another communicator said: "We need your prayers here, just as we needed them on earth. It is one of the saddest mistakes to think that when we die the tie is practically severed with those on earth, and that loved ones left behind have no longer any *power to help* those who have "gone on before.""

The first message was from a husband in spirit life thanking his wife for her prayers. All of us *can* have that power to help, some, naturally, a little more than others, according to development, though the strongest power of all is *love*.

The worst barrier of all, when a transition has recently occurred, is the dark, desolate wall of grief and gloom that surrounds those left behind. Oh, I know only too well how difficult it is to transcend this vacuum of personal loss, when everywhere we look there is a poignant reminder, whether it be a pair of beloved slippers, a pipe or a powder puff which will never be used again.

But we have to *live through* this period by continually calling on the power of the spirit to lift up our consciousness, and to give us the strength *not* to let our thoughts dwell on the mundane things, on ourselves and on the ache which seems to bore physically through the centre of our solar plexus. We must bear in mind that this not only causes a barrier, but also distress to those we love. It is therefore selfish and a form of self-pity, however understandable.

How comforting is this further message from the same communicator to his wife. He told her that during sleep her soul gladly floated away from her physical body and the material world, along with "ministering spirits" into "one of the beautiful spheres of light and love." There, even if she did not remember it on waking, they had been together.

He said: "As psychic development proceeds, you become conscious of these journeys. The memory of what you have seen and heard is a priceless possession, a foretaste of the glory of the life-to-come. But it is not always wise for these spirit journeys to be too well remembered. The contrast would make life unendurable, so in mercy it is often veiled from your minds." This happens often, maybe, but not always, as I know well myself.

In cases of sudden transition, such as in a "fatal accident," there is usually complete continuity of consciousness. I remember when Hughie Green, of television fame, had a bad car smash. He described later how he (the *real* he) had been close by, watching the ambulance men and other helpers extricating his unconscious body. The only difference, in his case, was that he returned to his body, and woke up in hospital.

Exactly the same thing was experienced and told many times by pilots in the war who were shot down into the Channel, consciously jerked out of their bodies at the impact which rendered them physically unconscious, before they were rescued and "lived to tell the tale." But thousands of those who have been *permanently* separated from their earthly bodies have also "lived to tell the tale" — from the world of spirit.

Mrs Alice Gilbert's son, Philip, was bicycling through the new Forest one night when his wheel hit something in the road which threw him off with a crash. He told his mother (whom I know personally) that he picked himself up off the road, wondering why he did not even feel bruised by such a thud. Looking round, he noticed that all the forest trees seemed to be lit from within, with myriads of tiny cells of light running up their trunks. It was a beautiful sight.

While it was dawning on him that he must be out of the body (for he had fortunately gained much knowledge from his mother, who had been receiving psychic training over the previous two years) he suddenly saw his grandfather standing there, to greet him.

Then he knew for certain what had happened — and somehow was not even surprised. His "soul" had always known that his earth life would not be a long one. For the last two months after leaving the Merchant Navy in which he had served when very young, during the war, he had just put off deciding what he was going to do, meanwhile enjoying a holiday at home with his mother.

(I don't beleive there are really any "accidents" or that anything

44

happens "by chance." This thought may be a comforting one to those who allow themselves to be tormented by thinking, "*If only* this . . ." and "*If only* that . . .")

Philip was delighted to see his grandfather, who had "died" several years before. But his first desire was to go back to the house where his mother was awaiting his return. So his grandfather accompanied him to the front door. Philip tried his hardest to press the bell, not unnaturally with little result. Yet his mother, upstairs, *did* hear "something." Opening the window, she called out, "Is that you, Philip?"

Then he experienced the frustration of not being able to shout back to her: "Yes, it's me! *And I'm all right!*" He knew the shock his poor mother was to face a little later, and prayed that her knowledge and faith would sustain her. Then his grandfather took him away to his own bright home, to introduce him to his new world of experience.

Yet every day he, and others, gathered round his mother. Owing to her trained gift of reception, he was able to communicate with her from the third day after his "death," and on over the years. He gave her an enormous fund of information which subsequently formed the substance of remarkable books, now, unfortunately, out of print.

As Philip quickly became established in his new sphere of activity he took on the job of helping other sudden arrivals. He told his mother: "I find myself more and more busy, for events, railway smashes, air accidents, seem to be incessantly precipitating crowds of bewildered persons over here, but most of them are more or less routine.

"People are very ordinary in most cases. One just appears to someone, usually in one's uniform, talks to them, tells them they're dead, studies their reactions — usually amazement at finding they are more alive than ever— and, according to their intelligence, one gives them a lesson in thought control and skimming" — floating swiftly.

"Some take to it like a duck to water. Others are stupid and surrounded by a mass of firmly fixed thought images into which one cannot penetrate. Most want to go and help their families, or someone they love. One has to explain the difficulties they will encounter" — meaning the inability to make their presence felt, seen or heard.

This desire to visit the family or a loved one before anything else is so natural, isn't it? The longing to assure them, if they possibly can, that they are still "there," alive and free, and still loving them; not extinguished and lost to them for ever.

Some time ago a man's spirit form appeared to Catherine. He told her his name and that he had passed over from a heart attack on the bus going to work. As his children went to the same school as our son Gavin, he was most anxious we should contact his wife, give her and the children his loving thoughts and reassure her that he was all right. Then he would be content to go with his helpers to have a recuperating sleep.

Having promised to do this for him, we felt bound to take the risk. I looked up the address in the telephone book, for I had never heard of the family, and wrote her a carefully worded letter, explaining that we lived with a most gifted medium. I told her what had occurred and of her husband's great desire for her to have his message of comfort, love and assurance which we felt obliged to pass on.

Our spirit friends subsequently told Catherine that she was secretly elated on receipt of my letter, but unfortunately she showed it to a friend who was advising her in her unhappy situation. This man took it upon himself to ring me up and literally "tore a strip off me". He said he had told the poor woman to burn my letter at once, and that it was a terrible thing to contact the newly dead, "as it held them back from progressing to their rightful place in the world to come."

In fact the very opposite is the case! Firstly, the man who "died" was a stranger to us and had contacted us, or rather Catherine. Secondly, he was only ready and willing to "progress" *after* he had first done his best to send a message to his wife, for this was the foremost thought in his mind. I am glad we kept faith with him, for I am sure his message did comfort his wife, despite the unnerving abuse I received from the family friend.

One cannot over-emphasize the importance of sending out loving thoughts to those recently passed over, as well as prayer, especially on behalf of those who were either entirely ignorant of any after-life or had very hidebound or orthodox ideas on the subject.

The following communication is typical of so many. It is from another husband to his wife and refers to a mutual friend who had recently passed on: "*I don't think you have any idea of the extent to which your thoughts helped her. We are extra sensitive to the thoughts of mortals, especially in the early days when our minds hover between the earth we have left and the new land on which our feet are not yet firmly planted. In that between condition we need constructive, helpful, loving thoughts.*"

Another communicator says, "Prayer rings up the legions of unseen helpers and guardians . . ." And still another message from one in the spirit world says: "In this land we are much more sensitive than whilst on earth. When thoughts are directed to us by mortals we have a direct call from those currents of thought thus generated.

"We are practically always able to come in close contact with the person who is thinking of us. When near, and acclimatised to his conditions, we can impress thoughts and ideas upon his mind. He will think they are his own normal thoughts!"

I beg those people who are suffering the pangs of separation from those they love to realise, and *know,* beyond a shadow of doubt, that there is no real separation — except in the physical sense. This last is hard to bear, I know, but must inevitably be minimised by the knowledge that life is continuous whether in or out of the dense physical condition.

We are not bodies with spirits, but immortals who temporarily take on a mortal body, with all its limitations. It is like donning a very heavy overcoat for a period and for a special purpose, and then casting it off, to be free again.

How wonderful it is to *know*, even though we may be walking at this moment in time through a deep, sombre valley where the sun does not seem able to penetrate, that a glorious reunion will be ours in due course, as surely as the sun rises after every cold, dark night. It is as certain as that.

TRYSTS

Dear one, from the dawning
Of the day
When I must slip away
Into the Morning,
Into the Summer Land,
I will wait
Beside that gleaming Gate
To take your hand.

And often, when you sleep,
We will walk
On emerald grass, and talk —
Our Trysts we'll keep.
You will be brave and strong
 With me so near;
Nor will you doubt or fear —
It won't be long . . .

(First published in *The Spiritual Healer* magazine.)

THE SCIENCE OF LOVE

It is really laughable — were it not so often annoying — how truths one has known for so long are suddenly "discovered" with great astonishment by "experts" in some field. Thereupon new bodies are set up to consider the matter, new journals appear and, inevitably, new laboratories for further research into whatever it is.

Soon after my husband and I started dairy-farming nearly 25 years ago our herd surprised everyone by consistently being top of the County in the National Milk Records, and went on to yield the highest average for Jersey cows in the United Kingdom for six years running. The County "experts" organised a Farm Walk, on one occasion, bringing a crowd of

47

people to see our herd and system of management.

"To what factors do you attribute your very high yields?" asked the County Officer — who had never so much as lifted a dung-fork in his life, let alone calved a heifer in the small hours. He expected erudite answers about food rations, intake per gallon, and so on. But my husband, addressing the crowd, replied: "Well, I consider the most important factor *is to be liked by one's cows*."

There was dead silence while the County Officer's mouth fell open. It was obvious that he considered us slightly round the bend, and thereafter we were spared any further "walks," and continued to top the records unmolested.

Now comes the sequel: I read recently in the farming press that a new body has just been set up, cumbersomely called The British Society for Agricultural Labour Science, and their new journal is obtainable from Work Science Lab., Dept. of Agriculture, Reading, Berkshire. What are they investigating so laboriously? Why, the influence of a herdsman's personality on milk yield!

It has now been established "scientifically" by "the study of two herdsmen in depth" that one consistently obtained 20% more milk than the other. I quote: "It seemed that the herdsman *whose cows liked him* got the extra milk." The piece ends with the words: "But *why* the cows liked him the report did not say."

I can tell them quite simply, without recourse to any "study in depth" or any science — except the Science of Love. In other words, this herdsman obviously loved his cows, as my husband and I loved ours — personally and individually. We cared for each one's individual character and needs — and how different they all were! We could even read their thoughts.

For love *is* a science. It is *the* fundamental Law of the Universe, and there is nothing in existence, in any dimension or in any form, that does not respond to its application, or react to its demonstration. Even an engine. If the average tractor-driver had used my husband's 25-year-old Ferguson, it would have been sold for scrap about 15 years ago, whereas it is still as willing and game as ever. He loves it and would never part with it.

Whether it be a car, a mower or a tractor, if one drives it with the same feeling, understanding and consideration (I could say, companionship) that one rides a horse, it will last indefinitely. Perhaps some would think me odd, but when I put my 15-year-old mower away after mowing a large expanse of lawn, I cannot help giving it a pat and saying, "Good old mower!" And having arrived home safely after driving through the night, I find myself patting the wheel of my little car and saying: "Good girl!"

Why not? One is told from the spirit world that when metal and wood or other materials are made into something, whether a house, a machine or a ship (and here every old sea-captain will agree), that object takes on a "personality" of its own. So that, in the aggregate of its assembled parts, it, too, within its limitations, responds to the Law of Harmony and Love.

Plants, being far more sensitive than minerals, naturally respond to this law in a more spectacular manner. The late Dr. C. E. Last, author of *Man in the Universe,* produced meticulously checked records and conclusive photographic proofs showing the difference in growth between prayed-for and unprayed-for plants.

The Rev. Dr. Frank Loehr, of Los Angeles, a religious scientist, wrote a book called *The Power of Prayer on Plants.* Mr W. B. Higgs, a Scottish agriculturist, spent over 40 years studying the significance of the power of prayer, and proved beyond doubt its practical application to his large agricultural practice. And a South African surgeon, Dr. J. D. Pearson, likewise proved the difference between pots of seeds which he blessed, and pots of identical seeds which he ignored.

One could quote innumerable examples, for this is surely a wellknown fact. We can also prove it for ourselves. Prayer, or blessing, genuinely and sincerely practised, is a vibrational out-going of a divine and compassionate Force — which is Love.

There is scarcely need to reiterate, therefore, the effect of outgoing love on the vastly more sensitive animal kingdom, and the response evoked by it, both in terms of physical well-being, mental stimulation, and emotional reciprocation. This naturally varies according to evolutionary capacity, but can be of an unsuspected degree in the (seemingly) most unlikely of creatures.

The effect of true, compassionate love in human beings can be miraculous indeed. It is literally true that "Love makes the world go round," for if the outpouring Love of God, the Creator, the Great Spirit, were withdrawn for a split second, the world and the entire manifested universe would disintegrate and cease to exist — except as primordial potential. We *are* because God *is.* And God is Love.

We must always keep in the forefront of our consciousness that all matter, and all form, is *materialised spirit.* One could say that, having "incarnated," and descended the downward arc of *in*volution into dense, slow-frequency spirit (i.e. matter), the whole planet Earth, together with all the life to which it offers hospitality (whether mineral, vegetable, animal or human) is struggling now to climb the *e*volutionary arc towards *spiritualised matter.*

We are privileged to live in most vital times. A great stirring is taking place, on all levels. As White Eagle tells us, the Spiritual Heirarchy is drawing very close in response to the cries and invocations of a large section of Humanity.

Do not let us be despondent or depressed or negative in our thinking, because, when one stirs up a pool by much movement, the slime and mud is disturbed and many dark, obnoxious and evil things come to the surface. This must be so, and rightly so. Only when darkness and evil are brought to the surface and seen for what they are, can they be overcome by the Light.

All the teaching from the spirit spheres which is coming through in innumerable places throughout the world at this time, speaks of "the great awakening," "the great changes which are even now taking place," "the working out of the Plan," the growth of the New Age, a new release of energy which will precipitate the Earth into the Fourth Dimension, the raising of vibrations, both physical and spiritual, and so on.

One teacher says: ". . . the knowledge being spread now is preparing for the change into the new dimension the world is now entering, that of the fourth density." Another says: "Your world has now reached the end of its span of turmoil, of its revolving away from God; and now coming into full force is the might of God and the gradual process of uplifting has now begun.

"The preparation that has been going so long in time, here in this outer world, is now ready, and *with assistance from those in tune,* will make firm contact with the Earth. The linking up of the two worlds will become stronger now . . ."

And again: "We, from the Other Side, grow ever nearer to you; the veil gets ever thinner." And ". . . the line between science and the realms of other worlds will become extremely thin.

"There will, too, inevitably, be world turmoil and unrest. Try not to let your thinking and hope turn from the positive at such times; try to hold within you the knowledge that all that is happening is part of the final working out of the pattern. Try to learn to see beyond the immediate agony and suffering, both of the world and of the individual."

Stress is also made on the linking up, even if only in thought and aspiration, with all the groups and centres of light spreading like a network over the globe. Belong, if possible, to one such group — it matters little which, so long as the object is not so much to receive (for this comes automatically) but to *give,* to "send forth the Light," to concentrate on the blazing Christ Star pouring its light on to the world and irradiating the hearts and minds of mankind.

A teacher says: "It is often difficult for you to imagine the way in which the spiritual attunement of individuals and groups can affect physical conditions. We can only assure you that it does . . .

"Perhaps the most important word to remember is the word Harmony. Strive to become harmonious in all levels of thought and living, and you enable yourselves to work and be worked through . . ."

"It must often seem that what one life can give and do is insignificant. This is not so at all, for what one life — one soul — gives is magnified and expanded many times by a constant mirroring process. What you give forth consciously to the cause comes to us upon a ray of harmony and light and, as we use that ray, so it is taken up on ever higher and higher planes, and is expanded and magnified many times . . . each individual is of the utmost importance to us."*

You may think I have come rather a long way from cows. But the Law of Harmony, and what I like to call the Science of Love, applies equally to all life and to each moment of living.

It matters not in what circumstances we are placed, or how "insignificant" we feel ourselves to be. A cripple in a bed-sitter can contribute to the awakening of the world, to the thinning of the veil, to the spiritualisation of matter, and to the upliftment of mankind.

So, may I suggest that we ponder over the prayer of St. Francis, and strive to make it our own:

> Great Spirit, make me a channel of thy Peace;
> That where there is hatred — I may bring Love.
> That where there is wrong — I may bring the spirit of Forgiveness;
> That where there is discord — I may bring Harmony.
> That where there is error — I may bring Truth,
> That where there is doubt — I may bring Faith,
> That where there is despair — I may bring Hope,
> That where there are shadows — I may bring Light,
> That where there is sadness — I may bring Joy.
>
> Grant that I may seek rather to comfort — than to be comforted;
> To understand — than to be understood;
> To love — than to be loved:
> For it is by giving that one receives;
> It is by self-forgetting that one finds;
> It is by forgiving that one is forgiven;
> It is by dying that one awakens to eternal Life.

Gildas Communicates by Ruth White and Mary Swainson (Neville Spearman Ltd.)

THE PROBLEM OF POSSESSION

"Like one possessed". How often this expression is used in common parlance — and how often it is literally true! Far more often than anyone would imagine.

Of course the materialist would deride the possibility of any such thing, for a materialist is unhappily in the position of a man living on a very large estate surrounded by a high wall. In his preoccupation with the life of the estate he has quite forgotten that any wall exists, so he does not even seek for a door in it.

When, from time to time, he hears people talking of a world of activity beyond his domain, he thinks they must be either mad, lying, or deluded by strange fantasies. The thought that *he* might be deluded, or ignorant, and his life most limited in consequence, would not occur to him. However clever he may be at his job, this wall not only limits his own life, but limits his field of service to others — especially should he be a psychiatrist.

For the percentage of people in mental hospitals suffering from possession must be very large. Theirs is indeed a tragic situation, for if the possessing spirit were removed, these people would be perfectly normal. Moreover in so many cases the plight of the possessing entity is equally sad.

For what is possession? Put simply, it is this: we all have a vital or etheric body the same shape as our own, which usually protrudes a couple of inches. This is what is usually seen by clairvoyants and mainly denotes our state of health, vitality, or lack of it, and general condition. But *beyond* this, each person lives within an oval, egg-shaped "aura," or evelope, or magnetic field, generally extending two or three feet from the body (though vastly more expansive in the very highly evolved, about whom we need not concern ourselves at present.)

Within this aura are bands of colours which, when tranquil, reflect the spiritual status, and range from the muddy dark reds and browns of the low-evolved up the scale to the clear blue, violet, pink, amethyst, primrose and fresh green mixtures of the truly evolved, which is indeed a lovely sight.

This oval aura constantly changes with the thoughts and emotions, the higher variety augmenting the beautiful colours, the base or evil ones doing the opposite; while sudden fear, jealously, or "seeing red" with rage, for instance, floods it with lurid colours and jagged shapes, and sets it all a quiver with agitation.

Now it is this ovoid envelope which can, in certain circumstances, be invaded by an earthbound spirit, or even more than one (like the poor man whose possessing spirits made him shout to the Nazarene "We are legion!"). Who are these spirits?

There are many categories, and among them some merely very "earthy" people who have passed over suddenly, do not realise the fact since they are still "alive," are quite ignorant of any after-life, and immediately cling to or possess the body of anyone who has what is called "a leaky aura." (this is caused by various factors).

In some cases it has been known for the possessing spirit to imagine the body is quite his own, and be furious because he feels the *real owner is the intruder* who will not let him alone, so is constantly trying to drive him or her out! When this occurs a perpetual tug-of-war is going on in the patient, who fluctuates between one personality and other, "hears voices," argues back, has fits of temper, depression and so on, and whose life is made miserable and out of control.

52

Dr. Carl Wickland's classic book *Thirty Years Among the Dead*"* gives innumerable case histories of possessing spirits who were removed from patients (often in the first instance by electric shock treatment) and then took over his wife's body — Mrs Wickland being a first class trance medium. In this way he was able to talk to them, hear their stories, convince them little by little of the (to them) amazing fact that they were "dead," and to open their spiritual eyes sufficiently for them to see other spirits who were trying to help them — sometimes their own mothers — and thus persuade them to go with them.

All these "interviews" were recorded verbatim over the years, numerous names and addresses given by possessing spirits being checked and found to be correct, as were the details given of events prior to their "deaths." Often the patient would be present while Mrs Wickland was entranced, and have a conversation with the spirit who had formerly been his or her most unwelcome guest.

Many were the causes of these spirits being earthbound and leaching on to a living person. Some had been either drunkards, drug addicts, criminals or suicides; some vicious, entirely selfish and coarse; or merely ignorant and frightened at finding themselves "living" but without a physical body. Sometimes the possessing spirits had themselves been possessed during their own lives, and this was often so among the suicides. One explained that he had not wanted to take his own life, but "a man was always with me who forced me to do it — and then, when I saw my body lying on the floor, he laughed."

In such a case the victim, having taken his life "while the balance of his mind was disturbed" — in other words, during a kind of black-out when "something came over him" — is so outraged and resentful at being cheated out of his body by some gloating low spirit, that his one aim is to get back, and as he cannot get back into his own body, quickly finds someone else's to attach himself to, and live through. Thus the pattern repeats itself.

It must be remembered that the physical and astral planes intermingle, and by the law of attraction we all attract spirits of higher or lower degree, according to what we ourselves are, and in line with our habitual thought patterns. If we try to live on as high a level as possible by keeping a check on our undesirable traits, "forgiving those that trespass against us," offering kindness, wishing to serve our fellows, never harbouring ill-will, we automatically attract those from the bright spheres to aid us in our endeavours.

Quite simply, we offer no attraction to low-grade spirits, and open no door for them either to enter our auras or to impinge their influence upon us. If they put in an appearance in passing, they are soon sent packing, to seek more fruitful ground for their vicarious pleasures and malicious

---

(The Spiritualist Press).

enjoyment. But where there is hatred, anger, ill-will, vice, drunkenness, cruelty, criminal tendencies, etc. there they will be found crowding in, feeding on these loathsome emanations, egging on the weak to give in still further to their weaknesses, and obtaining gleeful satisfaction thereby.

One spirit teacher tells us: "These souls do much harm wherever they find an atmosphere into which they can proceed to instil their own particular form of poisonous misdirective force. Therein is shown the great danger of allowing *small* faults to creep up on one until, suddenly, evil and chaotic influences pour in, and disrupt even the good endeavours of the — at first — *careless* people.

"It can be seen that not only the earth people then become sufferers, but that evil or ignorant earthbound souls are also retarded from progressive direction; for these souls cannot break themselves away from the scene of action which appeals to their base, crude thought forms; and any help which is offered by strong, highly placed spirits, is often brushed aside."*

The fearful cruelty of the savage and dehumanising wars that are taking place in various parts of the world at this time is not only creating thousands of earthbound spirits seeking revenge, but is in part created *by* them! This is a sobering thought. Violence begets violence, in *all* spheres. This is explained most dramatically by the leader of a band of high spirit workers. Their task was to deal with the aftermath of a massacre . . .

Another high spirit of much power had been able to draw the victims away, still dazed, from the hideous scene on Earth, and now this great mass of people were lying down or wandering about in a stupor on a barren, rocky plain in the astral world, over which hung a cloud of mist, in which streams of dull red and murky slate-green moved. There were 3,000 men, some 2,500 women and about 1,000 children. I will quote (all italics are mine):

"These people had been vilely done to death. They were not very highly attuned spiritually, except some few of them. Were they to be suddenly awakened out of their stupor there would be an outburst of frenzied rage on the part of some three-quarters of their number. These would swamp the others and *the upshot would be a panic and a stampede in fear and hatred back to the scene of their massacre. Here arrived, they would, in turn, enrage their still incarnate fellow-countrymen and the slaughter would be renewed by them against their ill-users. This would be avenged, and so the horrid tale of woe would be prolonged.*

"Our objective was to prevent this catastrophe. But the means to that end were not so clear. Every one of these victims was a free-willed being. Free-will is sacred, and may not be gainsaid. Each of them must be given opportunity to choose which way he would go, and what he would do.

Poised for Flight transcribed by Madeline Dingley, Oakdene, High Steep, Jarvis Brook, Crowborough, Sussex.

And this choice must be made with full knowledge of what had come to pass. We must not hinder that choice, or in any way deflect it out of the line of freedom. All we could do would be to ensure that the choice be made in conditions favourable to wisdom.

"In their present state these people would not be able to use their reason, but would be blinded with rage and terror. For were they fully to regain their bearings at this moment, the last emotions felt in the flesh would break out in the spirit . . . *Then that violent uprush of unholy emotions would transfer them back at once to the earth-plane* which would, by its strangeness, affright them. For it would be weirdly strange to them viewed for the first time from the spirit side. Yet they would sense their murderers . . . Then would ensue one of those hell-scenes on Earth which, whether enacted singular or in company, so perplex men from time to time as to motive, and the extent of the fiendish cruelty attaching thereto. We on this side see the origin of such events."

There is no space here to relate the lengthy process of their gradual awakening, or the methods used to achieve this, after great thought, inspiration and guidance from still higher spheres. Suffice it to say that they began with the children. One by one they were roused, and led to a specially "created" fresh meadow, full of trees and flowers, in the company of a gay, smiling, most highly evolved spirit boy.

Later, they tackled the women, also one by one, *most* of whom were so taken up with finding and fondling their children, waiting for them in the meadow, that hate left them. But unfortunately not all of them, for there were a few in whom lust for revenge outweighed maternal emotions . . .

The men created far the worst problems, and even with the help of the most spiritually evolved among them, who had been wakened first and, after much discussion, lent their aid, there finally remained a hard core (among them some women and some priests) so consumed with hatred that they refused to turn away from earth to explore their new surroundings, but returned to do what harm they could; and the communicator adds: "before gravitating to their own hells for winnowing and refining. *Yet only to those of like mind with them in wickedness would they be able to do hurt.* These are they who make your Earth a place of sorrow, my son — to make sad the heart of an angel — where it should be a very pleasant place."*

How vitally important it is that mediums and sensitives evolve *spiritually* as well as psychically — for there is a world of difference between being spiritual and merely being psychic. Subtle temptations can assail even the most highly motivated without constant self-examination, not least of these being vanity, and a sense of power. Such character defects can easily be seized upon by an unscrupulous

---

*Outlands of Heaven. (Vol. V of The Life Beyond the Veil) by G. Vale Owen. (The Greater World Association).

earthbound spirit seeking to undermine any *good* work.

The saddest thing of all is when a gifted, dedicated medium over many years will not accept the fact that his or her gift may be declining, perhaps through age or health, and out of vanity is tempted to indulge in even *one* deception. That one deception can cause incalculable damage, for it immediately casts doubt upon the integrity of all that has gone before, and can shatter people's faith in what has heretofore been completely genuine. It is like an infidelity in marriage. One slip or lie which has been discovered immediately makes the partner wonder: how many others I don't know about?

Many, many people of all types and states of evolution are psychic without being aware of it. They have "a loose vehicle of vitality" and, being quite ignorant, this can result in what is called "a leaky aura." Being unaware of it, they cannot protect themselves, and would not know how to, anyway. (This is often so among criminals and those addicted to lust and vice). They are especially vulnerable through their own character weaknesses unless they make determined efforts to reform.

Even in giving way to despondency, depression and continual negative thinking we are laying ourselves open to the undue influence (if not worse) of low spirits seeking to leach on to any morbid state or atmosphere. It therefore behoves us all to hold the good, the beautiful and the true always in our minds, to lift up our hearts in loving goodwill, to turn to the light, to try to give *out* light, to spread happiness — and never to lose our sense of humour! There is no laughter, not even a smile, in the lower regions. Joy, laughter, and love belong to "heaven."

THE RESCUE OF THE EARTHBOUND

Everywhere one turns in the Spiritualist scene one finds reference to innumerable healers, healing services and healing circles. It is excellent that this is so, for there can never be enough dedicated healers. But it does accentuate the fact that there would appear to be a shocking lack in another most important sphere of service: rescue work.

Is rescue work only done in private home circles, and therefore seldom heard of? I believe this to be so — insofar as it *is* done — for the members of our own spiritual service group on the Other Side have repeatedly bemoaned the almost total lack of facilities and means of co-operation open to them for use in this vital work. In fact our spirit friends have told Catherine, our medium: "If only there were *millions* like you, there would still not be enough!"

But unfortunately rescue work in our own home circle had to be abandoned after Catherine's coronaries, and indeed all trance work virtually ceased, and all psychic work drastically curtailed owing to age and health which is very sad, but inevitable in the circumstances.

There are now an increasing number of priests who undertake exorcism, usually in cases of haunted premises, but occasionally in cases of living people possessed or obsessed by the intrusion of unwelcome guests in their auras. Though this latter departure should be welcome (I mean the growth of work in this field, not the departure of the unwelcome guests), it is also fraught with dangers and difficulties, in my opinion. For the mere fact of being an ordained priest, of any denomination, does not give the power to exorcise — *unless* the priest possesses the necessary "gift." And although some priests undoubtedly have a latent psychic gift, there are few who would have any understanding of what they were doing in "casting out" so-called evil spirits. Into what state would they be casting them, without themselves having a working knowledge of the various conditions which pertain in the next spheres of life? They might well cast them, metaphorically speaking, from the frying pan into the fire — or into another person's aura.

The 58-page report of the commission set up by the Bishop of Exter on exorcism, which has taken 10 years to compile, makes it obvious that the official Church (irrespective of many enlightened individual clergy) not only wants exorcism to be "a closed shop," but takes a ludicrously medieval view of Spiritualism, listing in its types of hauntings: "Demonic interference, usually at desecrated sites . . . *and in connection with seances*."! (My italics). So it seems that intelligent and knowledge-able clergy are still voices crying in the sandy wilderness into which the ostriches of Officialdom continue to hide their heads.

I should like to see a dedicated Rescue Circle sitting weekly at every Spiritualist Church in the country, as well as in all Groups which meet regularly. That this is not so can only be attributed to the fact that there are not *nearly* enough trance mediums available. I often think this, in turn, is largely due to the iniquitous burning and drowning of psychics in the past, for the psychic gift is mainly hereditary, being related to certain factors and enzymes in the make-up of the physical body. Thus we, and countless souls in desperate need, are suffering from the ignorance and sins of those dark times in our history.

Though many sightings of "ghosts" are merely the momentary tuning-in to a thought-form imprinted on the ether by some violent emotion of fear, hate or anguish experienced in that place by someone in the past, yet very many persistent, noisy, or generally troublesome hauntings are all too factual, and are caused by earthbound entities caught up in a web of recurring "dreams" and unable to escape owing to shock, intense emotion, ignorance of what has happened to them, or in some cases of guilt-ridden people, the stark terror of "Judgement."

These latter ones feel safer in their own self-created prisons, clinging to old sites, associations and earth experiences, rather than risk breaking loose only, as they fear, to be brought to some awful Judgement Seat for their "sins," real or imaginary. It is terrible to think how many ministers of the Gospel of Love are responsible, especially in time past, for sowing the seeds of fear by teaching an abominable hell-fire creed, and preaching "the vengeance of God."

Incidentally, while reading a book called *The Restless Ghosts of Ladye Place* by Harry Ludlam, which contains a number of authenticated hauntings, I was struck by the lack of imagination (and therefore the selfishness) of the people disturbed by these hauntings. In nearly every case they were only interested in getting their rates reduced, or being found other accomodation — never sparing a thought of compassion for the plight of the haunting entity!

Even on the very rare occasions when a sensitive was called in, and the "ghosts" appealed for help (in one instance two lovers: ". . . help John for me! Help us to rest!") no one appeared to make the slightest attempt to *talk* to the earthbound spirits, explain their condition to them, let them get their story off their chests, or give them the necessary help to be released into their proper spirit spheres.

All too often "psychic researchers" are called in — in the mistaken belief that they are Spiritualists, or psychics! They are rarely either. And, researchers are apt to turn even ghosts into "guinea-pigs," merely to prove or disprove a theory.

How wonderful, then, to turn to that beautifully written and most moving account of the successfully performed rescue of an earthbound young woman in *The Heavens are ringing,* by Ivan Cooke.* This intensely interesting rescue case was achieved many years ago through the mediumship of Grace Cooke, (among countless others she performed), with the co-operation of her guide and teacher White Eagle, and others from the spirit side of life. The actual conversation with the unfortunate girl was conducted by Ivan Cooke, and other sitters.

Driven to a frenzy of loneliness and despair by the cruelty of others, over a hundred years ago, she had smothered her much-loved babe, and then thrown herself out of the window. Her sense of "wickedness" was only matched by her terrible fear of God, even of Christ, and it is significant that in this case a Minister of the Church was also earthbound until he had seen the joyful release of this poor soul and her ecstatic reunion with loved ones in the light . . . I advise anyone interested in rescue to read this compelling and revealing little book.

It is as well, when considering such cases of earthbound spirits, to remember that "time" as we know it does not exist for them. In fact released spirits usually express utter astonishment that so much earthly time has elapsed — and are quite often fascinated by the changes that have taken place! This was certainly so in one of our rescue cases — that of a

---

White Eagle Publishing trust.

delightful young couple killed while eloping by carriage in 1764. They had been earthbound in our Pond Field ever since. In those days the road, which winds down a very steep hill towards marshy ground, had not been built up by banks as it was later. In fact only in the last year or so has it *again* been widened and somewhat straightened out, being considered dangerous. And this couple were being chased . . .

I described the case in my book *Tales of Two Worlds*. The girl, Louisa, frequently came back to visit Catherine in her gratitude, and was fascinated by seeing cars, and even such "modern" domestic items as rubber hot water bottles! She told us where the old smithy was, (which proved correct), and described the life and doings at her home, a beautiful stone mill-house in a nearby valley of the Forest, the picturesque remains of which have recently been broken down as being unsafe. Likewise the large lake, in the centre of which was an island she loved to row out to, has in recent years been drained by the breaking of the huge dam, for local people who used to swim there have told us that too many got drowned in the currents.

She told us where to look for the remains of the cottage by the stream, where their old housekeeper lived with her husband who caught trout for their breakfast — and there I found it, the red-tiled kitchen floor, almost hidden by grass, the cottage having been demolished. How pleased she was, too, that I brought back a slab of stone from the mill, and that my husband transplanted some of the flowers she loved, so we now have a patch of "her" blue and white "soldiers and sailors" in our glen. Of course she is now united with Trevor, her loved one, in perfect freedom.

Not all earthbound spirits are either noisy, or cause any disturbance, or are "local." Many are attracted by a medium's light, and are unconsciously directed to this light by those higher spirits anxious to help them but who are unable to penetrate their consciousness direct, imprisoned as they are by their own mental darkness which creates a barrier around them. As our guide said: "We strive to enter, *but we must have help from mortals.*" We are so much closer to them in vibration, being on the earth plane.

It is therefore up to all mediums to offer all the help they can when any wandering spirit is clairvoyantly seen. Such was the white-robed nun whom Catherine saw on three occasions in our garden. She asked her guide about her, and was told: "She is Sister Anastasia, one-time Prioress of Dingley Priory, earthbound since 1867. Can you help? She was attracted by your light."

I will not repeat the story of this rescue, which I told in *Tales of Two Worlds,* except to say that when this gentle Sister returned to give heartfelt thanks she said through Catherine in trance, and I quote from our tape-recorder: "May God bless you, my sister, for your help to me. I am now safe, and among friends. *There are few to help such as I, on earth* . . ." She has become our loyal friend, and is happily engaged in the

Children's Realm. Indeed, I have myself "met" her and talked to her, when taken on an astral projection to that Realm, but that is another story.

Many, many are calling for help, and mediums are few; mediums are very busy people, and already over-worked, and all may not be suitable for such work, anyway. And if the earthbound spirit enters the medium in trance, and is violently emotional, the sitters must be experienced and responsible, as well as the medium's band of spirit helpers and protectors. But it is such *worthwhile* work, and brings such *joy,* not only to the released spirit, but to those who have been used as instruments, in whatever capacity they have served.

Ivy Northage, the well known medium, deserves to be most warmly congratulated for creating a school to develop mediums. May she not neglect the vital subject of rescue work in their training! Meanwhile we can *all* help by remembering the earthbound in our prayers — and those who may well become the *new* earthbound every day: the suicide, accident and murder cases we read of in our newspapers. Before we turn over the page, let us send forth a quick but sincere prayer for light to enter their darkness and confusion, for such a little act of love, by many, is most potent and can breach the dark walls to enable angels of mercy to enter. We cannot be reminded to often by our spirit teachers that no act of love, no selfless prayer, is ever lost; and as White Eagle says: "There are so many of them (distressed spirits) which must be touched by you earth ones."

RESUE FROM THE LOWER ASTRAL

In the last chapter I touched upon the rescue of the earthbound, albeit very briefly, for the subject could fill volumes. The same applies to rescue from the lower astral. These spiritually dark regions are filled with those whose earthly lives have been dominated by the lower self, with all that this implies in terms of vice, depravity, cruelty, greed, negativity, rebellion, pride, hypocrisy, hatred, bitterness, selfishness, the lust for power over others — in fact one or many of all the things that are etched on the *reverse* side of the coin whose other face is Love.

Yet however low the human spirit sinks, even to the depths of solitary darkness where there are no longer any victims to torment or "get the better of," there comes a time — and that time may be hundreds of earth years — when rebellion at its own self-inflicted state sets in.

I know of a case where the turning point came by just *one* outgoing thought, not of self, entering the mind of one obsessed with pride, arrogance and power. That thought was the sudden memory of sunlight on the Nile . . . and with that memory, a piercing nostalgia for the light, an anguished cry, utter humiliation, and the start of the slow climb through gradual self-awareness, remorse, suffering . . .

That was long, long ago, for that once-proud, over-ambitious, intellectually brilliant high priest (at whose approach the "common people" had to step off the side-walk), who plotted to become more powerful than the Pharoah and was knifed by his competitors, who left his body to the vultures, is now one of the great Teachers from the high spiritual spheres, so filled with the love of the All-Father that he appears as a shining, vibrating light to those good people in the lesser planes of beauty unless he "cloaks himself down" to make himself visible to them.

Through this Teacher's remarkable trance instrument I have been privileged to listen to countless tapes of difficult rescue cases, some of them spanning weeks and months, which were brought to this particular circle at the instigation of the leader of a rescue group on the Other Side. This leader, Black Hawk, had deliberately turned his back on the glories of his own sphere to dedicate himself to this noble and arduous task. He is but one of millions.

It may be asked why it is that co-operation from people still living on earth is so often necessary and indeed vital in obtaining desired results at a given point. The answer is twofold: firstly, the vibrational gulf between the ministering spirits and those in the darker regions is far greater. Though help is always at hand, these self-imprisoned souls are unaware of the closeness of ministering angels — for this is what they call any discarnate people who are trying to help them. When they (the imprisoned ones) have *reached* the point of seeing them, their brightness and aura of light in contrast to their own darkness or greyness makes them think of them as "angels." Often these "angels" have themselves been rescued and brought into the light, and then, when they are strong enough, long to help their erstwhile companions. Under the protection of a band of higher spirits, and often with the co-operation of a rescue circle on earth, they help to wipe their own slates clean by this willing form of service.

The second reason why earth people are necessary is that we possess the semi-physical "vehicle of vitality" in our total make-up, sometimes described as "something of the earth," or "earthly vibrations," and therefore very much nearer to those souls who need help, for they themselves have retained this "vehicle of vitality" whereas it should *normally* have been discarded about three days after death. The shedding of this semi-physical etheric body is called "the second death," or "re-birth" into freedom. (It occurs to me in passing that this may well be part of the reason why it was "on the third day" that Jesus was able to manifest his transmuted body of light, then freed from the "vehicle of vitality.")

Many of those in lower astral conditions still do not realise, even after hundreds of years, that they are "dead." They have continued to lead the same (usually degraded) life in astral conditions which are to them, of course, as "real" as earthly conditions are to us. One very snobbish, titled, arrogant but impeccably well-spoken Regency "buck" who "found himself" in the sitting room of this particular rescue circle, (having been whisked, so to speak, into the trance instrument), thought it strange indeed that ladies were present, and would not deign to converse with the leader of the circle till he was allowed to address him at least by the title of knighthood, not being in the habit of talking to those of lesser degree!

As of old, he occupied himself with "gaming, wining and wenching." Asked how long it was since he was at his country estate, he became a little vague: "Some time . . . some time . . . but I'm well content where I find myself, thank you. Except that I am mightily plagued by some low Sicilian fellow whose pretty little wife once pleased me in passing, don't yer know, and he is for ever after me to kill me. Fortunately he has not yet found me. Apparently he imagines I was in love with the girl, or some such nonsense! How could a gentleman of quality be in love with *canaille!* The insolent fellow must be mad. But I admit I find it an inconvenience, you understand."

It takes tact and ingenuity on the part of sitters to start to convince such a man (who had no love for anyone, even his mother) of what he called "the astonishing proposition that I am dead!" Week after week he came to converse ("It makes a pleasant change, for I confess I often find my usual companions a trifle boring.") The circle persuaded him to seek out friends of theirs (helpers on the spirit side) between his weekly visits, and even to ask for one called Black Hawk, who they told him he would find interesting. ("Ha! A noble savage! That should prove diverting. Rest assured, however, that since you inform me he is a friend of yours — strange as it appears to me — I shall comport myself like a gentleman.")

Eventually he was brought round to accepting the truth, but only after sinking to lower conditions among people he found intolerable. After an interval, during which the circle wondered if they would ever hear from him again, a very changed, humble, pleading, suffering voice spoke to them. Almost too ashamed to speak, he hardly dared to hope he still had their friendship after the pompous, dictatorial and condescending way he had treated them formerly.

Concurrently, the case of the Sicilian consumed by revenge was also dealt with. Finally, the two men met, and the Sicilian was enabled to join his patient and loving little wife at last; while the former nobleman, having been purged somewhat of the dross, started to help others in like condition to what his own had been.

This case, so sketchily told, took a long time and was very complicated for it also involved "Mother Meg," that dragon of a brothel-keeper who catered for such as the nobleman, and where ignorant, weak girls were kept in subjection, not having the courage or will-power to escape from her clutches even if they wanted to — and not all of them did.

This woman had been carrying on her old "service to the gentry" since the time of Charles II. She proved a tough, violent case at first. Once the spirit operators had to withdraw her instantly from the medium as she tried to strike one of the sitters in a rage. Her language was abominable. She was finally softened by their finding the one chink in her armour: that she had once been a mother . . . Somewhere in the spirit world were those who had been her children. Suddenly she wept for the first time in centuries.

"Mother Meg" is now no more. Instead, a glowing "Sister Margaret" sallies forth on rescue missions. She has been through the mill, she knows it all — that hard, bitter crust, and the greed, and the power. But now those souls she succours say of her: "Sister Margaret is an angel!" One of her girls, too, touched by the redeeming love of Mother Meg's "chuckerout" in her old establishment, was also brought into the light together with this tough but goodhearted admirer who genuinely loved her. She, also, returned after a period to persuade the other girls that beautiful realms of freedom did exist, if only they had the desire and will to reach them.

The potential is always there — that diamond of divinity which has been brutally battered, or encrusted with filth, or embedded in the hard rock of sin. As this circle's Teacher said so often: *"The cork must rise — eventually."* But how worthwhile it is to help it to rise sooner rather than later, sometimes *so* much later (during which time others are dragged down.)

I strongly recommend anyone interested to try and get a copy of one of the most remarkable books I have ever read.* This is all the more fascinating since the brilliantly-acted television series, "The Six Wives of Henry VIII" has brought this cruel and violent period vividly to mind.

Canon Pakenham-Walsh, a most lovable character who passed over in 1960 at the age of 92, became strangely obsessed with the Tudor period as far back as 1917, and especially with Anne Boleyn, about whom he wrote a play to prove her innocence once and for all. (This obsession was not in fact so strange, as it turned out, for here indeed was a case of affinities incarnating at different times, as was confirmed by him subsequently in communications received since his transition.)

By the most extraordinary series of apparent coincidences and "chance" happenings, while knowing nothing of psychic matters, he was led by the persistent Lady Anne into becoming the earthly pivot around whom the eventual rescue of Henry VIII (and others) was at last effected — 400 years after his life on earth, during which interval he had spent much time "sleeping" in a kind of nightmare.

Most unusual was the fact that during these years this whole affair not

---

A Tudor Story by Canon W. S. Pakenham-Walsh. (James Clarke, 1963).

only took the Canon to a variety of unusual places (as evidential "tests" set by Anne), but was conducted through the agency of *several* high-calibre mediums one after the other, none of whom had any knowledge of the other's previous part, and all of whom were astonished by the personages contacting them and using them, and indeed keeping them very busy.

As can well be imagined in such a period of intrigue, plots, fear, weakness, (yet often incredible bravery) and acute suffering on every side, it was inevitable that very many other characters of the time were involved and made their appearance also, some in the light, some yet in darkness, but all bound to each other, whether by the bonds of guilt, hatred or love. The one person who, though quite free, could not achieve true happiness until she had helped Henry was his first wife, Katherine (of Aragon) who truly loved him.

There is no space to write further of this intricate and absorbing story, except to say that, once again, children had a softening influence. The episode when Henry, having been at first incredibly arrogant and indeed alarming, has progressed enough, — by true penance, suffering, slow self-realisation and striving to assert his higher nature, — to be shown his two sons whom he longs to see, is very emotional.

These two sons are, of course, Edward VI by Jane Seymour, and the still-born son born to Anne Boleyn — still-born prematurely through the shock of finding Henry closetted with Jane — and the main cause of her immediate incarceration in a country castle while still ill, followed by removal to the Tower, farcical trial, and execution only 4 months after this unfortunate birth. Henry married Jane the very next day. (His two sons were of course shown to him as young boys, though naturally they had matured and "grown up" in spirit life.)

The mediums who played such a large and vital part in this long drama were, in order of appearance, Mrs Clegg, Miss Kelly, Mrs Hester Dowden, Mrs Blanche Cooper (through whom, in 1925, Anne spoke to the Canon in the direct voice) Mrs Crawford Smith, Mrs Monson, Miss Martin, and finally Mrs Estelle Roberts through whom, in 1953, Anne told the Canon (whom she always called "my Champion") that the book of these events was now complete.

She urged him to make Henry's request known to the people of England. That request was that he should not merely be thought of and remembered as he was in the dark days of his earthly life — the excesses, cruelties and sensualities of which, incidentally, people still like to gloat over! — but (and I quote his words): "I beseech thee to give heed to my request, let there be some record made that those who come after shall read and know that Henry, once King of England, did repent . . . A while ago I was enraged, torn with distress at what I had been taken to see, that horrible picture of my past . . . 'Tis my punishment — I accept it — to see these ghosts out of my sinful past, but as I grow stronger in the knowledge and understanding of the Love of God I shall learn my lesson and strive to

64

win back other souls who have erred in like manner as myself."

On this occasion he was surrounded by his queens, Mary Wyatt, Wolsey, Sir Henry Norris, Sir Thomas Boleyn, Sir Thomas More, Cranmer and many others, and he says: "Surely this group of those to whom I, as King and man was both cruel and unfaithful is of itself sufficient proof that my repentance is no vain boast. There was a day when these now gathered round me shrank with horror and flew terrified at my approach, so strongly did my evil deeds still — I must use the words — stink in their nostrils. And now, by the mercy of God . . . my tears of anguish have washed the stains of sin from my robes . . . ."

Let us now think of him thus. And also remember that this long and painful transformation and eventual triumph of his higher self only came about through being brought into contact with earth conditions, and earth people, through earth mediums.

OUR REAL SELVES NEVER SLEEP

Everyone talks about how busy they are; how much there is to fit into a day — or try to fit in, for an awful backlog always remains. "If only the day were 48 hours instead of 24!" we complain, and I confess I am among the worst offenders in this respect, at least with my mortal mind. We think our daily chores and activities and work so important that we often tend to regard sleep as a necessary nuisance.

Yet our activities during sleep are really far more important. We are our true selves during the sleep of the physical body. The mind never sleeps, nor does our etheric body. It merely withdraws, and our minds continue to function in another dimension, in other spheres, and in a variety of ways, according to the people we are.

Mrs Alice Gilbert's son Philip, an advanced soul who left his earth life through an accident as a very young man, as mentioned in a previous chapter, had many interesting things to tell her on this subject in his daily communications to her. After seeking information from a higher entity, he says:

"Sleep life is in some ways a mirror of post-death life. People who are not very 'spiritual' — that is, who have no conscious aspirations towards evolving into Universal Harmony, people whose whole preoccupations are material, to do with earth affairs (and there are millions and millions, the greater proportion of mankind, so far) never get in sleep further than the lower astral plane (not the lowest, unless they're very evil.)

"There they wander, in a confused blur of their own and sometimes other people's thought-images and symbol pictures, with now and then an encounter with the less evolved. They meet their real self with its inner desires. So psycho-analysts are quite right when they claim to judge a person's repressed wishes by his dreams, so long as they allow for the fact (and few do!) that not all the memories brought back from sleep *are* from the lower astral. If the patient is clearly of an idealistic or highly intelligent type, then his 'dreams' may be true visions.

"For people who are beginning to evolve emerge from the lower astral in sleep, and enter the reality of post-death life. They travel astrally, and their subconscious mind picks up impressions . . . But very rarely do they remember anything of this . . ."*

In this last statement I feel that he errs somewhat, for one only has to read Dr. Robert Crookall's books to realise that innumerable people experience most vivid and detailed conscious astral projections, including the departure of their etheric body from the sleeping physical, and its return.

I myself have been singularly fortunate in this respect on very many unforgettable occasions, and have described something of these projections in *Tales of Two Worlds*. Once, too, as I merged with the physical body, which then awoke, my etheric sight saw the outstretched hand, palm upwards, of the spirit friend who had "seen me home" — such a shining hand!

Another time, when just returned from a visit to the gardens surrounding a Teaching Centre, the fantastic, brilliant, glowing, scintillating colours of those abundant banks of flowers still shone before me for a brief moment before fading away — as if the lights had suddenly been dimmed on a brightly lit stage. It is impossible to describe their unearthly irridescence.

Some years ago I was conscious of receiving much teaching during sleep, and for this I had to be asleep by midnight — in time, as it were, to join my class. I must also have studied books in the Halls of Learning, for so often I was "still reading" as I awoke, endeavouring, in vain, to hold on to the words as waking overtook me.

In this I am in no way exceptional, (heaven forbid that I should give any such false impression!), but am merely one of "the lesser sleepers" referred to in the following interesting excerpt from a book of teaching which was given to me many years later:

"The travellers from Earth, when sleep overtakes the body and the inner self is released for this travel, are on many planes of intellectual progression. Some are of high degree . . . Their work takes them into the high spheres, during earth sleep, and during this refreshment of spirit, new inference is put into perspective concerning the duties willingly undertaken during the present earth life.

"Therein is the reason why Leaders return: to accept another birth and life on earth so that good can be constantly performed by them, in a

---

Philip in Two Worlds by Alice Gilbert (Andrew Dakers Ltd.) unfortunately out of print.

particular setting and series of duties.

"The lesser earth sleepers, with minds and real selves in flight to other lands are to be found either in training zones or spheres, working on particular subjects; or in travel to even farther spheres, wherein the continuance of training is taken up during observation of life in diverse conditions.

"The Earth — could this but be seen — is a vast terminus, in constant use for the comings and goings of visitors, guests and relatives — home returning and revisiting alike. One day the scene will become visible to the outer eyes, not, as now, only acceptable to the inner consciousness when 'awake in sleep.'"*

Naturally, this is not regularly so, for if people are *mentally* (not physically) tired, their etheric body does not rise above the astral or near-earth plane, and they bring back a weird and confused "dream," often reflecting symbolically their inner conflicts, worries and anxieties in a series of thought-images. Sometimes these reach far back into childhood traumas and conditionings which still lurk below the surface and can be "triggered off" by some daily happening or emotion.

How very different is the true projection! Especially a "journey" arranged for us for a special purpose; even, sometimes, as a warning of some great change in our lives. Here, symbolism is also used, but this time by our higher helpers or guides, to "break the news" gently, as it were.

An 85-year-old reader has given me his kind permission to quote a remarkable experience he had one night. Before doing so, I would like to say that he and his dear wife had been most happily married for 56 years, and for 38 of those years had worked closely and harmoniously together in a small Health Food Stores, where, as he put it, "the smallness of the business gave us time to help the troubled ones that came to us with their problems." His dream, or rather astral projection, was as follows, in his own words:

"I found myself in a delightful shady glade: the tree-tops were out of sight, but I was greatly impressed by the stately grace and strength of the trunks, standing like columns of living marble, yet very much resembling the red pines of America.

"My attention, however, was soon focussed on the round pool of clear water right in front of me, and the two feminine figures some yards away on my left, one of whom was my wife. Her companion I did not know, but there was something most impressive and dignified about her appearance. She was tall and beautiful, with a long dress of dull gold which, in sunlight, would be very bright.

"As I wondered who she could be, I was surprised and horrified to see my wife lie down and begin to drink the water of the pool. If the water was

---

Poised for Flight transcribed by Madeline Dingley, Oakdene, High Steep, Jarvis Brook, Crowborough, Sussex.

clear, I felt it was not safe to drink, and fear came over me as I tried to call to her: 'Don't drink that water!' But my voice would not come — some external power kept my lips from moving. The situation was now dangerous, and the only way to prevent my wife drinking from that water was to run round the pool and drag her away before it was too late.

"Again some mysterious power frustrated my attempt, for instead of running round the pool, I found myself on high ground, looking out towards a landscape of rare and breath-taking beauty. The scene was completely changed from the glade with the pool and its trees, and my feelings also were very different. My lips were no longer sealed, and I called out gleefully: 'I've been here before!'

"Before me was a land of mellow sunshine filled with hills uncountable, their peaks rising up to the azure sky. They resembled sparkling pyramids alight from within with colours all their own — sky-blue, irridescent green, and rainbow purples prevailing. From various centres I noticed wisp-like streams of vapour floating gently across the hills, and somehow I knew that where the vapour came from, the dwellers in that glorious land lived in townships and communities.

"I continued to gaze in rapture and delight on the amazing beauty of the extensive landscape, so full of refreshing, vibrant air and clean pure light, and I woke with it all vividly impressed on my mind. The thought never occurred to me that such beauty had a message of sadness and loss for me until three months later, when the dearest one of all passed rather unexpectedly, leaving me bereft, dazed and lonely . . . Now I believe the wondrous land I saw from a distance is the home-land in spirit of my wife, where she will be rewarded for her very honest and selfless life on earth."

This was not only a gentle warning, to prepare him for the coming separation (though his mortal mind did not wish to accept it as such at the time), but also extended to him a most wonderful message of comfort and encouragement — for in other astral projections which he had experienced many years back, he had visited what he calls "his Land of the Hills," and had truly "been there before."

The beautiful female figure in the gold robe was his wife's guide, who would watch over as she came "to drink the waters of Lethe," and we have since been able to assure him that she has been sleeping peacefully for a while, being rejuvenated and re-invigorated by the healing rays directed upon her, and the healing vibrations of unseen music.

However, my old friend (for he has become my friend though we have never met) passed through a great ordeal, which is but natural. He wrote, "To be compelled to go on alone seemed like getting a savage sentence for not committing a crime." His sense of loss and loneliness was augmented by the fact that during the period of his wife's "sleep" he neither felt nor experienced any contact with her, waking or sleeping.

I begged him to be a little patient, for I knew that where there was such a bond of true love and harmony there can be no real separation. I knew that she would soon be preparing their new home "in the Land of the Hills," to have it ready for his arrival presently, as any good wife would do. And I knew she would somehow make her presence felt by him, as soon as she was able to do so, if only he could keep on keeping on.

Imagine how happy I was to receive a further letter and to learn that he had now had unmistakable evidence of her loving presence beside him in their home, and several clairvoyant glimpses as well, including one most precious one.

"I feel elated," he wrote, "which will keep me going until I have *earned* further blessings. It is far from all sadness now, and I see a purpose and meaning in two people separated, instead of going over simultaneously, as she always hoped . . ."

Also, he has twice been shown the vision of an archway, reaching from the floor to the ceiling. This is assuredly the archway (though with no view beyond it at present) through which he will one day step into that familiar Land, and a blissful re-union. Meanwhile, in allowing me to write a little about him, he hopes that others whose dear ones have gone on before, may find comfort.

In the next chapter I would like to tell of the prodigious amount of "work" which many people undertake, during the sleep state, in helping those less fortunate ones in the astral regions. Never let it be said that the time we spend "sleeping" is a waste of time! It can be supremely important.

GOING ON "NIGHT DUTY"

It's strange (and yet not so strange) how often I receive a letter or hear or read something "by chance" just at the right time. It works both ways, too, for I constantly receive letters from readers who had been troubled by problems or unvoiced questions who say: "Your article came at exactly the right moment. It was just as if it had been written *especially for me!*"

I think we all tend to procrastinate. The date tells me I must get down to writing an article. But the sun shines and I think: I'll just tidy my border, or I'll just clean the windows, or just do this or that. And then it is tomorrow. Urgent work piles up, and again it is tomorrow — until panic seizes me! Last night I wondered how to start this piece of writing — and this morning by first post came a letter from a reader *on the very subject I intended to write about!*

My unknown friend has been a Scout leader most of his life, and earlier this year a medium told him: "I see spirit children round you, and feel you help them a lot, often in your sleep state." As he had been told this on several occasions, this latest reminder that he might be doing "a night shift" in Another Place cast his mind back over the years to the few remembered excursions he had experienced during the sleep state.

Still by far the most vivid occurred as long as 30 years ago. He says: "There I was, walking across grassy meadowland, talking to a companion on my right. I've no idea who he was, though I was chatting as if on the friendliest terms. 'What lovely grass you have here,' I remarked, attracted by its short, very fine texture. 'Yes, it is rather nice, isn't it,' my companion replied.

"I looked down and was somewhat startled to find I was wearing my scout uniform. 'Is scout uniform worn here, too?' I asked. 'Yes, it is sometimes — on appropriate occasions,' was the reply. This brought me back to the purpose of my visit. 'What am I doing here?'

"'You see those boys over there?' We had come to a gentle rise and I could see two boys a little to the left, halfway up the slope. 'We want you to talk to them.'

"Although some distance away I could see they were 'little horrors' and realised this was going to be a tough assignment. 'Surely,' I said, 'you are more used to this sort of situation. Things like this must happen all the time.' 'No,' he replied. 'This is a job for you.'

"'Well, at least you will come with me?' I hoped that the sight of some personage might overawe these lads and bring some semblance of order into the proceedings. 'No, this is for you — alone.' And with that my companion turned to the right and I to the left. Well, I thought, I've come all this way, so I might as well have a go.

"Here I was, in at the deep end. I pitched in. It was, as I had forseen, a difficult session, but after some time I seemed to make contact and was getting across whatever it was I was supposed to be talking about. This is the strange thing, I never did remember any part of this conversation, though I suppose one could guess what it was all about. I don't remember returning, either, but when I did wake up it was with the feeling of a job well done."

A job well done. How satisfying! Far, far more people than one would ever imagine are enlisted for these "night shifts" during deep sleep. Many ask in prayer to be used for this work if and when possible, though it would seem that the majority have little or no recollection of the astral body "extra-mural" activities on which they have been engaged. The reason given for this, by many communicators from the Other Side, is that we have enough to cope with, experience, remember and assimilate in our daily life without retaining the details of our "night life" as well.

It is mostly, therefore, from our friends or helpers in the spirit spheres of life that we obtain information or confirmation of our excursions. As this information comes from a wide variety of sources, and has been recorded over a period of nearly a century, its validity cannot be denied.

In *Claud's Book*, published in 1918, Mrs Kelway Bamber's discarnate son communicated the following to his mother: "When your body sleeps, your soul comes over here and we spend hours together . . . Thousands of people come over in this way every night, and are more awake while here than on earth in their mortal bodies. To do this, people must be spiritually evolved to a certain degree . . . Sometimes we work amongst those who have just wakened in the spirit world and are bewildered. We explain to them where they are and bring their friends to see them.

"It seems curious to you that you should be able to do this even better than I, as you are still in a mortal body; *but that is the very reason.* You see, you are the 'half-way house,' as it were, (possessing the semi-physical vehicle of vitality) for along that little cord that connects your soul and body are travelling thoughts and desires of earth. You are therefore more in touch with the earth and so feel more familiar to one who has just come over."

Again, in *A Star of Hope,* a book published in 1938, Constance Wiley was told: "During your hours of sleep you were working in our world, and did much to help the cause of the mission on which, with others, you were sent; it was a mission of importance to some who had been projected *very suddenly* into our world. You have a very convincing way which helps, *especially because you are still in the flesh.* Though this may seem strange to you, it is so.

"They have, you see, so recently been in the flesh and had no preparation or thought of 'passing,' that they cannot realise death has taken place . . . Then it is that people like yourself, who desire to serve, are of great help in convincing them that they have 'passed on,' and help them to understand and listen to those who are sent to be their teachers. Tell all you can that they work for others in this way during their earth-lives, *if they truly desire to serve, and pray to God to permit them to do so.*"

I myself have one particularly vivid recollection of being taken to visit a woman who had just passed over after a long illness. She was in a very dazed state, lying in a white bed with her hands on the smooth covers, but totally unaware of the spirit helpers around her. Yet when I came to the foot of the bed and smiled encouragingly at her, she saw *me,* and responded at once. She "came to life," and began to wake up to her surroundings with intelligent interest.

In a previous chapter I told of the passing of Philip, Mrs Alice Gilbert's son, and his subsequent communications to his mother.* She has been used frequently for this "night work." On one occasion Philip told her that a mother who had lost contact with her boy during the war, had passed over and was distracted. He said: "I realised it was a job for you. Meanwhile I had taken Grandpa (in the spirit world) to see her, but she could only see him as a faint warm light. But *you, being still on earth,* even though you were functioning in the astral plane, she could see, and you

---

Philip in the Spheres, Aquarian Press. 1952.

71

talked to her. When at last she grasped what had happened, you took her to her boy . . ."

In her previous book, *Philip in Two Worlds* (now unfortunately out of print) she records many fascinating instances of her co-operation during the sleep state: "At night you trip along, and we work very hard. You have a regular round just now — about 10 people whom you visit regularly — every one ex-concentration camp. That sort of trouble seems to attract your attention even more than those who have died in battle or accidents." (This was just after the war.)

In this connection, the following is most enlightening. Philip tells her: "Last night you brought through a memory, rather blurred by thought-forms, of our work together — rather grim, for we had been to the lower strata and had coped with some of the Nazi gang. We struggled together to subdue some of the Belsen crowd — the very worst, and most determined, who are trying to establish a certain domination over some of their discarnate victims, who are linked to them by deep hatred.

"For *hatred* creates a strong link, just as love does. Those victims who had strong personalities, without any specially spiritual or high ideals, sometimes learned to hate with all the strength of their souls the thugs who terrorised them. This is scarcely to be wondered at, or blamed — and yet, in the astral world, hate, because it causes intense pre-occupation of the mind with its object, draws, by inevitable consequence, the victim and the tyrant together in a dreadful bond.

"By hate, I don't just mean indignation, dislike, defiance, but the real emotions of deep, brooding revengeful ill-will for retaliation. On this some of these poor wretches fed. They passed their days in phantasies of revenge on their oppressors, so that these images became part of their spiritual make-up, and afterwards they have to seek out the hated object, and a hideous battle of wills ensues. *Such victims were waiting — round those gallows!* (After the Nuremburg trials.)

"Yet, although their minds had become a sewer of hatred, many of these people had done in the past kindly, loving acts, and so we are able to help them. It is an unpleasant job, and you don't often go on it. But it was felt that you could help two women who had seen their babies gassed, and had so brooded with this unhealthy hatred that the little ones were not able to be brought through this dense and murky aura of vindictiveness they had created.

"You managed to persuade them that their children needed them, and little by little you cleansed their minds, whilst I and others stood on guard, fighting off the evil thought-emanations which sought to penetrate your aura.

"You see, I'm realising more and more that the words of Christ contained deep, universal, *scientific laws*. 'Do good to them that despitefully use you,' and 'turn the other cheek' does not mean weakly giving in to oppression. It means 'Don't think and brood evil revenge and

72

hatred, because if you do you are actually forging a link, in the astral world, an evil link which you will find difficult to break, and the stronger you are as a personality, the stronger link your thoughtform will create."

While speaking of the war, it is good to know, (if the word "good" is understood correctly in this context) from the people Philip met in the spirit spheres, how many honest, decent Germans, young and old, were actually shot by their officers for refusing to take part in cruelty.

They chose the only right way: refusal to participate, refusal to compromise to save their mortal skins. And — though this was not at all the object of their noble conduct — their actions gained for them their freedom in the immortal spheres.

Not long ago we asked our young teenage son, Gavin, what he would do if faced with the alternative of committing some horrible act or being shot. Without a moment's hesitation he replied: "That's easy. I'd be shot." Long may he, and other youngsters like him, regard this "problem" as non-existent.

It is not only discarnate souls whom astral travellers from the earth plane are able to help during sleep. One night Philip took his mother, in her astral body, round his old haunts in the Middle East, and together they rescued a young Merchant Navy officer who had been fooling around. He had a very fine inner self, but on this night was blind drunk and wandering the streets. Philip's communication goes on:

"Two thugs were round the corner, but we made him veer away and emerge to sanity. Then we poured thoughts into his mind. I almost managed to materialise to him, *as his etheric body was still opened by the alcohol, and so helpless against the incursions of discarnate entities.* In our case, we were benevolent, so he was lucky, and has learned a lesson."

VICTIMS OF THE ATOM-BOMBS

It seems almost incredible that it was nigh on 30 years ago that the atom-bombs were dropped on Hiroshima and Nagasaki. Perhaps as one grows older time becomes non-existent, a meaningless method of measuring a sequence of events.

When one is 15 or 20 a lifetime seems infinitely long to envisage. In the despairing moments which assail us for one reason or another when we are very young, we wonder how we are ever going to get through it! Yet when one reaches 65, "time" races by, and all the pictures in the kaleidoscope of one's life are as vivid to the mind's eye as if they had happened only "the other day."

At any given moment, if I so wish, I can listen to the drone of the V1 — the drone which abruptly stops. In the silence I begin to hear a swishing sound, faint at first, then louder and louder and still louder. I hear myself think: "This time this is *it*." "Something" tells me to sit bolt upright in bed. Why? Merely because I don't want to be killed lying down? Or is it a prompting?

I hear an ear-shattering explosion. Everything is blasted to smithereens; and, eventually, when there is nothing left to fall, my head is still, by a miracle, sticking out of a blackened rubble heap in the sudden quietness of a Sunday morning. The realisation that I am alive numbs any pain. I am even surprised at discovering blood which must be my own, since I am all alone.

Only "the other day," that August of the War — *if* my mind makes it so. For all is in the mind. And this bears a resemblance to "time" or "timelessness" in the world of spirit — the world in which thousands of people found themselves as the result of a gigantic holocaust, and because their heads were not above the rubble, but under it — in Nagasaki and Hiroshima.

So the fact that a quite amazing number of these Japanese victims were being brought in large batches (several batches per session) to a rescue circle in South Africa in 1970 is in no way remarkable from the point of view of the time lapse of 25 years. (Though remarkable enough in other ways.) The appallingly sudden shock of the fate which had overtaken them, without any warning of a raid such as we in Britain were accustomed to receiving, produced a chaotic state of mind, as can be imagined.

They did not know what had happened. Many did not know whether they had "died" or not. All were suffering from shock. They found themselves wandering about their old homes, lost, bewildered, lonely, homesick, frightened. If they were alive, what had happened and where were they? If they were dead, where were their honourable ancestors?

Then there were those who had not been killed at once, but were fully aware of the horrible extent of their burns — of pain, terror, hunger and thirst. These things remained fixed indelibly in their minds, and even though they had vacated their maimed bodies they continued to go hither and thither seeking help for their burned bodies, still suffering hunger and thirst, still utterly confused, in a timeless dream-state of the mind.

In this condition it was not possible for spirit helpers to penetrate their consciousness or to make themselves seen by them. Even those who came to realise they were "dead" were not much better off owing to faulty preconceived ideas. They were earthbound.

I have a friend in South Africa who played an active part in this very splendid rescue circle. They sat on Sundays and Thursdays and did invaluable work. To give an idea of the vast organisation on the spirit side, I will quote from the guide's explanation given on one occasion to the sitters:

"We would like you all to be able to see what goes on here on a

Thursday night. We will describe it to you if you will all hold hands for a while . . . That is lovely. Well, now, on a Thursday night we bring along a large group of what is called The Brotherhood to protect you all. Then we have a group of helpers who collect as many lost and wandering souls as they can persuade to come. Once we have collected a lot, we leave them in a room just next to you — it interpenetrates E.'s house. We have a group of others who stay with them, and when you start your circle we all surround you — as D. has been able to see. (Clairvoyantly.)

"Then we have several more groups who surround the whole of the town. They have to be there to protect you from undesirable entities coming near the circle. We then have a very large gallery that seats about two thousand. In the gallery are seated many of the people you have already helped. They in turn help others. Also present are many of your loved ones who all take a very great interest in this work. And then we also have people here who are learning our methods of communication between the two worlds. So you see, my friends, there are very many interested and involved."

Now the majority of the Japanese were Shinto, and had been taught that when they died they would be met by their honourable ancestors. Accordingly the spirit helpers "built," in the astral, a beautiful Shinto shrine in the shape of a Pagoda, approached by broad white steps, and all suffused with a wonderful blue light emanating from behind the shrine.

The sitters were informed about this by the guide, and told to do their best to direct the thoughts and attention of the earthbound ones to the light and to the Pagoda, telling them that if they went up the steps towards it they would find their honourable ancestors waiting to greet them. For different groups, such as Buddhists and others, appropriate shrines or conditions were built up.

Each batch of victims had a spokesman who utilised the medium, a man. How, you may ask, could these people who knew only Japanese either speak or understand English? The answer is that it is the *thoughts* behind the words which are transmitted, both ways. Mediumship is a highly technical and complicated process which it has taken hours to explain on some of the teaching tapes we have from those in spirit qualified to instruct us, so it cannot be explained briefly. I merely refer to it to forestall what might be an obvious query in the minds of readers.

The proceedings followed much the same pattern, time after time. The Guide would say: "We would like you to know that the people you have already helped to the light are now in turn helping our friends on this side to collect as many wandering lost souls as they can. We know you will do your utmost. So may we bring the first batch along? Please remember they are looking for their honourable ancestors, and we have them here waiting to help. Now over to you . . ."

Here are some typical remarks made by the various spokesmen of the various batches: "What is this place we have been brought to? . . . We are

75

all very confused, and some of us are badly burned by a terrible thing that fell from heaven . . . we do not know what it was . . . Please help us . . . we are so badly burnt. We are very hungry and thirsty . . . We do not understand your words . . . We do not know you . . . Yes, we are Japanese, but how do you know that? . . . Yes, we are from Hiroshima, and we are all very homesick . . . What is that noise? (a car hooter outside) Oh! we are very frightened . . . we are not able to see . . . Why do you help us? We are not of your nation . . . Be very careful, we do not ask for love from other nations. We are the Japanese race, and we must stay like that . . . We are all lost, we do not know what is happening . . . No, we are from Nagasaki . . . what happened to our honourable ancestors? Why weren't they here to meet us? . . . Yes, yes, we can see a light now . . . and white steps . . . many we go and look? But please wait here for us . . . Oh! what a beautiful Pagoda! What a lovely place! . . . May we please stay here? . . . Oh my goodness, my honourable father is here! . . . We are all going now, we are all very happy, we have found them at last . . . Thank you, thank you . . . God bless you too, but we have a different God . . .''

All these typical excerpts were interspersed, of course, with explanations, answers, encouragement and directions from the sitters. At later sittings many group spokesmen came back to render their gratitude for the help they had received. One of them said:

"We would like you to know we appreciate your loving kindness more than we can express. We were all hovering around our homes and couldn't understand what had happened to us as the force was so tremendous and so sudden that we did not realise we were no longer on earth. Our teachings were all wrong — up to a point, that is . . . We could not be helped, and our ancestors could not contact us until we were brought to you. My friends, there are not many who can help those who were in our state of chaotic mind. We thank you for your love to us from a foreign nation. And in turn we will help many others if we will be allowed to use this circle. We are going now. Thank you and may the God of all heaven bless you.

On one occasion there was the sound of a train passing near by, and the spokesman who had returned to give thanks, said: "We never thought we could hear that noise again! This is really too amazing, we can hear the train so clearly." (Through the medium).

What is truly amazing, however, is that on the 15th November 1970 the circle members were told by the guide in charge that they had now helped between *seven and eight thousand* victims to the light! On querying this astonishing figure, they were told that it was indeed correct.

Now I am always wary of mentioning communicators with wellknown names. For one thing, people who know little or nothing about Spiritualism tend to ridicule the subject by pointing out, quite erroneously, that those who communicate so often purport to be the famous.

At the other end of the scale there are those who dismiss it, without investigation, under the equally erroneous impression that "nothing worth while seems to come through, but mostly inconsequential messages from someone's Aunt Sally." (It is difficult to win!)

Needless to say, both types of critics are unaware of the all-embracing teaching which is given in private circles of integrity and dedication on every subject one could imagine, and even on subjects one could *not* imagine. In any case, it is a little unfair on those whose names were wellknown during their lifetimes if they are precluded from communicating or being accepted as communicators on the grounds that such communications will be automatically suspect!

In view of the work achieved by this particular rescue circle over a long period, and especially because the work dealt with the victims of the atom-bombs over Japan, I do not find it surprising that one of those who became interested in it was Winston Churchill. The following is one recorded excerpt which, to my mind, seems very typical of him:

"Here I am, my friends. We are all very interested in the work you are doing. It is really an eye-opener to me. If I had been told of this in former times I would have said you were a bunch of nuts." A circle member asked him why he had not spoken to Lord Dowding who would have enlightened him. "He surely would have done, my friend, but Dowding and I didn't see eye to eye. We do *now*, make no mistake about *that*. He sends you all his love and thanks you for the help you are giving. He was always so interested in this sort of jiggery-pokery!"

On being asked about General de Gaulle he replied: "My friend de Gaulle is still getting over his funeral. They really went to town over the poor chap, same as with my funeral. It really isn't necessary for all that flapdoodle."

Asked about a wellknown colleague who had "died" fairly recently: "We are not sure about him ourselves. We are not sure where to find him, we mean. He is still floating somewhere around his old haunts. Probably he still goes to his Club every night as he used to."

Questioned about Hitler: "Hitler is still wrapped up like a cocoon. He will not be let out of his little cell until he sends out a glimmer of light. Stalin, also, is not with us. He is still earthbound and influencing leaders of the black States and also the Arab States. But we will win in the end. Goodnight, and God bless you all from Winston S. Churchill."

(This was recorded on November 12, 1970.)

WHERE THOUGHTS ARE SEEN

Recently I had a delightful letter from a man in Australia. He expressed the charming wish to "make an appointment" with me for when we are both in the spirit world. An active Spiritualist for a great many years, he felt an affinity through reading my articles and as it is impossible for him to come to the Old Country in his declining years he hit on the much happier and more sensible solution of "making a date" for later on! In his own case, he hopes to depart in the reasonably near future, for his dear wife awaits him, whereas I hope to stay on the earth plane for a longer period. However, in due course I shall endeavour to keep this appointment. Why not?

My engagement book is already rather full in this respect — though thank heavens there will not be the Time factor to harass me! I have already made so many dates with all and sundry: friends whom it is not possible to see owing to physical distance on earth; all my friends, family and contacts already in the world of spirit; and also those of my friends who simply cannot bring themselves to believe that any part of them will so much as exist after their span on earth finishes. "Alright," I say to them, "but I shall make a date with you, nevertheless. I shall find you out, rouse you from the stupor and bewilderment you may well be in at such an unexpected turn of events, and one day we'll have a good laugh — *and I'll expect you to have the good grace to say to me: You told me so!*"

After I received this letter I fell to thinking about how one would contact someone one had never seen and only knew of by name, for one could not visualize the person in one's mind's eye. One method is, of course, by the power of thought. In his *Post Mortem Journal** .T. E. Lawrence (of Arabia) tells us: "One is part of a great universe of thought which can be tapped without the mechanical interchange of words, either heard or read . . . I have been deliberately experimenting and trying to reach the thoughts of other minds, especially those who most inspired me on earth. Sometimes I succeed, sometimes I fail. As one might expect, the basic law is affinity. One can only hope to contact minds with which one has or could have had affinity, a relationship of kind with kind, however different in development. Appreciation of a poet or writer may argue a certain degree of affinity, but that particular soul may have progressed beyond one's reach and so one draws a blank. On the contrary, in rare cases he may have retrogressed."

**Post Mortem Journal, Communications from T. E. Lawrence through Jane Sherwood. Neville Spearman Ltd.*

He goes on to say that the principle of affinity leads to unexpected encounters. He instances the (to him, at that stage of his spirit life) strange experience of being caught up, while alone in his spirit cottage, with a kind of conference in which several people were exchanging and developing ideas in ways which interested him. He found himself joining in and asking questions which were answered, and it suddenly dawned on him that one of the unseen people was his medium friend, and that he was in touch with the thoughts of a group he had once worked with while "dictating" a previous book through this medium. (Thus there were two of the group living on his own plane, one on a higher plane, and one earth-dweller.) Though none was in the bodily presence of another, a satisfactory way of communicating had been evolved, simply on the basis of affinity. Rather like a radio programme in which people situated in different places or even countries can talk together during a common link-up interview.

No, I don't think I will find much difficulty, when I have attained and learned the freedom of thought control in the next world, to send out a call to my sympathetic correspondent now on the other side of *this* world. For obviously we are on the same wavelength — even in little things which made me smile. Commenting on an article in which I mentioned saving a furry caterpillar from being run over, he at first thought "this is surely a bit much" until he suddenly laughed, remembering how *he* had spent ages rescuing "those little silverfish things," that seem to haunt warm cupboards, from a hopeless predicament trapped in a cold, slippery bath! The picture evoked by this particular rescue operation endeared him to me at once.

Also his sense of humour. Again referring to a recent article, he described a woman who never ceased talking about 'I'. "It's bad enough that she exists, without her constantly reminding one of the fact!" he wrote. Only a spiritually developed person is able to poke fun at failings and foibles with *love* and *humour* — not impatience, irritation, resentment or anger. We all have our maddening habits . . .

Friends ring up from time to time just to let off steam, usually about the trifling inconsistencies or behaviour of those they love most. People rise above themselves (their lower selves) when faced with a *real* crisis or problem in their lives. It is the repetition of pinpricks which get on our nerves and get us down. One day, when someone rang up seething with exasperation over the most ridiculously small, but repeated annoyance which had gradually grown out of all proportion, my husband pointed out that this was indeed a situation of cosmic importance, surely affecting the future of the universe! She had to laugh in the end, albeit a little reluctantly at first.

Such are the humorous paradoxes of us human beings whose uncontrolled minds dart about from one level of consciousness to another, from the sublime to the ridiculous. We start the day, perhaps with a prayer or invocation, determined to make every effort to conduct our thinking, feeling and doing on a happy, serene and tranquil level. And then, through anxiety or tension or the bustle and pressures of mundane living, we lose our perspective and allow ourselves to become irritated by trifles. Molehills become mountains, and the proverbial "hole in the bucket" becomes a matter of major importance, throwing us off balance, and causing the most horrible little specks and darts and vicious little arrows to flood our auras, not only affecting ourselves but penetrating and wounding the auras of those about us.

If this is so on earth, where the slowness and coarseness of the vibrations make us less aware of it, in the next sphere of life emotions are a visible, tangible and inescapable reality. They cannot be hidden, or glossed over by a conventional phrase. The discharge of hatred, anger or intense irritation can cause grievous injury to the one against whom it is directed, which is why, as Lawrence tells us, "the angry, the sadistic, the brutal and the jealous have of necessity to foregather in their own place, because the atmosphere they engender cannot be borne by others, nor can they themselves bear the more rarefied conditions of the higher spheres. Cure of these disorders comes gradually, and as they are cured they are able to graduate into better conditions and higher planes of being. The path upward is always open and there are willing hands to help and encourage any who aspire to tread it."

Lawrence himself, owing to the false personality he had taken such pains to build up during earth life, and his disregard for the art of human relationships, had much to learn at first and, with others, was in a home under a highly spiritual teacher called Mitchell. "Mitchell is endlessly patient with us when control slips and impatience or anger fume out of us. He knows how to take the horrid emanations into his own clear being and transform them there. If he returned them in kind the resulting state of all of us would not bear thinking of. But in thus accepting and transforming the waves of negative emotion we sometimes send out he shames us into fresh effort. *For he suffers*. The delicate fabric of his body is harmed and hurt although he tries not to flinch when he is scorched by our beastly reactions.

". . . The conviction is brought home to us that unless we can clear ourselves of evil emotions it will not be possible for us to remain among the decent people on this plane. The alternative will be to leave it and find homes in conditions where the astral bodies of the inhabitants are coarsened by habitual indulgence in anger and hatred, and where the air they breathe is infected with their hot and murky emanations. 'Your big difficulty' " Mitchell tells him on one occasion, " 'is a scorn of slowness and impatience of mediocrity and, if you will forgive me, a really horrible feeling of superiority to most of the pleasant and ordinary people you are meeting here. They cannot avoid recognising your reaction to them and so they keep away from you.' "

He told Lawrence to look at himself, and this is what he saw, in his own words: "Shafts of keen blue light struggling to issue from a core of dark and muddied colour — a tumult of angry, murky shadow at the centre and, as a response to his criticism, angry dartings of red flying off from it. It was not a pretty sight. 'You see,' he said gently, 'we have to clear all that before you are ready to go on.' The shock broke me down. All my pride and unconfessed arrogance were shattered. I saw myself as less worthy than the least of those to whom I had been condescending . . ."

Later he says: "I have become wary of impatience and anger; *their manifestations are too repulsive*. The slightest shift in feeling makes a corresponding change in appearance, as well as in one's own feeling of well-being . . . It really amounts to this, that one is not safe in this place until all the twisted, negative emotions are cleared out of one. Then it will be possible to live fearlessly and freely, knowing that one cannot send out any harmful emotion. Hence Mitchell's drastic treatment."

In this astonishingly honest record, Lawrence gives us a most salutory account of his purgation before he was able to attain the sunlight of happiness and the pure air of freedom, service and sociability. "So differently am I orientated since I got my own inner tangles sorted out that social intercourse with all manner of men is now my chief delight . . . My friends on earth would find me altered; far more *blessedly ordinary,* and free, thank God, from the accursed legend which was for so long my prison."

Oh, how important it is to get our "inner tangles" sorted out *here*, on the earth plane! To take the trouble to analyse our emotions and reactions, to become aware of them, and see them objectively from outside the ego-personality. How much better, when we pass over, to be able to give support, strength and help to the myriads of "Mitchells" instead of finding ourselves their reluctant and rebellious pupils, scorching their love with our unruly and petulant emotions!

I think that the cultivation of the God-given sense of humour is so often our best ally in becoming self-aware, and in the regulation of our less pleasant traits. The ability to see how humorous, and even ludicrous we really are, in so many ways, is a good stepping stone. It also makes life so much more pleasant and harmonious for everyone else, besides ourselves. And those "unconsidered trifles" which are such sources of irritation, annoyance and resentment must be our first targets in this training.

Self-awareness starts like a grain of mustard seed — over very small things. I often smile when I remember how, over a period of years during my youth, my mother would always return from a day's shopping in London with exactly the same remark: "Of course it was rather expensive — but to buy the best is much cheaper in the long run." She really made herself believe that this was her valid excuse for extravagance, until we made a joke of it. Thereafter she never got further than "Of course . . ." before we all chorused, "We know! It's much cheaper in the long run!"

and everyone burst out laughing, including herself.

I'm sure our friend often smiles now, instead of exploding, when she remembers the phrase "cosmic importance"! For the fact of the matter is that however insignificant the cause, the effect of *accumulated* negative thought or emotion *becomes* of cosmic importance because it creates a cloud through which the Light cannot penetrate. Imagine the ear-shattering noise if every member of a large orchestra continually played the wrong notes — all trifling little notes if played singly, by themselves, in each member's home. But we are all members of a vast orchestra, and it depends on each one of our individual notes whether the symphony is a disaster or whether it approaches in beauty, melodiousness and aspiration the intention of the Master Composer, which is to reproduce on earth the glorious vibrations of the music of the spheres.

THE STORY OF ALF

The question is often asked: what about those who are suddenly pitched into the next world without ever having given a thought to the subject of "death", — or, indeed, a thought to anything much? A young fellow, perhaps, who was quite uneducated and un-read, concerned only with the necessities of earth-living, making ends meet for a wife and kids in a time when poverty was still a harsh reality in pre-1914 England?

Such was Alf, a little Londoner with ginger hair, a cloth cap and a "choker". He was a coster. He sold fruit and vegetables from a barrow up Paddington way. On very special occasions, just for Shows, he could afford to hire "a moke," a brown lady donkey called Daisy. He had a very soft spot for Daisy. He tried to make it up to her for the pretty rough treatment she sometimes received from others who had her from the man who kept ten donkeys for hire.

It was a tough life. Things weren't too happy between himself and his "Missus" and, as he put it, "The word Gawd didn't mean nothing more than a swear word — like Gor' blimey." He had been into churches but the parsons never made sense to him, which was not altogether surprising.

Then came the War. Like lots of other young fellows he joined up "to have a bash". The Sergeant-Major never succeeded in turning him into much of a soldier, but he was soon sent to France. Before the end of 1914 he was in the mud of the trenches, "like rabbits in a burrow". One day five of them were in a dugout together. They never heard it coming. They never heard it explode. But a direct hit from a shell blasted them instantaneously "into Kingdom come". *Only they didn't know it.*

Alf's story, as told by himself whilst controlling the trance instrument of the late Norman Hunt's remarkable home circle (of which I am privileged to possess 120 hours of tapes) provides *one* answer. Just one — for every case is individual. But from each one, however different, there is something to learn.

Alf was a good-hearted little bloke. His main trouble, as he said, was that — like hundreds, thousands of people — "he didn't *know* nothing." His story is a long one, so I will only give verbatim excerpts:

"How did we know we'd been killed? The answer is, we never knew we *was* killed. Next thing I know, we were walking down a road together, talking. One of us says, 'What's happened? Wasn't like this a little while back. What's happened to the War?' We says to ourselves: 'Funny! Must have got hit. Knocked a bit silly-like, took back to hospital, now we're having a rest camp or something, and come to our senses. 'Cause there ain't no mud — and there ain't no Sergeant-Major!'

"There's this road, the sort of road you would have thought horses and carts might have been down, a bit rutty, grass here and there, trees both sides, flowers, dicky-birds a-singing and all. Nice warm day. I says to my mates, 'I wonder if there's a boozer down this way. I think I could do with one.' We keep a-going, and we don't have to walk very far. We come to a bend in the road and there *is* a boozer. Proper little country pub. We go up three steps, all white, into the parlour. Nice place! Comfortable chairs, nice little girl, fair-hair, behind the bar.

" 'What d'you want, boys?' she says. She comes round like a proper lady out behind the bar and serves us our drinks at a table where we sit down. Cheers! And we talks. We scratches our head a bit. We didn't none of us quite know what had happened, or where we was. Well, we drink up our beers. 'We'd better walk back,' we says. 'We must have come from somewhere and we'd better get back there, wherever it is.' So we start walking back the way we come.

"One bloke suddenly turns to me and he grabs my arm, and he says: 'Here, Alf, you know what's happened to us?' 'No', I says, 'that's what we're a-trying to find out.' 'Mate,' he says, *'we're dead!'* 'Ha! Go on! *You* can be dead if you want to — *I* aint! Nor you aint — don't be so daft! Dead? We've just had a good pint, we're walking down the road on a nice sunny day — what d'you mean, dead?'

" 'You see that light over there, over that hill?' he says. 'No! I can't see no light, mate'. He says: 'I tell you, we're dead. And I'm going over to see what that light means, because it's got something to do with us being dead. What about you others, are you coming?' 'No', they says, 'we're going to stay with old Alf. We aint dead, neither!' So off he goes, and we don't see him no more. Now that one had a bit of education. He'd done reading and that. And that's how he'd come to the idea as how we was dead.

"There are some gaps in my memory, but I went on in them there conditions — not walking down the road, but doing more or less what I

83

wanted to, and wondering about some leave, and when do we get home to Blighty, and what about the old woman — because it was all earth thoughts, you see, Guv'nor. It never even dawned on me as to how it was *always* a sunny afternoon! There weren't no rain and there weren't never no night. But at last I come to the idea that maybe that bloke was right. We *was* dead. That's why there aint no more war and no more Sergeant-Major.

"Well, being dead's got its points. Nice summer afternoon, nothing to do but enjoy yourself and walk around, and have a little sleep when you want to, and you can go to the boozer. And you can have your fags. And that went on a long time . . . and I began to get a little bit tired of it. Nothing to look forward to. Nothing 'appening. And then I began to wonder . . .

"I thinks to myself: supposin' as we *are* dead, who'd be the bloke to ask about it? Ask a parson, I reckon. He's the bloke wot's supposed to know. I wonder how I can find a parson. Parson? I says to myself, don't be a bloody fool, Alf. How much did you have to do with parsons when you was alive, if you *are* dead?

"I wasn't exactly unhappy — I was never unhappy there — but kind of discontented, unsatisfied. I wasn't in Heaving and I wasn't in Hell and I wasn't on earth. I wasn't nowhere. I met people, lots of people, but they didn't seem to know more than wot I did, or if they had an idea they couldn't make me understand. So I goes and sits under a tree, by myself, and I starts to think.

"You've all got to come to this here thinking, sooner or later, *all* of you. And if only people would do their thinking *before* they come over here, and try to put right what they *can* while they're still on the old earth, they'd save themselves a lot of trouble.

"You keep fast hold on your memory. And it's much clearer. Things you've forgotten come to your mind. Things you maybe *wanted* to forget about, or maybe really forgotten. But here they all come back to you. You'll find there are a few things you could have put right, things you put off, and never done. If you suddenly get killed you can't tell someone you're sorry — not unless they go to someone like these people they call mediums — and how many of 'em do that?"

So Alf 'did his thinking'. About the way he'd treated the kids sometimes, about his marriage, about old Charlie down the road who he'd always been meaning to go and see and never did, and a few things he didn't like thinking about very much. And he found that it was the little things that mattered — not the things he thought he'd get 'copped' for if he'd been found out, but little, mean, thoughtless things, like thinking of Number One too much, not caring enough.

But then there were the good things to remember, which gave him a warm feeling of satisfaction, the good, kind things. And he thought it all out, by himself, just (as he put it) "between me and Gawd, because nobody else can do your thinking for you — and you've got all the time there is."

Alf tells us: "If now I'd had a little idea — not so much as wot you've got, but just a little idea — and if I'd been told to holler out for someone to help, then I would 've set up this 'ere holler and I'd 've got help, because I'd have turned my eyes that there way. But I never knew.

"So I have to wait till one of the blokes wot I'm knocking about with, someone I'd met there, wot's been doing his own bit of thinking, he sends out a holler. He gets somebody to come down . . . Then this lady comes to see me, a jolly person, a fat girl. She says, 'Alf, it's not you I've come for, it's this Frenchie. I've had a request from someone wot knows this Frenchie, to give him a helping hand, and I can do it. Alf, I can see by the look of you,' she says, 'you've had enough of it, and you're ready to come out of it.'

"I says, 'Missus, I don't know who you are, but if you can get me out of this here . . .' She says, 'Alright, Alf. Come along with me'. And she takes me and old Frenchie by the hand, and we start off a-walking, and she's a-talking, and — I don't rightly know how it happened — I finds myself here, where I am now.

"Then I has to start a-learning — where I am, what I'm a-doing, what I've got to do, and learning how come I've come up here, and why I never come up before. I done my bit of thinking and I got it all straight. I never put everything right, because I couldn't, but I was very willing, and I'm still very willing to put right whatever I can, in some way or other. And I tells that to some of the people I meets up here.

" 'You mean that, mate? Want to do a job of work?' 'Yus,' I says, 'I reckon I'd be able to work out a bit of my trouble if you'd give me a job'. 'Alright, there's people down on the old earth, Alf', they says (because they all knew my name) 'that don't know no more than wot you did. Would you like to give a helping hand, maybe, so that if only one or two of them don't have to go through that there, d'you reckon that'd be a bit of a job?' I said, 'Blimey, lead me to it! What do I have to do?' 'Well, this aint no pick-and-shovel work. This is *mind*,' they says."

So Alf went to what he calls "a teaching place, where people like Mr Abu (the advanced spirit teacher of Norman Hunt's circle) come to talk to people like me . . . and I went to these here places for a long time, and I learned a lot about using my mind, how to do it, and wot it were for.

"And then this girl, the same one wot brung me up from down there, says, 'Alf, your teacher tells me you're all ready to start your job. You know what to do. You know how to do it. You've got enough strength of mind to keep out them that's not supposed to come, and to help in those that is, and can't manage it on their own. I've got a link-up with a bloke down there wot's one of these — instruments, they call 'em. Will you work with him and with me? And I can introduce you to some very nice people that I've known for a long time, and you're going to like them and they're going to like you. It's only opening and shutting the door, in a manner of speaking, but you'll be doing a real good job.' "

And that is how Alf, the little coster who'd been blown to pieces in 1914 finally became the invaluable and much-loved "doorkeeper" of the Norman Hunt circle 35 earth years later. And because Spirit works in a wonderful and mysterious way, the jolly, fat lady who "brung him up," as he put it, was the instrument's dear wife who had passed on suddenly while he was yet in a stage of being developed for his superb mediumship to come. (His name was W. F. Rickard, affectionately known as Rick.)

"Well, that's how it came about, Guv'nor. Mind you, I know *now* I wasn't a 'wicked one', no. I wouldn't have been where I was . . . but I wouldn't like to have been, now I know a bit more, because where *I* wasn't unhappy, there's them that is, and they're harder to get at. I've been through my little bits of remorses and that. If I hadn't I wouldn't be here where I am.

"And now you tells me it was 35 years . . . It don't *matter*. It's not the time that counts, but the condition. Don't be sorry for 'em about the time, only the *condition*. When you get up here it rams home this 'ere Love, like nothing else can. I don't know nothing about Gawd — Gawd bless Him — you don't need no picture of Gawd. Just *live*, proper . . . with love and that. And I understand when they say *Gawd is Love*, because we're a-living in it, Guv'nor! *We're a-living in it!*"

Note. In the early fifties Norman Hunt visited the Paddington area Alf had described in some detail, and came across two old women who remembered Alf "Ginger" Harris, and his barrow of vegetables.

JOSH, THE SEABOUND SMUGGLER

It is often the task of the sitters in a rescue circle to break the news to the communicator that he or she is what is called "dead". In the normal course of events this has to be done skilfully and at the right time, after confidence has been built up. Even then it can be a long time, in some cases, for this extraordinary idea to be accepted. After all, if you have believed that death means extinction, it is something of a shock to be told, while engaged in an animated conversation with a group of friendly people in a sitting-room, that you are dead!

It was a refreshing change for the sitters of the Norman Hunt circle when a ship's Captain, Master of a privateer, who had been roaming the seven seas and the waterfronts of the world for over 150 years, broke off conversation (through the trance mediumship of W. F. Rickard) to announce to them — in case they did not know! — "*I'm dead, you understand?*"

I have always had a soft spot for Josh Whitehead. Pirate and smuggler he may have been, but he had a strong sense of morality for all that. Let him speak for himself. Norman Hunt, with his quiet friendly voice, had a knack of gaining the trust and confidence of those who were brought to his weekly circle to be given a helping hand. His remarks are printed in italics, for clarity.

On this occasion a lovely air of Bach was being played on the gramophone while the medium went into trance. The music was suddenly broken into by a harsh voice, deeply tinged with melancholy. The manner was brusque and laconic. "What d'you call that? 'What shall we do with the drunken sailor?' What kind of music are you playing? That ain't my kind of music."

Well, I'll turn it off. "I'm obliged to you. I'm much obliged to you." *Did somebody suggest that you should come along here? Or what brought you?* "A ship's Master goes where he thinks he will. At home in any Mess. This one's as good as any, but I didn't like your lily-livered music. A good shanty, and the lazy lubbers'll pull — after the marlin spike's been at work, and you've rolled three or four of 'em in the scuppers — the rest of 'em will work all right!"

But you're not still thinking about that now? What else do you think about? "I'm thinking about a nice little, tight little wench. A nice little tight little house, where I can get all the grog I want, and every night all watches in bed." *Yes, that life must have been pretty tough.* "Somebody had to keep Boney away. Hundred and fifty tonner, fifty-four carronades, privateer. Bit of smuggling on the side, contraband . . . and why not? It's a long time since I was afloat, but your memory's just as keen."

What other memories have you got before that? "Blue water under the sun, grey water under the clouds, the white burning sands and the palms. Little native girls, little native boats. Water as clear as crystal . . . sharks . . . and oysters and pearls." *"Did you have anything to do with pearl fishing?* "Contraband. Privateer, I said. You go your way about the seas; you please yourself what you pick up and how you pick it up. But if I could do a turn . . . something to keep Boney off, why not?"

Why not? "Why not? I'll tell you why not. Half a dozen round shot in my hull . . . all hands . . . hundred and fifty tonner. Square rig foremast, square rig mainmast, rigged mizzen. Crew, lazy lubbers, fifty-five of 'em . . . all hands. Boney took no prisoners."

What was the name of the craft? "My craft? The *Sally Widger*. As tight a little wench as you could ever find, and as tight a little craft as you could wish for . . . The name of my boat *and* of my wench. My name? It doesn't matter now. They called me Josh." *What are you doing now, Josh?*

"Rolling around. I'm shipping aboard craft strange to me, and covering the seas as I used to cover them before. And I'm seeing bloody, dirty business most everywhere. Josh and his crew were tough men. We had to be tough, we led a tough life, but we weren't dirty. I go along the waterside now — I'm dead, you understand?"

Of course; what is called "dead". You knew that, didn't you? Going down didn't stop you "living". "I know, I know. That's why I get free passage. Can't charge a dead man fares! I go along the waterfront all around the seas . . . In my time, the waterfront was a rough place. You'd have your sailors, your English tars; you'd have your matelots, you'd have your marinos. For no more than a word you'd get the back of a fist. Now? Dirty little white-faced *rats!* Sneaking round corners and sticking a knife into honest men. Twisty business, dirty business! For stinking money, not earned fair and square."

What part of the world are you talking about? "Do you know Rio? You try Rio on a dark night when the moon's new. Down on what they call the new quay — not there in my time. You'll see things going on that would make an honest ship's master spew. We were rough and we were tough; we weren't dirty, my friends. And why am I come here to tell you all this?"

Yes, please tell us. Perhaps you are tired of rolling around? "I'm not tired of rolling around so long as I'll get there in the end . . . but will I? Where's my ship? Rotted by now. Where's my crew? And crew's First Mate? Where's Boney? Gone with the rest."

But you are the proof that it is only a part of them that has "gone with the rest"; you are here! "There's only me left." *No, those chaps are somewhere, you know; in the same world that you are in.* "They don't answer my hail. Can't call up the bosun to pipe 'em aboard any more. Signed on under another master . . . and I'm thinking it's time I signed on too . . . somewhere else."

Have you met your wench yet? "Wench has gone with the rest. There's other wenches I've come across. I'm not concerned. I was never a womaniser. I took my fun where I wanted and when I wanted it, but I wasn't a womaniser. Rough, tough, but never dirty. Josh Whitehead had a clean name, tough but clean."

Had you any special friend? A mate? "Mate? You couldn't make a friend of your mate, it wouldn't do. Ship's Master is a lonely man . . . got to be a lonely man. It's 'Mr Mate, jump to it'. 'Yes *sir!*' You can't make friends with your mate."

How many years did you have on the water? A long time? "All my life. I wasn't a King's ship . . . my own craft. As a boy I was an apprentice before the mast . . . up the mast as well, and down in the bilge. I tried it both ends, forrard and aft. I've drunk bilge and I've eaten pineapples off the tree . . . down there they grow, on the ground, on little bushes . . ."

Well, we think you must be a bit tired of it all and we should like to give a helping hand if we can. You'll have to sign on under a new master. "I'll not sign any King's Articles. I'm a Master Mariner." *And a straight one. That's the point now.* "But I can't bring myself to sign on as a Third Mate. I've been offered the post."

What sort of post is it? Do you know anything about it?

"I haven't been told the ship's name; I haven't been told her destination. I haven't been told anything about her, but I've been told by some cocky little articled clerk — that's what he looks like to me — there's a berth open to me as Third Mate, as soon as I like to take down my gold braid and touch my cap to my own First Officer. Three times I've refused that berth, but I'm getting almost tired enough to take it. He was a good First Officer, he knew his business. But it's going to be mortal hard. What can *you* tell me about the craft — anything?"

Not about the craft, I'm afraid. You said a little while ago that you were dead. What do you think that means? "Loneliness, wandering about. Times when memory is pleasant and warm; times when memory is bitter." *But you are looking astern all the time. You have got to keep a lookout over the bow as well.* "Waters ahead — I've got no chart for the waters ahead."

But perhaps you've got a First Officer who has. Why not take it on? "Tell me the vessel's name." *I should think "Happiness". It sounds odd but I believe it's true. And the port is "Rest" and "Peace".* "Peace? There's no peace." *Take it on, and try it out, Josh. It's no good going on as you are. It doesn't get anywhere in the end. You can't die again, you know. Why not make a new start?*

"How can I put my name underneath that of my own First Officer?" *What do you think it means, putting your name under?* "It means 'Yes Sir!' " *It means that I, Josh Whitehead, am what I really am, inside me. If I'm clean and straight inside, well, good enough. It doesn't matter what I call myself — not on the new seas you are sailing. That's the difference, Josh. It wasn't like that on the old seas; you had the gold braid and that was good enough.*

"Tell me, is there any prospect at all of getting any further information about this craft? I'd like to know, if I can, the conditions aboard . . . hard tack?" *Of course you would. This funny little "clerk"* . . . "No, no, . . . shrimp! Shrimp!" *Well, never mind. You've got to stand on whatever you really are, Josh, and not on anything in the way of rank.*

"A man spends forty years of his life — forty-three years — twenty of them in command; fifteen in command of his own vessel. That man builds pride in himself. He'll doff his cap to no man. He's master of his vessel and he's master of himself. Now I'm to say 'aye, aye, Sir!' "

But it doesn't matter now. You are you, whatever you are.

"If I thought I could meet my little wench at the end, I'd have a go. We were going to be spliced, but every voyage I put it off. I'd got a little bit more to do, a little bit more to get, and I had easy money in fighting Boney — prize money, don't you see? I got my prize all right — down below."

If you haven't forgotten her, she won't have forgotten you. She's waiting for you, without a doubt. "I've never forgotten her. I kept that wench waiting for me. Sally Widger . . . Twenty three last time I saw her — a slip of a girl." *London?* "London! What have I got to do with that hell hole? Bideford . . . and Pompey. (Portsmouth) Tidy place since my time."

Again Josh went off on his reminiscences, comparing the easy life of a privateer to the hard slog of "the liner men" who endured "nine solid months on hard tack and salt horse." Again and again he preferred to chat about sailing, and ships, and again he had to be brought back to the matter in hand — the problem of his pride. "My First Officer. *He* stands in the way with gold braid all over him!"

The gold braid doesn't make him into anything special. "It makes him master of the ship!" *But not the master of the real you!* Then, suddenly, he seemed to make the decision. His love for his little wench won over his pride. "Damme! If he can take me to Sally, I'll sign!"

I think that's why you've come to talk to us. "Have I got to go back to this little shrimp?" *He might not be such a shrimp after all! Ask him his name. We know a little chap called Alf. He might look a shrimp but he's a good little bloke. Tell him "the Guv'nor" asked you to speak to him.* (This was a reference to Alf, the doorkeeper of the circle, who often played his own part in cases of this sort. Now he was evidently playing the part of the clerk.)

"I've got to sign the Articles blind? I can't see my craft. I don't know my cargo, how it's stowed, where it's stowed, or where we're bound for . . . I was never a man for taking a step in the dark. But I'm very tired of rolling round."

You'll find Sally. If you loved her and she loved you, you will be joined again. There's very little doubt she is ready and waiting for you. "Do you think she knows about me? About me *now*? She loved you, didn't she?* "She did. But does she know about me now?" *You've got to make a move, and she's got to make a move towards you. How else can you get together?* "And I've got to sign on to get there?" *If you've been told that, you'll find it's true. These people don't tell lies.*

A silence ensued. The sitters waited. Had he gone? But Time is quite different in that other dimension. In those few earthly minutes Josh Whitehead had *acted*. His love for this wench had finally made him sink his pride, abandon his gold braid, and accept the inferior position of Third Mate under his own First Officer. He had "signed on the dotted line" . . .

And suddenly his voice burst out of the medium in a shout of delight: "*Can you smell it? Can you smell the breeze? She's a-coming . . . she's lifting her forefoot . . . she's throwing the spray . . . she feels it . . .*"

His new ship had put to sea! One could almost feel the spray as she dipped and rose again on the waves. One could almost see the white wake behind her as she ploughed her way, all sails filled, across that other ocean. And I'm quite certain that when she put into the peaceful port they were bound for, young Sally Widger was on the quay, as bonny as she was when Josh last saw her more than 150 years ago.

90

A LESSON FROM AN ANONYMOUS LETTER

I am always intrigued by the psychology of people who write a letter full of "righteous" indignation, purporting to be on the side of the angels, and yet have not the courage or integrity to sign it with their name and address. It must be, of course, that in their heart of hearts they are ashamed to do so. What other reason could there be?

The reason I feel constrained to "answer" it before it is burnt is because it is signed with the legend: "*A True Christian*". This made me think that perhaps we can all learn a little from it in various ways, lest we, too, fall all unwarily into the trap of spiritual pride — which immediately renders us the very opposite of a "Christian", whose hallmark is humility. Indeed, it is a daring person who aspires to term himself or herself a *true* Christian, for I think it is safe to say that no such person exists on this earth plane.

What is a Christian? The teaching and example of the Nazarene later led to his being called by the Greek name *Christos*, meaning "the Annointed or Christed One," and thereafter to his followers becoming known as "Christians". But this Christianity as taught and demonstrated by the Nazarene has only ever been tried, to date, to a very minimal and superficial extent. This is quite evident from the state of the world.

Nor did the Nazarene incarnate on this Earth to start a new religion, but to expound and supplement the Ancient Wisdom, and, to this end, to be the medium for the Cosmic Christ Spirit which overshadowed him. He also demonstrated, in a way none other had done before, the fully materialised spirit body after physical death, thus becoming, in a sense, the Father of Spiritualism. He also demonstrated the goal which humanity will one day achieve in aeons to come: when the atoms of the physical body become so filled with spiritual light that when the soul which informs the body vacates it, the atoms of the body will be transmuted into the ether within three days.

He also added a new aspect to man's relationship to God and his fellow-men — new, inasmuch that this aspect had become totally submerged in the corrupted religions of that time. He replaced the wrathful, vengeful Jehovah (and other primitive gods) with a God of Love, a God who IS Love.

He taught that compassion, understanding, service and love were not the weaknesses they were deemed to be in a hardened, cruel era, but were the most important attributes of a human being, and formed the surest and quickest path to the "mansions" of the Father.

To heal the sick in body and mind; to succour the weak and those in

91

darkness; to comfort the mourner and uplift the weary; to release earthbound and possessing spirits; to hate evil but to love, (even if we cannot like) and show positive compassion to, the wrong-doer; to refrain from judging, for without knowledge of another soul's evolution or karma no judgement is possible; to serve others rather than self; never to do to another what we would not like done to ourselves; to recognize God in all manifesting forms, even to the stones under our feet. These are just a *few* of the things he taught.

He also gave us a blueprint to aid us in discovering and knowing *ourselves*, so that mankind, through self-knowledge, might advance spiritually a few steps further up the mountain which leads from the vaporous valley of distorted shapes and shadows to the clear dawn Light. Above all, perhaps, he taught that what matters much more than our *believing*, or subscribing to this or that "religion" or ritual, is our *becoming*. Belief is static. Becoming is active. And until we come to know ourselves quite ruthlessly and honestly, and then do something about it, we cannot *become* anything. We remain automata, the robots of the lower mind.

Anyone, therefore, of whatever religion or none, who is able to demonstrate in his or her life some or all of the teachings of the Nazarene, albeit to a limited degree *but from the heart*, can be termed a "Christian". It is a non-personal, universal concept. It is the fundamental Law of this universe. It is the Law of Love-in-action.

But where, where is the love in the proclamation I received from "A True Christian?" Here I must explain that a certain Mr H. who lives in a Midland town, apparently claims that he has on a number of occasions seen and spoken to a vision of a lady in blue, whom he calls the Blue Madonna, and that she has cured him of a serious illness. If this is really so, Mr H. has been greatly blessed, both by his clairvoyant vision and by his healing.

Why, then, is my anonymous correspondent incensed to the point of fury? Let me tell you. First, because (and I quote) "not only does he make this claim on his own behalf. He also has the effrontery to make a similar claim for a *mongrel dog* belonging to him!" (Whoever Mr H. is, and whatever he is, I just loved him when I read this!) Secondly, because it seems that Mr H. is unfortunate enough to live in "a back street slum". The writer also informs me he is "a drunkard", and adds, with true charity, "It is my opinion he should have stayed in the gutter where he rightly belongs."

Thirdly, because he is not attached to any church, and is said to be an agnostic. "Why," asks the writer, "should the Madonna make herself known to such a man? Why should she choose to appear in a filthy back yard?"

Fourthly, because the writer apparently knows where and to whom "the Madonna" (or Mary, as I am sure she prefers to be called) would or would not choose to appear: "It would certainly not be in such a place as this. She would have chosen a place — *and a person* — more fitting."

Fifthly, because Mrs X. "a highly respected medium (?) and other church authorities, after having met and listened to Mr H.'s outrageous story, promptly dismissed him as a liar. I agree with their sentiments," the writer goes on, "and urge all good Christian people to join with me in denouncing him . . ."

I think I have quoted enough to give the gist and tone of this communication. Of course it is easy to say that the unhappy person who wrote this is sick, and leave it at that. But this sickness is of a kind which does infect people, in some form or another and to a large or small extent, more often than one would suppose, and certainly more often than is good either for ourselves or others.

None of us can plead Not Guilty to passing judgements, from time to time, on people about whose lives, or spiritual evolution, or karma we know absolutely nothing. It inflates our egos to do so. It is so much easier to see the mote in our brother's or sister's eye than to look searchingly into the mirror to find the beam in our own.

This does not mean that we should not be *discerning* about other people, or shut our eyes to their problems or mistakes, or ignore evidence which indicates that they are treading an unfruitful path which they will surely have to retrace sooner or later, here or hereafter. Sometimes we can give them a helping hand — if they will accept it. If not, they must proceed on their way; in which case sincere prayer for light to surround them and penetrate them is doubtless the most helpful course.

So I offer my hand to the writer of this letter, since it is written to me, in the hope that something I say might help, or ring a bell somewhere upstairs in this person's higher mind.

My friend, why should it be an affront if a dog should share a psychic experience, and in so doing be healed of a complaint? Domestic animals are much more clairvoyant than the majority of humans. They cringe in fear, with coat or fur raised, in the presence of unpleasant entities or vibrations, but absolutely bask in the radiance of a good or elevated spirit.

Many are the times my attention has been drawn to the presence of a discarnate friend by the purring gaze of my cat, directed over my head or shoulder, and following the movement of my unseen visitor. And most dogs are very psychic indeed, which makes them, as we know, good subjects for spiritual healers to treat. Is not a dog infinitely precious as an expression of the One Life — mongrel or not? (How many mongrels there are amongst us humans!) Is a dog less worthy than a sparrow, not one of which is overlooked by the Father?

And how can any man's spiritual status be evaluated as "low" simply because, through circumstances we do not know, he has the misfortune to live in a slum area, and, it seems, also to suffer from a serious illness? Men have been driven to drown their sorrows by drinking with much less reason, especially if they are very sensitive to the cruelties and sufferings of the world. One has only to recall many of our most inspired poets.

No one "belongs" in the gutter, either physically or metaphorically. If people temporarily find themselves there, then they are objects of compassion, not contempt. It was the callousness of the Eastern religions in this respect which the Nazarene challenged. We should seek out the reason and if possible, help them out of it. If we "pass by on the other side," like the Levite in the parable of the Good Samaritan, we may well find ourselves in a similar situation in our next incarnation.

Why should Mary make herself known to this man, and in this place? I do not know, nor can anyone else know. But I do know that this dear woman, who bore much suffering in her earthly life, has not removed herself beyond our ken to some impossibly high Heaven, but plays her part in aiding the work of the Great White Brotherhood of which he who was her earthly son is the Master of Masters.

Whether or not it was she who caused Mr H.'s vision, she has certainly made herself known from time to time, and also succeeded in imparting much information through the dedicated trance mediums of certain spiritual groups whose reputations are beyond reproach. Was poor little Bernadette considered "a fitting person?" Indeed not. She aroused the fury of the "righteous" and was called a liar by those who considered *themselves* to be more "fitting" recipients of such visitations than an uneducated girl from "a back street slum."

Just suppose, for a moment, that this man who lives with his mongrel dog had done Mary a very great service or kindness in a previous life, those many years ago in Palestine, or perhaps on the flight into Egypt, or here in Glastonbury. Nothing is beyond the bounds of possibility, and no one is in a position to contradict such a possibility. Just suppose, for instance, that he was that inn-keeper (no doubt quite fond of the bottle behind his bar) who took pity on the plight of a pregnant woman and offered her his stable when everyone else had turned her away? Is it not interesting to think on these things?

And are we not apt to forget, my friend, that the Nazarene was often castigated by the Pharisees for keeping company which was not "fitting?" Sitting down and talking to "publicans and sinners," they said. In other words, helping those who were most in need of his help.

And was it not one who had formerly been a rich courtesan, a harlot, — one, moreover, whom he had once delivered from possession by seven earthbound spirits — who was the *first* to see the risen materialised Master on that first day of the week?

So, my anonymous friend, would it not make the sun's rays shine more warmly on us all if we refrained from casting the first stone? And if Mr Derek H. and his dog *did* see what he says they saw, and *were* healed, as he says they were? And if it was not so (and it is indeed a strange experience to invent) then let us pray that it may yet be so.

THE TRAMP WHO WALKED WITH ANGELS

The following incident was related to me by a friend. In the early 60's, just before an old Spiritualist Church in Brighton, Sussex, was demolished, and while the cottages next to it were empty, also awaiting demolition, a wellknown tramp took up residence in the derelict cottage by the church entrance.

He was known to all and sundry as "Sunshine Joe." He had no fixed abode. Indeed, he suffered from claustrophobia when some kind person obtained a furnished room for him, and found he could not stay in it. This claustrophobia was made more acute by undergoing two months in a prison cell after he had been had up for begging — an unfair charge, it would seem, as he never begged but was an industrious pavement artist. However, having no address, he was not eligible for Social Security, and many Spiritualists gave him little parcels of food.

One day Ivor Davies, the President of the Church, and his wife Gertrude invited him in to a Sunday service. He accepted the invitation but would not sit with the rest of the people. He sat behind a heavy curtain at the back of the hall which Mrs Davies draped back sufficiently for him to see the medium.

It was a lovely service. The hall was brightly lit, the singing was good, and an excellent trance address was given through the mediumship of Mrs Gladys Burtenshaw, followed by a demonstration of her clair-voyance and clairaudience.

After contacting two people in the congregation, Mrs Burtenshaw said she wished to speak to "the dark gentleman hiding behind the curtain." (With his long unbrushed hair and beard and weather-beaten face, Sunshine Joe certainly did appear dark).

At first he did not answer, but when my friend, who was near him, quietly told him to speak up, he replied in a refined voice, "Yes, Madam!" "You knew I was going to speak to you, didn't you?" said the medium. "Yes, Madam," he replied. "I felt someone touch my shoulder *before* you spoke to me."

"There is a highly evolved spirit here," continued Mrs Burtenshaw. "He tells me he knew you when he lived in this life, and his name is Joseph." "Yes, Madam," said Sunshine Joe, "he was the Master of the Workhouse where I was brought up."

"You think you walk alone," she went on. "*You are never alone. You walk hand in hand with the angels.*" (Mrs Burtenshaw was referring to the White Brotherhood, who are sometimes called angels or white angels by many people.) She repeated the words slowly, in a tone my friend could only describe as holy, as if she had been raised in spirit to vastly higher realms and was full of wonder. She remained quiet for a few minutes. Then she resumed the demonstration of her gifts.

But it was no good. Almost at once she stopped, and turning to Mr Davies on the platform, said, "I am sorry, but I cannot go on. I cannot climb down from the heights." And she sat down. There was a stunned silence.

After the service finished, Sunshine Joe slipped out from behind the curtain at the back and was the first to leave. But as the rest of the congregation moved towards the entrance my friend listened to their remarks as one person after another commented in amazement: "Fancy going to *him*, and not to us!" Oh shame! Verily the last shall be first and the first last! The lesson to be learned from the anonymous letter writer mentioned in the last chapter has apparently still to be digested in many quarters — even in a Spiritualist Church, it seems!

Sunshine Joe still walks around and sleeps rough, but I'll wager that he is a beacon of light to many poor souls with whom he comes in contact. If his old friend Joseph and the "angels" walk with him, then they cannot but be helped. How much nearer to the Great Spirit is a tramp who earns the name of Sunshine than a dictator who brings misery to millions!

DREAMING TRUE

Dreams can often be utilised as a means of communication by those near and dear to us who have passed from this life. And are there not countless instances in the Bible of people being warned in a dream, or given advice or instructions in a dream? The Magi were told "in a dream" not to go back to Herod when they left Bethlehem. Joseph was told "in a dream" to take the child and depart for Egypt; and so on.

Of course it *seems* like a dream to the waking consciousness, but in reality the sleeper has left the body during the sleep state and has actually met and communicated with those on another dimension. Very often the communication is not given in words, but in pictures and symbols. In the following story the man's father (in spirit) tries to prove his identity to his son by showing him pictures of his childhood home and places they had been for holidays. This is built up in a series of dreams in order to make his son really take notice and, so to speak, wait for the next instalment!

After spending a year in the Persian Gulf, where he had been working as an industrial geologist for an oil company, a middle-aged man called Leslie French arrived back in England.

He had lived a roving life for the previous twenty years and had lost touch with many of his relatives. He wrote to his parents only rarely. His mother had died in 1957, and on arriving back in London in August 1961 it was to find that his father had died the previous week in Liverpool. There were a few pieces of furniture, some books and a box of papers left to Leslie in his father's Will — everything the old man possessed. There was hardly any money, just enough to cover the funeral expenses.

A few weeks later, while staying with a cousin in Surrey, and waiting for his next foreign assignment, Leslie French had a series of dreams. Every one concerned his father, and they were usually set in Leslie's childhood — the garden, a field, the seashore, and, on one occasion, a railway station. In *all* the dreams his father had a message to give him about money.

In one dream he told his son: "I have taken good care of you. There is a new Will, and I will tell you more about it in good time." In another dream he said, "It is in a numbered deposit box, but it is not the right time to say any more. You must be patient." In the last dream the message was simply: *"Mrs Cockroft, Finchley."*

What all this meant, Leslie had not the slightest idea. Actually he was in little need of money as he was a bachelor and well paid by his firm — but the dreams and messages contained in them intrigued him so much that he spoke about them to various friends. Finally, one of them put him in touch with an acquaintance called Jack who was interested in Spiritualism.

"I expect you won't be able to make anything of it," Leslie said to Jack, when they met. "I've probably been eating too much for supper!" "On the contrary," said Jack, "I can make quite a lot of it. For instance, *Mrs Helen Cockroft happens to be a medium, and she does live in Finchley!*"

So he arranged for Leslie and Mrs Cockroft to meet one November afternoon — three months after his father had died. The appointment was not in Leslie's name, and Mrs Cockroft had no means of discovering anything about her unknown visitor.

Yet a few minutes after they were all settled in her consulting room, she turned to Leslie and said: "You have come to me about a series of dreams which feature someone, now departed, who was very dear to you."

She went on to say that every dream had included a message concerning finance, possibly a Will. "The matter is complicated, and I am not able to see any more at the moment," she told him, "but if you come back, I will try again."

At this first meeting the medium was doubtless exercising her gifts of ESP (extra-sensory perception) and no actual contact with Leslie's father seems to have been made. I mention this for a purpose. The following week Leslie visited Mrs Cockroft again, this time by himself. She told him that in the meantime she had made a strong contact with his father and had received from him the number 2231 and the address of a famous Oxford Street store.

Maddeningly, Leslie had to leave for Amsterdam to supervise an oil-drilling, and was away two or three weeks. But during that time he had a *further* dream. This time his father seemed very pleased and told him: "You have done a very good job. You did right to visit that lady."

Now all that remained was to ring up the store and ask what the number 2231 meant. He was told that the number could possibly relate to a strong-box in the firm's safe-deposit, but that the information was confidential and could not be disclosed.

However, the following week Leslie visited the store to meet a member of the Board of Directors, taking his solicitor with him. The company admitted that the box (number 2231) had been rented by a Mr French, but in no circumstances could it be opened without his authority. Of course, after they had verified that Mr French senior had died, and that Leslie was heir to all his property, they agreed to open the box.

In the presence of Leslie, his solicitor, and two representatives of the firm, this was carried out the following Friday. Inside was a signed Will and an insurance policy naming Leslie as beneficiary, and realising, on the death of the insured, the sum of £5,000.*

In my opinion this kind of evidence — even on such a simple and mundane level (for of course anyone who has only passed over so recently is still very concerned about the welfare of his family and other earthly matters) — absolutely refutes the notions of some occult groups and societies that a medium can only "re-vitalise" the disintegrating etheric or "vital body" or "astral shell" of the departed person, and that the individual in question is not present or communicating.

If this rather fantastic notion were so, such a revitalised "astral shell" could not possibly carry on an intelligent and very personal conversation on many subjects, including its own experiences after "death," could it? One might as well say that all the appearances of the Master Jesus after the crucifixion, when he continued to give important teaching to his followers in their "home circle" in the upper room loaned to them by his uncle Joseph of Arimathea were merely appearances of an astral shell!

I believe I am correct in saying that, in normal circumstances, the "vital body" (which kept the physical body activated) disintegrates in about three days — the individual, of course, being fully alive in his or her spirit body, as real and solid to them in their dimension as ours is to us in our dimension. I have heard, however, that sometimes these sloughed-off astral shells can be seen round graveyards, having the tendency, in certain cases, to be drawn towards the old physical body for a while. This gives rise to the idea of "haunted graveyards," but *such* "ghosts," when seen, are *not* the individuals.

As for the criticism often voiced by certain occultists that mediums read a sitter's aura, and pick up thought-forms: well, if a sitter consults a

---

With acknowledgement to the monthly Telegraph magazine, South Africa, in which this true story first appeared.

98

medium or clairvoyant who does *not* go into trance, but who "gets" things about the sitter — maybe troubles or worries, family situations, work, people, or even what is likely to occur in the near future, and so on, this *does* come through the medium's very wonderful gift of clairvoyance and the ability to read the aura and see symbols which can be interpreted (sometimes being aided clairaudiently by the guide or control in attendance.)

This is indeed a very wonderful gift, like psychometry, or any other form of ESP at a high level. What is wrong with this, I may ask? It is this ESP that scientists everywhere are now getting so excited about!

No medium would even pretend that this was anything to do with communication, *unless* someone in spirit definitely showed himself or herself, and gave messages to be passed on to the sitter. (As in the case of Joseph and Sunshine Joe). In which event the medium can describe the person in detail, report what the person in spirit is saying, and the sitter can reply, thus carrying on a conversation.

There is a tendency for people who have not studied this vast subject thoroughly, or had the opportunity of much experience, to want every detail "cut and dried," put into pigeon-holes and neatly labelled! But we are dealing with the cosmic!

In conclusion I would say "God bless mediums." Theirs is a privilege — usually earned in previous lives — a responsibility, and an opportunity for service which is unequalled. May they "love, cherish and obey," and never debase or exploit their gifts.

STRANGER THAN FICTION

A Spiritualist friend of mine whom I shall call Florence, gave me permission to recount the following strange story in which she played a major part. I only wish I had known of it many years ago when I was a scriptwriter, for it contains all the ingredients for a film!

The scene is a very ancient Manor House in Sussex. The main characters involved in this particular episode in its long history are:
Mrs X — a Spiritualist friend of Florence's.
Fiona — Mrs X's unmarried daughter.
John — Mrs X's son-in-law.
Mrs B — a medium.
Florence.
The local doctor.
The head of a mental hospital.
Perhaps I should add that the above are the "living" characters.

Not unnaturally the old Manor House had a reputation locally for being haunted, and although John laughed scornfully at such an idea, he was grateful, nevertheless, at being able to buy the place at a greatly reduced price on this account, and Mrs X, her two daughters and son-in-law took up residence in the January, a few years ago.

Within two months John was startled out of his sceptical attitude, for on entering his study one day in March, he saw the grey-robed figure of a young girl gazing mournfully out of the window. She turned, and looked at him. Whereupon he fled, white-faced and shaken.

In May, Florence and a mediumistic friend, Mrs B., were invited to tea in the family's new home. Neither of them knew anything about the supposed hauting. After walking about the grounds and along the "Priest walk," they were shown round the house. During their tour of inspection Mrs B saw clairvoyantly many figures from the past, including many monks. (They discovered, later, that the house had indeed been the home of monks centuries ago, until the dissolution of the monasteries by Henry VIII. Subsequently it had for a long time been a Church of England vicarage, but this has no bearing on our story.)

It was Florence, however, who surprised both Mrs B. and the four occupants of the house while they were inspecting the cellars and speculating about the house's history. Suddenly she felt she was a military man, cooped up in that cellar and unable to escape. So great was her agitation that she broke into the conversation to tell them of her acute sensations.

It was now her turn to be surprised when *they* told her that she had been pacing to and fro, to and fro, quite ignoring them. Yet she was quite unaware she had left the group, or indeed moved about at all, and was able to repeat their conversation which part of her mind had been listening to.

There was a mystery here which had to be resolved, and when Florence and Mrs B. were departing after tea, they both felt a work had been left undone. Accordingly they asked if they could return the following week, with the intention of holding a circle in the house in the hope of being able to help a very unhappy condition.

Events took a dramatic turn, however, before the week was out. The unmarried daughter, Fiona — an extremely sensitive young person — was found lying unconscious on the floor of her bedroom. The local doctor was hastily sent for, and in his presence she "came round," crying bitterly, and saying she could not go on living because there was nothing to live for any more . . .

The doctor forthwith had her admitted to a mental hospital as a potential suicide. Her alarmed mother presumably concurred, being at her wits' end, and not suspecting at that juncture that this untoward happening was in any way connected with the house — or Fiona's bedroom.

When Florence, Mrs B and two other Spiritualists who had accompanied them to act as "power houses" arrived on the day appointed

100

for the seance, they had no idea what had occurred, and assumed Fiona was at work. Perhaps not wishing to upset them just before the sitting commenced (at which none of the family were present) Mrs X did not tell them about Fiona till *afterwards*.

So the circle, consisting of Mrs B, Florence and the two other Spiritualists, sat privately. Almost immediately Mrs B. was entranced by a most unhappy soul. She rose from the chair and went to the window, sobbing. Encouraged by Florence to try and speak to them, the unhappy entity said her name was Lucy, that she was waiting and waiting for a letter from James, her loved one, but it never came, and that *she could not go on living because there was nothing to live for any more* . . .

Florence ushered the entranced medium back to the chair, and tried to explain to Lucy that her James was no longer living on earth, and nor in fact was she. Much time had passed, and if only she could try and understand her real situation she would be helped to find her loved one.

But Lucy, too cocooned in her despairing state of mind, could not understand what they were trying to tell her, and Florence called mentally for help from the medium's spiritual guide, Abdul. In the twinkling of an eye, it seemed, Lucy was displaced from the medium's body, and Abdul took control.

He told Florence she should have no fear, that he would now be able to take Lucy up to the Light. Although the Manor House was a good house, and many prayers had been said there by many occupants, those in spirit were too high, vibrationally, to penetrate the impenetrable wall of dark gloom with which Lucy had surrounded herself in her one-track longing for word from Lieut. James Day — who, *unbeknown to her, had been held captive in the cellar of her own house, and battered to death there*, during the Civil War in the 17th century!

It had needed a focal point, a medium on the earth plane, to make contact with the poor girl who had been earthbound for so long, (though time would have been meaningless to her, more like a recurring dream state). Asked why she had never obsessed or possessed anyone in the house over all those years, Abdul explained that she had been too wrapped up within her own consciousness, waiting only for James, to notice any of the occupants *until now*.

Then Abdul, entrancing the medium still, stood up, arms raised high. The arms were held out in welcome, and words were uttered in some foreign tongue. He appeared to encircle someone in his arms, and a look of ineffable happiness spread over "his" face . . .

The medium's consciousness returned as Abdul vacated control of her. She looked around, saying she could see Abdul and Lucy surrounded by a throng of white-robed figures, and they were going through a door.

The sitters were overcome by a feeling of wonder and gratitude that they had been used to help her release. Indeed, Florence and Mrs B. must assuredly have been prompted to invite themselves to the house again to hold this seance. And who knows whether John, the erstwhile sceptical son-in-law, had not also been prompted by spirit to buy the Manor House in the first place — to be startled by the vision of Lucy at his study window?

But what of Fiona? After the dramatic sitting had concluded and the four who took part in it joined their hostess, Mrs X broke the news to them that Fiona had been removed to hospital that very week, and recounted the baffling circumstances which were so distressing.

Immediately Florence heard what Fiona had said on recovering consciousness in her bedroom (which turned out to be Lucy's bedroom), she realised the words were absolutely identical with those uttered by Lucy while entrancing the medium!

It became obvious that Fiona, a hyper-sensitive girl, had been overcome by Lucy's anguish in the bedroom they "shared," and had temporarily been "taken over" by Lucy's personality, and her unconsciousness had been, in fact, a trance state.

Florence despatched a letter to the Medical Superintendant of the mental hospital in which she attempted to explain the "haunting;" Lucy's words which were identical to Fiona's; that the unconsciousness had been an entrancement; that the patient was *not* a potential suicide or melancholic, but was hyper-sensitive and had been obsessed by this earthbound personality.

This was indeed more than a mouthful for the Superintendant to swallow, and the reply was a curt one! *But*, a few days later, he discharged Fiona with the words: "There is nothing wrong with you. You are *never* to return here." What had happened?

It transpired that once again Fiona had slipped into unconsciousness, and remained so for three days and three nights. She lay quite peacefully in her bed, looking happy and well-nourished. No drugs had been administered. The staff were non-plussed, but it must have been realised that what Florence had written was the truth, for the patient had followed exactly the same pattern of unconsciousness as before she was admitted. But this time she awoke as her normal, happy, bright self! *As happy as Lucy now was* . . . Fiona continues to hold down a good job. But Abdul has advised her, through his medium, not to investigate psychical phenomena as she is too sensitive and would be unable to protect herself.

So concludes this strange but true story, with the following interesting additions:

1. Florence later discovered, from the Public Reference Room where she went to look up the history of the Manor House, (a) that Lucy and her family had lived there in the 17th century, and (b) that a young soldier had been battered to death in the cellar during the Civil War. These facts were quite unknown to her or to anyone else concerned at the material time.

2. The week after Lucy's rescue had been effected, Florence and her friends attended a service in a Brighton church, and the clairvoyant

demonstrator, who was unknown to them, came to her and said she had just completed some work for spirit, and to look to August (three months ahead) for a result of this work.

3. In August, at a circle in her own home, Florence was told by the medium present that a young girl dressed in a long flowing robe, mittens, a poke bonnet, and with curls hanging down over her shoulders, was walking over to her (to Florence). She gave her name, and said she was Lucy's sister, and thanked her for helping her sister to join her loved ones.

Who can deny that truth is stranger — and more wonderful — than fiction?

THE DOG THAT ASKED FOR HEALING

How our dear friend Francis — sometimes referred to by the Other Side as "the Light of Assisi" — must have smiled at Chum! For Chum was a dog of character if ever there was one: self-contained to a degree, never responding by so much as a tail-wag to a friendly greeting. Pearl Gorvin, the healer, wrote me the following delightful story about him:

"A few years ago I lived in a little seaside town in Northern Ireland. A neighbour owned a terrier dog called Chum. (A complete misnomer!) I made repeated attempts to become friendly with him, for he used to trot past my bungalow, on his own, several times a day. But he always ignored me utterly, never even turning his head. This went on for about *three years*. I even wondered if he were deaf.

"However, in time Chum developed a severe skin complaint; but he continued his lone walks, ignoring my advances as usual. His back was very sore, so I put him on Absent Healing. Then, one day, I heard a scratching on the back door, and went to see what it was. It was Chum! He had come up the garden path, up several steps, and stood silently before me.

" 'Well, Chum,' said I, 'come along in,' and he did just that. He stood perfectly still in the centre of the kitchen, and allowed me to give him healing — after which he at once trotted out again, and *never came back*. Neither did he acknowledge me. He just passed and re-passed as before, never turning his head in my direction, as 'un-Chummy' as ever!

"In a short time, though, the skin all down his back was quite healthy, the sores all healed, and that was all that mattered. I often wondered if it could have been St. Francis who sent, or brought, Chum for his healing."

Perhaps it was. That *someone* in spirit prompted or guided him to take the action he did is evident. And this someone was in turn drawn to do so by the absent healing prayers offered by the healer on this dog's behalf.

Thus, what often appears to be an astonishing, almost miraculous event is really a logical sequence of cause and effect. (In this case one could have wished that Chum would henceforth have passed the time of day with his benefactress, so put it mildly, for ingratitude is usually associated with humans!)

A most touching instance of gratitude and remembrance was told me by another reader, Mr. P. One day during the war Mr. P's daughter found a lame magpie on the doorstep of their home — doubtless guided there by spirit helpers. The leg was broken. She put on a splint, and dressed it. She named him Billy, and taught him many games, like knocking a ping-pong ball back to her from any part of the garden — a game magpies love, as I know from my own experience.

In 1945 they had a bad air-raid. Poor Billy took fright and flew away from his perch in the garage, and did not come back. But some *months* later, Mr. P. and his family were sitting in the garden when they suddenly heard Billy's familiar call from the garden fence. There he was — with his "wife!" After a friendly chat, and an exchange of happy greetings, both birds, calling loudly, flew away together. What pleasure he had brought to the family by letting them know all was well with him and, as it were, returning to say "thank you!"

Which naturally brings me to our own magpie, Joey, mentioned in a previous chapter. He has taken over both us and the premises. Our cat, Moppet, has accepted him and they will both sit together on the table. He insists on sleeping in the house, and if the door is open thinks nothing of walking up the passages in the morning to see who is getting up.

He has become very possessive about "his" kitchen window, however, which sometimes presents problems if anyone is staying in our cottage, next to the house. For people have a habit of talking to us through the window, and when this happens he persecutes them quite viciously! He is obviously defending his personal precincts, for he has been extremely friendly with the 30 or so visitors we have had since his arrival — *except* the two or three who have talked through the window, and these he henceforth regards as enemies wherever they may be. Even an umbrella opened as a shield will not drive him away!

What a welcome he gave me when I returned from a week in Scotland with young Gavin and a school-friend of his. We had started the 600-mile drive late in the day, meaning to spend the night on the way, but I decided to make for home instead. So we finally crept into the house at 4 a.m., careful not to wake my husband. But Joey knew I had returned, and at 8.30 in the morning he came through the open window of my room, straight on to the bed, and made little soft crooning noises while I kissed his head, put my hands round him, and generally made a fuss of him. This went on for at least five minutes.

He is really a *most* remarkable, and endearing bird. I cannot help wondering if he is indeed "half angel and half bird," for that great teacher known as "The Tibetan," (or the Master Djwhal Khul) tells us: "The bird kingdom is specifically allied to the deva evolution. Certain groups of devas (nature spirits and the like) who desire to pass into the human kingdom, having developed certain faculties, can do so via the bird kingdom; and certain devas who wish to get in communication with human beings can do so via the bird kingdom.

"These cases are not many . . . but in the cases which do occur these devas pass several cycles in the bird kingdom, building in a response to a vibration which will ultimately swing them into the human family. In this way they become accustomed to the use of a gross form, without the limitations and impurities which the animal kingdom engenders."

It is beyond my comprehension how people in some European countries can bring themselves to snare and kill thousands of song-birds during their annual migration south. Moreover, certain "fashionable" shops in London which import jars of little birds as pickled delicacies should be prohibited from doing so. Since it is illegal to snare birds in Britain, it should also be illegal to import snared birds. One wonders what kind of person really enjoys that pitiful mouthful of robin or redstart, thrush or pippit. Surely mankind has progressed somewhat since Roman emperors ate a thousand larks' tongues for "starters!"

The quality of fidelity in so many animals is truly amazing. Their psychic awareness also. How many, many authenticated proofs of this could I relate, if I had the space. How does a dog who literally "missed the boat" at Vancouver when his master sailed for Japan, select out of all the ships in the harbour another vessel also bound for Japan — and to the same Japanese port?

Yet this is what a terrier called Hector did, when he followed his master 5000 miles across the Pacific. Nineteen days later the ship he had stowed away in, the *S.S. Hanley,* was unloading its cargo in Yokohama when another steamer docked about 300 yards away, and some men from this steamer got into a sampan and sailed near the *Hanley's* stern. Muttering and quivering with excitement, Hector jumped into the water and swam to the small boat, where he was hoisted aboard — into the arms of his master, Willem Mante, who had thought never to see his beloved companion again! It is an incredible story, but a true one.

Moggy, a cat taken in by a neighbouring family when her mistress was taken to hospital, suddenly disappeared one night (though she had become great friends with this family). Her old mistress had died in hospital, and at the funeral a few days later the family were astonished to see Moggy sitting on a tombstone, watching the proceedings. She had come 15 miles, to a village she could not possibly have known, for her mistress's funeral!

Nor was this the only journey this most psychic cat undertook, for later on, when the young son of the family was taken seriously ill some *20 miles away,* he kept on calling for his beloved Moggy in his delirium. He and

Moggy had formed a great attachment. One evening when the boy's mother was sitting, helpless, at his bedside, she heard a slight noise. It was Moggy quietly jumping through the window! When the boy felt the cat on his bed, he fell into a calm sleep, and recovered from that moment. Moggy had received his calls telepathically. This in itself is not very unusual where there is the link of love. But this brave cat responded instantly by setting out to find him over strange country all those miles away.

I suppose the moving story of Bobby, the Skye terrier who has a statue erected to his memory in Edinburgh, is wellknown, especially as Walt Disney made a memorable film about him in 1960. It was in 1872 that Bobby finally passed over, to be united in the spirit world with the old shepherd he loved so much that he never left his grave for *14 years*, except once a day just to get a meal from a friendly restaurant-keeper. Such fidelity and devotion is fantastic, and surely makes us humans feel very humble indeed.

A member of a "rescue circle" in South Africa, called The White Rose Circle, has told me how many times animals have been instrumental in helping to bring souls out of the shadows into the light. One man, who had been a hermit in earth life, was helped to the Light by his beloved birds; another man by his little fox terrier. While others would not budge from their conditions until their horses came and fetched them . . .

Verily we are all members one of another, for all creations have One Father, and we should do well to remember and practice the advice of the great Russian writer Dostoevsky. "Love all God's creation, the whole and every grain of sand in it", he wrote. "Love every leaf, every ray of God's light. Love the animals, love the plants. Love everything. If you love everything, you will perceive the divine mystery in things. Once you perceive it, you will begin to comprehend it better every day, and you will come at last to love the whole world with an all-embracing love."

As this chapter is about animals, written in the month rightly dedicated to them in honour of the birth of their champion, the beloved Francis, who prompts the pens of all of us who plead their cause, especially in the merciless experimental laboratories of the world, I feel I can do no better than to end with "The Dog's Prayer:"

"O Lord of all creatures, grant that Man, my master, may be as faithful to other men as I am faithful to him. Make him as loving towards his family and friends as I am loving to him. Grant that he may guard with honesty the good things with which Thou hast endowed him as honestly as I guard his.

"Give him, O Lord, a happy and ready smile, as happy and spontaneous as the wagging of my tail. Make him as ready to show gratitude as I am eager to lick his hand. Give him patience as great as mine when I await his return without complaining. Grant him my courage and my readiness to sacrifice all for him, even my own life. May he possess my youthful spirit and joy of thought.

"O Lord of all creatures, as I am in truth only a dog, make my master always truly a man."

LEARNING FROM OUR "LESSER BRETHREN"

One day, when my son was smaller, we were playing hide-and-seek among the tall lush bracken, down in the valley of our wood. Here young larch trees rise from the greenery on a steep slope, with the stream gurgling over little rocky waterfalls just below. Sometimes one comes face to face with an inquisitive fox cub, too young to be scared by the sight of an odd-looking creature on two legs, wearing clothes instead of fur.

But the slope really belongs to the badgers. They have chosen this ideal site, with all mod. cons. for what is said to be one of the largest badgeries in Sussex. These charming creatures have excavated a network of enormous, complicated sets, scrupulously clean within the various chambers, and with well-worn surface runs to the nicely hidden community toilet a discreet distance away.

They are on friendly terms with the foxes, and have a gentleman's agreement about sharing in emergency. The local hunt is not allowed through our forestry unit, nor through our neighbour's 60 acres, so when in pursuit of a fox, have to call off the hounds when they come to our boundaries. Then, if my husband is working in the wood, he watches with quiet satisfaction as the old fox cocks a snook at them, lollops unhurried down the valley and disappears into a badger's set.

They are on friendly terms with us, too, coming up the garden to the back door for scraps, keeping the youngsters in order with grunts and sharp taps of the paw on their backsides if they misbehave. On one occasion, in the early morning, a very young one was playing with Gavin's inflatable boat tied up at the edge of the pond. He was soon picked up by the scruff of the neck by his anxious mum, who then proceeded to administer a reprimand with much grunting and grumbling.

One evening, going out to my dustbin, I saw a badger watching me intently through the archway. Although he disappeared, his curiosity was such that in a moment his long, white-striped face popped round the corner again for another long look. It was positively embarrassing! He has since become very tame and allows us to speak to him on his regular evening visit. How incredible that only a comparatively few years ago human beings not only enjoyed baiting captive badgers with fierce dogs, but first sawed off their strong lower jaws to put the poor beasts at a terrible disadvantage.

107

Anyway, while playing hide-and-seek, creeping low through the veritable forest of bracken stems, I came upon a large round nest, and in it, as if sleeping comfortably, was the skeleton of an old badger. He had known when it was time to go, and as no self-respecting badger would leave its heavy body inside a set, he had made a nest some little way away, curled up in it, and simply gone to sleep.

Why, I asked myself, have the vast majority of human beings forgotten or lost the art of dying, easily and gracefully, at the appointed time? How very few of us are able to continue and enjoy our normal routine or work, in full possession of all our faculties, and then feel suddenly very tired, sit down in the armchair or go to bed, and wake up in the spirit world.

This is what dying *should* be — and once was, long long ago, before man deviated from the laws of the Great Spirit, and by so doing created disease and filth, violence and crime, wars, hatred, greed, cruelty, wrong thinking, wrong eating, wrong doing . . .

This, I have been told by a wise, evolved guide, is what transition is like, *when desired*, on the ethereal planet Venus: the individual retires to a special place, and goes to sleep. In a short time even the "body" has disappeared.

This, too, we are taught from spirit, is how transition was in the *very* early life of the planet Earth, before it solidified and became heavy. Even in the Second Period of Atlantis, "death" was a self-induced process, undertaken when the Higher Self was convinced that it had served its purpose in that particular vehicle.

What a contrast, I thought, to the pathetic geriatric wards of our Hospitals, Homes and Mental Institutions where, so often, the spirit has all but totally withdrawn but is still held in leash by a malfunctioning, dissociated or diseased body which will not or cannot die, and sometimes is not allowed to do so by a zealous medical profession.

This sorry state of affairs derives from humanity having become emancipated from the directive of the group soul, individually independent, and therefore responsible for the results of free-will, reaping over and over again the effects of causes. Because of Man's increasing heaviness, contact was lost with the great Beings from the spheres who had once been his teachers and leaders.

Animals, on the other hand, even when "individualised" through close association with Man (thus achieving *personal* survival after physical death) are still, at the present stage, guided and informed by the group soul of each species, of which they are a part. We call this guidance the mystery of Instinct — knowledge without knowing, reason without reasoning. They know, but do not *know* that they know. Consciousness has not become *self*-consciousness.

When a small green caterpillar crawls under a leaf and spins himself into a cocoon, it is because the small still voice tells him to do so. He does not know why. He does not *know* that in the spring sunshine he will become a beautiful butterfly. But he obeys.

Those higher animals, however, who choose to throw in their lot with Man, giving him their allegiance and love rather than adhere to their own kind and group, have already taken a most important step towards *permanent* individuality at a later stage. And with individuality comes the question and problem of choice . . .

How do *we* choose? We also have a small still voice if only we would listen to it, and obey unquestioning, and without endless prevarications and rationalisations thrown in like spanners in the works by the lower mind.

How much we can learn from animals, the so-called "lesser creation," not only in the matter of dying but in our mode of living, if only we did not think ourselves so superior. We use rude and unthinking expressions when we sometimes refer to certain people "behaving like animals," or "living like pigs."

A moment's thought would tell us how totally untrue these analogies are. Pigs are extremely clean, when *allowed* to be, never soiling their straw but always using the furthest corner, or going outside if they have an exit. They squeal and roll with delight when given fresh, sweet bedding. The intensive, crowded, cruel imprisonment of factory-farm methods are totally alien and thwarting to the natures of all creatures so caged and crowded, and creates terrible mental tension.

As for "behaving like animals," this usually refers to people who are giving way to the utmost cruelty, depravity, savagery or lust — in fact behaving as no animal would ever dream of behaving, either domestic or wild. The use of the word "bestiality" is also a complete misnomer and an insult.

Are we really so superior? We cannot see in the dark. We have not the vision of an owl or a hawk. We cannot hear or smell so acutely. We cannot fly. We cannot find our way across oceans and continents without a compass. We are not such dedicated mothers. We are not so faithful to our mates or in our relationships. And how many human beings really die of a broken heart?

Should we not regard ourselves with a little less arrogance, and a little more humility, not to mention a little more sense of humour, perhaps? A comparison with animals can be quite a salutory exercise — especially in the art of growing old gracefully!

We are bedevilled by multitudinous diseases. Not so the animals in their free state. Even in a permissive, domesticated dog or cat society, has one ever heard of venereal disease among them?

And take the decline in conformation of human beings in advancing years. What do we find? All too often over-fat, flesh-eating men with pendulous stomachs, having lost nearly every hair on their heads and usually all their teeth, and odiferous with a mixture of sweat, whisky and tobacco. Sometimes incontinent as well.

Women, too, with uncontrollable "vital statistics" unless strapped up in various places, hobble about on enormous, diseased limbs — both sexes not infrequently suffering from loss of memory, and clarity of mind, or downright "ga-ga." Does one ever find this malformation and degeneration of body and mind in old animals? Never.

"But Nature is very cruel, isn't it!" people say, feeling squeamish at a cat eating a mouse or a lion bringing down a buck, while they themselves may just have returned from bringing down a hundred pheasants and are ready to tuck into a little lamb, or a pig, or a young calf! They quite forget the multitudes of vegetarian animals. In any case there is still a large majority of human beings who do not appear to think it strange or even disgusting that they feed every day on corpses.

Wild animals are much more merciful than we are. They do not fight to the death in a trial of strength or leadership; or over territory. When one is getting the worst of it, the matter is settled, and they part. It is only human beings who bomb and maim their young and burn them with napalm, or irradiate and exterminate whole populations of their own species.

Animals do not invent abominably cruel traps or spiked clubs — not to obtain food but merely to tear the fur off their victims. And those that kill for food usually do so very swiftly, to feed themselves and their families. No animal could take any pleasure in the ghastly affair of a bull-fight, "for fun."

So by what right do we kill them? By what right do we eat them? They were never introduced on to this Earth planet for this purpose, as every teacher from spirit will tell us. They were placed here for the purposes of their own evolutions, as we were.

By what right do we exterminate them? By what right do we imprison them and make their lives a misery in living food-factories? And by what right do we torture and experiment on them in their countless millions?

We are worse even than cannibals, for they only eat their enemies. But the gentle creatures we eat are not even our enemies. They have not threatened us in any shape or form. They do their best to please us by being docile and amenable to our often diabolical designs. They have no enmity against us, but on the contrary thrive on our affection and friendship when this is offered.

"But we *need* meat!" many people say, fearing that without it their bodies will grow weak. Nothing could be further from the truth. Have they forgotten that the largest and strongest animals are *all* vegetarian? The mighty elephant, the gorilla, the bison and the bull, the hardy camel, the massive shire horse, the fleet-footed deer — one could enumerate them *ad infinitum.*

From personal experience I can say that when I gave up meat some fifteen years ago the arthritis in my hip disappeared never to return. One feels a great satisfaction in having a *clean* inside, untainted by the fermenting flesh of dead bodies. And a greater satisfaction at not having killed a friendly creature.

Also, there would be so much more food to go round if we did not rear so many millions of "food animals" *to eat it up!* It is really a tale told by an idiot that instead of manufacturing and utilising our food direct from the soil, we feed it into animals, and then kill and eat the animals — thereby losing about four-fifths of the original produce and nourishment!

We owe it to *ourselves* to listen to that small still voice which whispers to us more and more insistently at a certain stage of our spiritual evolution. For as every cell in our bodies constantly renews itself, *we are what we eat.* Every cell partakes of the substance we give it. In this way, when we do not consume flesh saturated with the coarser vibrations of the less evolved (to which fear and resentment, often terror, are all too often added) the whole body becomes a more refined vehicle.

As it is progressively filled with more light, the vibrations quicken, and we become more psychically and spiritually receptive — and a more fitting temple for the unfolding and kindling of the Divinity within each one of us.

Fortunately the effects of the Seventh Ray, now that Earth has passed into Aquarius for the next 2,400 years or so, is already being felt by many, especially among the more sensitive young people. Chains of Health Food Stores, filled with a vast variety of pure and succulent foods, have become the "in thing," and are always crowded with the nicest kinds of people. Often they are run by Spiritualists.

I am convinced that the tide of dense materiality, including the cannibalistic cult of flesh-eating, has begun to turn. But, as always, the progressive and discerning *must* be in the vanguard and give a lead to the heavy laggards in danger of being left high and dry on the far shore.

The manifold ramifications of this theme could fill a book. But it is the function of a short essay merely to provide "food for thought," in the hope of helping not only fellow human beings who are seeking the lighted way, but also the animal and bird evolutions with which we share our planet, and from whom we can learn so much.

Let us emulate the little green caterpillar who hears the small still voice and obeys. Only thus can we emerge into sunlit freedom from our dark cocoon.

WE HAVE BEEN HERE BEFORE

It is often asked: if reincarnation is a fact, why don't we remember something of our past experiences on earth? The answer is, that quite a number of people *do* remember. I think it depends to some extent on the evolution of the soul. Silver Birch says: "There are many souls who know they have incarnated before. There are others who do not. Their souls may know, their consciousness may know, but it may not be known by the *mind*."

One is constantly coming across instances of "far memory" which cannot be denied or otherwise explained. The name of Joan Grant comes instantly to mind, for she was able to dictate, whilst in a state of shifted consciousness, many books about a number of previous incarnations, the most outstanding perhaps, and certainly the most beautiful, being *Winged Pharoah*.

Grace Cooke has written in detail about past incarnations in which she was connected with her present guide who now calls himself White Eagle, in *The Illumined Ones*. Dr Arthur Guirdham has written several books about his life as a Cathar in the Middle Ages. Christine Hartley's *A Case for Reincarnation* is extremely evidential; and now comes a book by E. W. Ryall called *Second Time Round**. Ever since childhood the author has experienced a flood of memories about his life as John Fletcher, a yeoman farmer born in 1645, with details of his life, friends and relatives and his death in the battle of Sedgemoor. Many individual details, in this case, have been verified by Dr Ian Stevenson, Professor of Psychiatry at the University of Virginia School of Medicine.

One could cite numberless examples, not least the remarkable revelations that came to light from readers of a national newspaper which requested people to write in about their knowledge and memories of past lives. But I am always struck by the many cases of very young children who remember most vividly, having reincarnated very soon after an early passing in the previous life. These vivid memories appear to fade from their minds as they grow older and become fully incarnate in the present life. (We are told from spirit that we are not *fully* incarnate till the age of 21.)

When Arthur Osborn was researching for his book *The Superphysical* †several magazines printed his request for instances of past-life memories, particularly children's memories. Three cases which he investigated are very interesting:

1. Mrs A. and Mrs B. are sisters. Mrs A. gave birth to a child whom she named Cressey, a fine, affectionate little chap. He died when he was 4 years old. Two years after his death, her sister Mrs B. gave birth to a boy. As he grew up his Aunt (Mrs A.) became very attached to him and mothered him even more than his own mother. One day, while playing with the child when he was nearly four years old, and being reminded of her own son's little ways, she began to weep. "What are you crying for, Auntie?" asked the little boy. "I'm crying because you remind me so

---

*Neville Spearman Ltd
† Fredrick Muller

112

much of my own little boy, Cressey," she replied. The child looked at her with astonishment, and said, "Why Auntie, don't you know I *am* Cressey, and have come back to you?"

2. A family in Minnesota, the youngest child of which died while at school, moved to St. Paul soon after. They did not return to their home town for several years, during which time other children were born to them. When they eventually revisited their old home, which none of the younger children had ever seen, the youngest child astonished her parents by the knowledge she showed of the streets, and she also *recognised and named* several of her "former" schoolmates, in spite of the difference caused by some 10 years growth since "she," in her previous life, had been to school with them.

3. The many well authenticated cases of young Indian children remembering their former lives are perhaps wellknown, so I will only refer to the case of the ten-year-old girl in Delhi who remembered many facts, incidents, places and people of her past life in a town a little way from Delhi. She gave the address where she had lived, *the name of her husband*, and the fact that she had died in hospital shortly after the birth of a son. Everything she remembered was verified after investigation, and when, on hearing of this strange phenomenon, her "former" husband came to Delhi (without, of course, the girl's knowledge), she recognised him immediately. This case was given by Mr Radhika Narain of Ramjas College, Delhi, who talked to this girl himself.

I cannot refrain from mentioning a woman friend of mine who had a home circle with a very gifted trance medium. A close friend of her's, whom I shall call David, had been in the spirit world a few years, and was a regular communicator at her circle. One day he announced that he would not be coming any more because he was reincarnating.

Two years passed; and then, to my friend's astonishment, David controlled the medium as he had done in the past. "But you said you were going to reincarnate!" said my friend. "I did," was the reply. "I died of starvation in Ethiopia at one year old."

Now David was (or is) an evolved person, and it would seem that he needed this brief but poignant experience to complete some purpose of his soul. Indeed, his reappearance on earth in the form of this unfortunate baby was so brief that one could say that he (the individuality of David) only took very partial possession of the new physical vehicle, so soon to succumb to malnutrition, and after this short interlude, retained his former personality.

When we had our own home circle with our medium, Catherine, we also had the experience of a communicator saying that he would not be able to come again as he was going to reincarnate. He told Catherine that he had been her brother in her last but one incarnation in the Himalayas. On the interesting tapes we have of his two or three visits, speaking through Catherine in trance, he expressed a rather pained surprise at what he saw now taking place in the twentieth century, and had some pertinent things to say about the modern mode of life!

He also said that he, like her, had experienced another incarnation *since* they were brother and sister in those far-off times, but that he came to her now as Rasamandas, her former brother. This ability of a progressed spirit person to adopt one or other of his or her former roles, as it were, when manifesting, links up with a most interesting little talk which the composer Liszt had with his musical medium, Rosemary Brown, on the subject of reincarnation. Mrs Brown includes this in her delightful and fascinating book *Unfinished Symphonies**, and as Liszt seems very anxious for people to understand and think about this subject, I will quote the following excerpt:

Liszt says, "What happens is rather like the putting out of a fresh shoot on a tree or a plant. On earth, you think of yourselves as complete beings. But actually only part of you has manifested through the physical body and brain. The rest is still in spirit but is linked and one with you. The human being can be compared to an iceberg. Very often there is only a fraction of the true soul which manages to show through and express itself.

"This is one of the things that we who have gone before want to help you to develop and understand so that people while they live on earth can manifest more fully and express themselves to greater degrees . . . All incarnations are absolutely voluntary. Nobody is thrust into the world against his will. No one *has* to go there. And this makes for justice."

Liszt explained to Mrs Brown that we are not really a unit at all. Each person is soul with many aspects. "Think of an atom," he said. "It is made of protons and neutrons which all go to make up the nucleus surrounded by electrons. That is what the soul is like. These separate parts are held together in the nucleus, but the parts can be isolated. And it is the isolated parts of the nucleus of the soul so to speak which can manifest as various personalities in your world.

"These are what the reincarnationist calls different incarnations — but they all belong to one soul which can choose which particular *part* of the soul it wishes to manifest. Let me try to put it very simply for you. Supposing we have a soul that has had a link with Egypt, and then put out another branch, as it were, to perhaps Greece. That soul could then appear as an Egyptian or a Greek. It is rather similar to having a wardrobe of clothes and deciding which ones to wear; or like an actor who plays different parts. The actor remains the same. It is only the playing of the role on stage which makes him seem different. His own private life goes on."

(This reminds me, in another connection, of a beloved teacher we know in the world of spirit who often refers to "my astral wardrobe" which he

---

**Souvenir Press*

uses when wishing to manifest to those on a lower plane than his own —
for unless he did so, and "cloaked himself down," he would only appear
to them as a bright light, which would not be very satisfactory for those
who love him but who are not yet advanced enough to see him on his own
plane.)

What Liszt had to say also links with what Silver Birch has said
through his own medium on this subject: "There is a consciousness
which is *you*, of which you in the world of matter are expressing but a tiny
portion, and there are portions of that same consciousness which are
expressing themselves in other spheres of expression. You and the other
expressions are all reflections of one inner spiritual reality . . . You
become increasingly conscious of more and more of yourself."
Ultimately, it is "a union of the different portions of consciousness
returning to complete the whole."

Our spirit teachers constantly refer to "old souls" and "young souls."
What does it mean? Put simply, it means that "old souls" are those that
have travelled the evolutionary path of experience, in and out of the cloak
of matter, for a long, long time, whereas "young souls" have more lately
started out on the path of individualisation from the group soul. All,
needless to say, are sparks of the Divine Essence achieving Self-
consciousness and ultimately God-consciousness, through experiencing.

Can anyone seriously imagine that an entity that is incarnate on this
earth for a few hours, months, or a handful of years in a state of babyhood
will *never* have the opportunity of experiencing the lessons that can only
be learnt in physical form, and which are so necessary for the spiritual
progress of that soul? Can anyone seriously imagine that the millions of
entities that start the development of their physical vehicles of expression
in the womb — and are cast out by abortion — will *never* be able to pass
this way again? Could this possibly reflect divine justice?

And what about those of our friends in the spirit world who come back
to us through trance mediumship and tell us details of their former earth
life or lives? How often, too, does this information supply clues to their
character and experiences in the life they have shared with us most
recently!

As Silver Birch says: "There are many souls *who know* they have
incarnated before. There are others who do not." For the latter, perhaps
it is more difficult to "believe" in reincarnation — the Law of Rebirth
which the Master Djwhal Khul, known as "the Tibetan," tells us *must* be
taught and understood in the New Age. For the former, the knowledge
can provide useful assistance in understanding what characteristics or
failings must be overcome, and in coping with the seemingly "unjust"
situations and conditions in life.

It can also aid us in helping others in distress to come to terms with and
accept, the karma they have "earned" for themselves, and thus, by
diminishing resentment, rebellion, and other negative traits, to help them

to work it out and release themselves. But always there must be love, compassion and understanding for the one who suffers, and the attempt at all costs to help him or her into the light. We must never ever be as the Levite in the parable, who "passed by on the other side"...

FALLING ON ONE'S HEAD

This is neither as humorous nor as odd as it sounds. C. V. Wood Jr., co-founder of the Mind Science Foundation in the United States, has this to say: "Within the Mind Science Foundation we have studied many persons who have had certain psychic abilities, and *in almost all cases* the ability developed after either experiencing a fall, or being hit on the head ..." (My italics.)

This rather startling finding is surely a great deal more than co-incidence. Although there are obviously thousands of psychics who have *not* fallen or been hit on the head, it seems strange indeed that of the many psychics investigated by this establishment a head injury had sparked off their psychic awareness "in almost all cases."

My own belief is that the answer may lie in the stimulation by the injury of the pineal gland. This is an appendage of the brain for which modern science can find no specific purpose, and considers it to be the remnant of a sense organ used in the far distant past, and which has become atrophied.

Brain researchers and neuro-physiologists concern themselves solely with the brain and its electro-chemical energies, seemingly under the impression that the brain and the mind are one and the same thing. They are fascinated, for instance, by the varying emotions and desires that can be produced by planting electrodes in the brain of both men and animals. It is certainly true that an electrode in the brain can bring to the surface early, buried experiences, in the same way that this can also be induced by certain drugs, or by hypnotic age-regression. On the other hand, interference with the brain can equally cause amnesia — loss of memory, (which quite often occurs following electrotherapy.)

But what scientists in general appear unwilling to grasp is that the brain is the *instrument* of the mind, and not the mind itself. Though there is an etheric counterpart of the brain, the brain itself disintegrates at physical death. The mind, of course, does no such thing for it is spirit, which cannot die. In fact after "death" it functions with far greater clarity. It is the mind which is the depository of memory, not the brain — often such an imperfect and limiting instrument, like a faulty radio which impairs the perfect reception of a piece of music.

As mankind became more and more enmeshed in the material world

116

the psychic ability (still so strongly developed, for instance, in the Australian aborigines) diminished, together with the pineal or psychic gland, often called "the third eye." And it may well be that a latent psychic ability can be jolted, as it were, into activity by a head injury in a certain place.

The injury, too, may have the effect of loosening the etheric body, for I have noticed that psychic people are much more easily caused to "jump out of their skin" at the slightest shock, sound or very loud noise, (a painful process which takes a little time to recover from), and are more easily able to leave the body, to astral travel in sleep.

Be that as it may, of all those whose psychic gifts have suddenly manifested after a fall or a blow on the head, one of the most astonishing is the Dutch "psychic detective" Peter Hurkos. Pieter van der Hurk (he only took the name Hurkos when he was active in the Dutch underground movement during the war) was born on May 21st, 1911 in Dordrecht, of humble parents. He was blind for the first 6 months from the effects of being born with part of the caul wrapped round his head and face. In Holland, as elsewhere on the Continent, to be "born with the veil" has always been regarded as a sure indication of strange and supernormal powers or, as we would put it, with a psychic gift. Yet Peter swears that he had no evidence of this until the fateful accident which befell him when he was 30.

He was a poor student, preferring to play truant in the woods, lonely and brooding. At 14 he ran off to sea as a cook's assistant, a life he did not give up till his late twenties, by which time he had married and had two children. In 1939 he settled down to work for his father as a house painter. Then came the Nazi occupation, when 70% of the Dutch people worked for the "underground."

It was on July 10th, 1941 that it happened. Working high up on a 4-storey building Peter leaned over too precariously to get his gallon paint-pot off a hook, and fell . . . He was unconscious for four days with a severe head injury (also a broken shoulder). An operation was necessary to save his life, and he has a three inch scar a little lower than midway down on the back of his head.

Recalling the days of physical unconsciousness he says, in his broken English: "But everything was so beautiful, the flowers, the mountains, the music. Like people singing far away . . . When I come out conscious, and I didn't die, I want to go back to unconscious, where it was so beautiful." His father always swore that Peter died, and "came back with two minds."

From the time he recovered consciousness, slowly and painfully, Peter "suffered" from spontaneous clairvoyance about people and events, near and far. He startled nurses and doctors alike by blurting out their personal secrets before he could stop himself. He heard voices and saw pictures. He had only to take a person's hand, or hold an object, to know what had happened or was about to happen, in exact detail. His psychometry was so acute that he scarcely dared to touch even a wall . . .

His new gift tormented him. He did not know what was wrong with him, and begged the director of a mental hospital, Dr. Peters, to help him get rid of whatever it was. But the doctor (who had previously been shaken to the core by Peter's knowledge of his double private life) could only tell him: "It is possible that what you have is something all of us have in limited degrees. In your case it is more highly developed apparently because of your accident and your brain injury. There are many things we do not know yet about the human mind and its capabilities. It is possible that your injury damaged certain functions of the brain and stimulated others."

Peter had to live with it — and has done so for the past 34 years. He has been investigated by many researchers, often exploited, lionised, abused, and constantly made use of by the police in many countries of the world to track down the most unsavoury and vicious criminals and to solve cases of missing persons.

This latter gift is not an enviable one when you have to tell a distraught father that his only daughter, aged 10, will be found in six feet of water by the last pole on the left side of the river by the boathouse. "He has never forgiven me," says Peter. Why, he asks, if he could "see" the tragedy after it happened, could he not have seen it before it happened, and so save the child? Why, why? echoes poor Peter, adding "I'm sorry, but I can tell only what I see." What is ironic in this instance is that the embittered father was Henry Belk, the man financially responsible for bringing Peter to America in the first place, to be researched by Dr Andrija Puharich and many others, including his own psychical research foundation.

The full account of Peter's amazing life can be read in Norma Lee Browning's book "The Psychic Life of Peter Hurkos," (Frederick Muller). The author knows him intimately. In fact he asked her to write his story for him and, though completely sceptical at first, she was finally persuaded to do so.

I am very sorry for Peter Hurkos. He once said he would give anything to be relieved of his "gift." He is a simple, uneducated man, and not a happy one. Although there appears to be a mania in the United States for research into ESP and into "what makes a psychic psychic" from a biological point of view, *no one* appears to have told him the slightest thing about Spiritualism, life after death, or any form of metaphysical philosophy which one feels would help him.

Perhaps the strangest thing about his psychism is that it seems strictly confined to extra-sensory perception, i.e. psychometry, clairvoyance on a mundane level, retrocognition and precognition. In spite of the voice which tells him things when he does not see pictures, there is no record of his ever being clairvoyant or mediumistic in connection with anyone in spirit. His gift is, so to speak, strictly earthbound.

Another psychic, the great Edgar Cayce, also manifested his extraordinary gifts of prophecy, medical diagnosis, and knowledge of patients' previous incarnations while in trance, or "sleep," *after* he was hit on the head by a thrown baseball in his youth.

In a semi-stupor, he instructed his parents to prepare a special poultice and put it at the base of his brain. He recovered next day.

A few years later, in 1900, having completely lost his voice through acute laryngitis, a vaudeville hypnotist asked permission to put him to sleep. Under hypnosis Cayce's voice returned loud and clear, and with a strange new quality of authority. The Voice said: "This body is unable to speak due to partial paralysis of the inferior muscles of the vocal chord . . . this may be removed by increasing the circulation to the affected parts by suggestion . . ."

From then on, Cayce was able to diagnose and treat every conceivable disease with incredible accuracy, though he had never studied pathology. It was as though a Great Healer had taken possession of his body. He was called, as is wellknown, "the sleeping prophet."

I would also like to mention, very briefly, the controversial Dr Lobsang Rampa, whose first book, *The Third Eye*, describing in fascinating detail his family, childhood and life as a Tibetan monk caused a sensation in the early fifties — and subsequent bewilderment when it was discovered that he was, in fact, an Englishman of humble background who had never even been out of England at that time.

His explanation to account for his extraordinary knowledge, also his clairvoyance, was that when he was climbing a tree, trying to photograph a young owl, a branch broke and he fell on his head, which rendered him unconscious. While he (his etheric body) was looking at his unconscious physical body lying on the grass, he saw a Tibetan lama gliding towards him. From that time on *he has been* that Tibetan lama, and that "personality" has written several further books about the lama's adventurous life following the Chinese invasion of Tibet, and also a book on psychic development, all of which have been best-sellers. His name was changed by Deed Poll to that of the lama.

Shortly after publication of *The Third Eye*, Lobsang Rampa visited the farm we had in Oxfordshire on three occasions. (Our cowman was rather taken aback to see a small, shaven-headed, bearded figure in the red and saffron robes of a Tibetan lama emerge from a large Ford Zodiac in our yard!)

On each occasion he brought a present of a "Catnip" for my cat, for he is devoted to cats. He ate nothing, but took tea. Remarking on a "cloud of worry" in my aura, I told him of our keen desire to have a child, that I had had nothing but miscarriages and was getting older every day. (I think I was then 46).

I do not pretend to know the truth about this strange man. I only know that, as he left, he said to me in a quiet, monotone voice: "You will conceive at Aries time, and you will have a son." In due course, when I was 48, our son was born. It was not for a little time that it dawned on me that he had been conceived under the sign of Aries — and I remembered the "Tibetan lama" with the grey English eyes.

Assuredly, "there are more things in heaven and earth . . ."

EGOTISM LEADS TO DESPAIR

I never, ever, iron my sheets without thinking of Mrs Farr. When I am tempted, through pressure of work, to be slipshod I think: "That would never have done for Mrs Farr!" and spend another five minutes doing the job properly. And while I'm straightening out the muddle they always get into, I smile, seeing her in my mind's eye enjoying the peace and beauty of the Summerlands of Heaven — and I see her shining. "God bless you, Mrs Farr . . ." I say, and wonder if she feels, just for a moment, a tiny warm ray of remembrance.

She lived in a cottage at the end of a grey-sand track, in a small clearing in the pinewoods. It was only a pram-ride from where I was born, and by the time the First World War started I could walk there with my Nanny who liked to visit her for a friendly chat. In those days, which seem like another incarnation, all the fine linen of the kind that was handed down for three generations, was taken by pony and trap to a private washerwoman.

The scented pinewoods have long since given way to a complex of housing estates, and the grey-sand track, so soft and silent for trotting hooves and rubbered wheels, lies buried beneath tarmac and concrete. Yet I am sure the etheric imprint of that humble home in the clearing still remains, with the rows of snow-white linen billowing in the breeze; and inside, the baskets, the steaming coppers, the big white-padded table on the red tiles, the rows of heavy black flat-irons, that hot homely smell, the kettle always singing on the hob. And that little smiling woman of uncertain age, taking such justifiable pride, and pleasure, year after year, in the meticulous perfection of her work.

Dear Mrs Farr, you could never have imagined in your wildest dreams, living in the obscurity of the forest, that well over half a century later the little girl who watched your labours in silent fascination would be thinking of you, and still inspired by your *example*.

You would never have believed that one day in the then so distant future — that future which was to embrace the agonies of two World Wars and many further agonies throughout many lands, and unimaginable scientific achievements, too, like radio, television, super-sonic flight and men driving a tractor on the moon — that the name of *Mrs Farr* —

Washerwoman would be read in print on the other side of the world.

Yet that's how it is. Though we might never move more than a mile from where we live out our seemingly restricted and unremarkable lives, we simply have no idea of the range and ramifications of our influence and example upon others — for good or ill.

And in the last analysis, when we reach the Other Side and our Recording Angel has totted up the score, it will not matter a tinker's cuss whether we flew from London to New York in a couple of hours, or climbed the mountains of the moon, or made a million.

What *will* matter is whether we learned the lessons we came to this earth to learn; whether we replaced hatred by love, bitterness by understanding; whether we kept on keeping on when the going was rough; whether we substituted service for selfishness; compassion for criticism; whether we gave or grabbed; whether we lightened someone else's darkness, or sweated blood for a fellow human being.

There is a pop song called "Where have all the flowers gone?" In the work we try to do in our little group "The Befrienders" for those in distress or despair, I often wonder where all the joy has gone for so many, many people. They have become a burden to themselves, and to others, through deep depression, rendering them totally inert, almost incapable of thought, certainly of action, often suicidal, and wrapped round by a seemingly impenetrable wall of cold, sunless gloom.

Nor has this anything to do with outward conditions, for a vast majority of those so afflicted are *materially* far better off than ever they were. The trouble lies in their *reaction* to conditions, and what arouses one's compassion is the fact that nearly all those who come to us, whether men or women, are simply not aware that they themselves have created the situations which they now find unbearable — usually over a period of years of misdirected thought, wrong values, wrong living, wrong feeling. They are literally living in the lower astral planes *now*, and there seems no escape.

Our aim is to bring some measure of light and self-awareness in *this* life, while there is still time, before they drift into the grey astral regions of the spirit world. For *then* they will find it even harder to shift themselves, and the dull, negative, enclosed thought-pattern will be even more difficult to escape from. I have been shown this terrible apathetic, almost mindless condition during a memorable astral projection to the lower spheres, under the guidance of one of our spirit teachers. I shall never forget it.

It is difficult to explain to people, for instance, that they are lonely and hopeless because they cannot love, are a hundred percent self-centred and consequently steeped in self-pity, repelling others by their demanding egotism. When a man sits and weeps at his own aloneness it is unfortunately a state he has created for himself by a life dedicated to a false goal.

One such was determined at all costs to rise out of the employee class to become an employer, to make capital enough to enjoy an early retirement, to buy a house and a life of ease in a country where the sun shines. He was obsessed by a passion "to be a success." To this end he worked on the fallacious principle that "he travels fastest who travels alone" — no ties, no responsibilities, no wife, no kids, no personal relationships except those of expediency or for the satisfaction of the senses, nothing "to hold him back." Now he is ready for that place in the sun — and nobody, not a soul, wants to know . . .

He has given one marriage bureau after another a detailed list of *his requirements,* but in his opinion they only produce "trash." There is not one iota of compassion for those women he brushes aside so unfeelingly. No thought that they, too, were lonely and had probably sat for an hour at their dressing-tables in their lone bed-sitters, trying to make the best of themselves in trembling anticipation at the ordeal of being "looked over."

It is too late now to get into his consciousness the truth in the lines of the poet who wrote:

I do believe that our salvation
   Lies in the *little* things of life;
Not in the pomp and acclamation
   Of triumph, or in battle-strife;
Not on the thrones where men are crowned,
   Not in the race where chariots roll —
But in the arms that clasp us round
   And hold us *backward* from the goal!

To seek for one's personal idea of happiness on one's own terms, to fit a formula of "*I want,*" never works out. Those who are scared of being tied, or committed, imagine they will lose their freedom to do whatever they want where they want and when they want. And when they have achieved this so-called perfect freedom they find themselves on a desert island, a king without a people, companionless, friendless, purposeless, unloved, eating dead-sea fruit. It is pathetic.

Ask such a one if he believes in God and the answer comes back: "How can one believe in a God who allows such terrible things to happen in the world?" (People do forget that Man was given the gift of free-will to make his own heaven — or hell, if he must. Nor do such people ever say: "There *must* be a God, because the world is full of such wonderful and beautiful and miraculous things!")

Yet there are many, alas, who would run away from heaven because they have allowed themselves to get into a state where they can't stand being happy! Every day, like reciting a mantra, they carefully enumerate all the things that are not as satisfactory as they might be, all the annoyances, difficulties, frustrations and unfulfilments of their lives, without being able to raise even a smile over all the really splendid and satisfactory things for which they should and could be most grateful.

122

They have come to *prefer* their dis-ease rather than make an effort to attain a balanced normality. They hide their light in black depression, retreating into the womb where it was safe and comfortable and dark and where no exertion was required of them — rather than reach out and grow in the sunlight which is always there in the blue sky, even if at times it is hidden from our limited vision by clouds.

Muscles cannot be strengthened without exercise, as every athlete knows. And this involves exertion and self-discipline. Likewise, our spiritual muscles grow strong only through trying to overcome the conflict presented by our personality or environmental difficulties. We have to learn these lessons in the schoolroom of earth living. *This* is where we grow through the painful adolescence of the spirit.

When we get to a point when we think we simply *cannot* go on another day with whatever the situation is, (physical, emotional, mental or whatever), and we *do* go on, we have grown that much stronger — and we have often gained the strength to *alter* what appeared unbearable.

Of course it is trebly hard for those who insist on denying the power of the spirit, who deny the existence of God, who cannot cast their bread on the waters and open their arms and their hearts and cry: "If you exist, *help me!*" This, as we know, is the first imperative step for any soul who wishes to climb out of the lower astral into the light. That, too, is why no group such as the Samaritans or the Befrienders can take on anyone spoken for by a friend. Those needing help *must* make the act of will to take up the telephone *themselves*. Otherwise it means they are not ready or willing to be helped.

The word SIN is not very popular in a permissive society. Nor is Self-Descipline. While old-fashioned GUTS has come to be regarded by permissives as a dirty four-letter word. Yet experience has lead us to believe that mental illness, of which we see so much (and of which depression is the first symptom) is in the last resort caused by sin — sins against the fundamental spiritual laws of Love and Light.

The Greater World Teacher, known as Zodiac, who during his life on earth gave up all to follow the Nazarene, was asked about insanity. "I answer out of my greater knowledge," he replied through his instrument, Winifred Moyes. "*No one who really prays to God with faith can lose the government of his mind.* The men and women who fill your institutions (other than by so-called accident) by their brooding, by their wrong thoughts, by their introspection, have brought about a condition whereby the spirits from the dark worlds can get into their auras, and once those spirits are in, they are tenacious; they will not give up until by suffering the link is broken."

And Dr. Carl Jung, reviewing a life-time of treating patients, said of all those over 35 years of age: "There has not been one whose problem in the last resort was not that of finding a religious outlook on life . . . *and none of them has been really healed who did not regain his religious outlook.*"

So, in the midst of the tensions and trials of modern living, when no one, it seems, has the time or tranquillity to really *live through* the experiences heaped upon them and which build up an undigested blockage more lethal than the traffic blocks in our city streets; when so many people are terrified of silence — a man just out of mental hospital said to me, "Don't you think there is *security in noise?*" which left me gasping — is it any wonder that my thoughts go back to the vision of Mrs Farr, so happy and contented while "slaving away," as moderns would put it, in the peaceful silence of the pinewoods?

I remember her not for what she knew, but for what she *was*. Not for what she did, but *how* she did it. Not for anything she said, but for the warmth of her smile. I cannot help contrasting her with the man who has three thousand books, and talks with erudition on Eastern philosophy, the Vedantas, the Upanishads, the illusion of matter, the reality of the subjective world, cosmic consciousness and karma till one's brain reels — but who cannot *feel*, cannot *give* of himself, cannot *love*, and is a very sick man, alone in the dark.

Not of him, but rather of Mrs Farr the Washerwoman the poet spoke in that same poem:

In Love, not Pride; in stooping low;
  Not soaring blindly at the sun;
In power to feel, not zeal to know;
  Not in rewards, but duties done . . .

How much we can still learn from her example. Because there was something about her quiet happiness which made many people, besides my Nanny, say to themselves when they were feeling low, "I think I'll go and see Mrs Farr . . ." God bless her.

COURAGE TO SPEAK THE HARD TRUTH

It seems to me that the true character of a person comes to the fore as the spirit is approaching the last lap of its earthly journey. It *can* be a very wonderful and serene experience *if*, no longer immersed in the cares and struggles of material, worldly responsibilities, the old person is able to rise above any ills or handicaps and remain out-going in thought, giving to others the benefit of their own life experience, whether it be by counsel, kindness, humour, friendship, prayer, or, quite unconsciously, by giving out the light of their being.

I have known many such. In spite of being crippled, or putting up with aches and pains of one sort or another, one leaves their presence with a warm feeling inside, uplifted by some undefinable radiance.

If the good can so shine forth, meeting the challenge which old age presents with grace and courage, maintaining a lively interest in people and events, the converse is also true, I am afraid! And just lately I have been appalled by the number of people whose lives are being ruined, their potentialities thwarted, and their spiritual development actually retarded by giving in to the tyranny, the selfishness, the ill-tempered perversity, and the egotistical demands of elderly relatives. They have allowed themselves to become absolute slaves, securely fastened by the ball and chain of an ageing bully.

The trouble is that all these victims (invariably women) are "good" people, and fondly imagine they are putting into practice, or trying their best to do so, the principles of kindness, forgiveness, service, charity and love. I would like to tell these good people that they are really doing *nothing of the sort!*

I would like to suggest to them that they look very deep within, and ask themselves (a) if there is not a tinge of spiritual pride in their own (often rather advertised) martyrdom, and (b) if there is not more than a tinge of sheer moral cowardice in their make-up which should and must be overcome for the good of all concerned.

I would also like to tell these poor souls that what they are doing is neither spiritual nor Christian, for two good reasons: firstly because, in these circumstances, kindness eventually turns into resentment, forgiveness into recrimination, service into dour duty, charity into bitterness, and love into hate.

Secondly, by indulging the whims of the tyrannical, feeding the ego of the selfish, egging on the sadistic by exhibitions of weakness, and encouraging the bossiness of the bully, they are in fact *making quite sure that the one they are ostensibly "caring for" will land herself or himself in the lonely, grey, lower astral regions* when the time comes to pass over to the other side of that little river which is approaching!

This is *not* kindness. Nor is sentimentality compassion. Nor is the fear of being thought "hard" anything but cowardice in case we are misjudged or disliked — for most of us long to be loved, sometimes at any cost. It certainly has nothing to do with the *real* essence of love. Let me recount a little true story:

Friends of mine, a married couple whom I shall call John and Joan, built an annexe on to their cottage for the wife's elderly mother to live in — a beautiful self-contained flat with every comfort, far superior to their own dwelling. They ministered to her in every possible way, and in every possible way she became progressively more demanding, more possessive of their time, more quick-tempered and rude, more outraged if they ever wanted to go out, until Joan literally trembled at the knees before summoning up courage to approach her. They became enslaved, nervous wrecks, and their marriage was consequently suffering.

One day they wanted to go out somewhere together, only to be met with the usual string of reasons why the old lady should not be left — including that hoary old chestnut: "I might be dead when you get back!" (She was in quite good health, incidentally.)

John, the soul of kindness, knew the time had come. He told her in no uncertain terms that he and Joan were going out whether she liked it or not, that she was a b.... selfish old woman, and many other colourful phrases, and that if she died before they got back it was just too bad, and she'd have to risk it. Whereupon he slammed the door and departed — supporting Joan by the arm for, hearing all this, she was in danger of fainting away!

When he went in next morning, the old lady was as perky as a sparrow. She even *laughed* (for the first time in years) as she said, "*Thank you, John. I never thought you were man enough!* You knocked the Old Adam out of me — I *needed* that! Of course the only reason I didn't want you both to go out was pure envy and jealousy. I hope you had a nice time."

From that day she changed, becoming considerate and responsive. John had many talks to her about life after death (for he and Joan were Spiritualists), and brought her to sit in our garden and talk to Catherine, our home circle medium. And when, later on, she did fade away one afternoon (while Joan was down the road, as it happened) she appeared straightaway in Catherine's room, in spirit, saying, "I know what's happened. I've gone over — and my first thought was of you. I'm not afraid . . ."

John's justifiable revolt was real "love-in-action." "I'd never have the nerve!" I hear people say, or "I doubt if it would work in *my* situation!" But then they have never *tried* it. Perhaps they think too much of their own image to risk it, even for the other person's ultimate good, not to mention their own, or their family's. It does take courage to slap someone's face to stop them lapsing into uncontrollable hysteria because, to be effective, you have to do it *hard* enough. And not in anger, but in love.

Such action "goes against the grain," as they say, especially if one is weak and easily intimidated. And here let me say that I have every sympathy with this attitude, for I have had to fight against it myself for most of my life, before I came fully to understand that *real* love demands strength, not sentiment, and that no human being has the right to tyrannise or dominate another human being. And certainly not to turn them into a willing door-mat. If you truly care for someone, you have to risk losing their love, even incurring hate, if the situation so demands — if it is *right*.

The Nazarene was not "meek and mild" when the situation called for the very opposite! It was not out of anger, but out of his agonised love for human beings, his longing to save them from themselves and bring them to the realisation of the Christ-Light, to rescue them from the darkness assuredly to come, that he told certain people (doubtless in far from tea-party tones) that they were "hypocrites," "whited sepulchres" and "a generation of vipers!" Indeed it is hard to think of *worse* things to be called.

Would-be do-gooders who merely offer sentimental sympathy, are doing no good at all. There is a time for sympathy and a time for action, a time for listening and a time for plain speaking. A time to agree, and a time to disagree. We *owe* this to those we care about, or are "caring for" — if we have enough courage and integrity.

I have often thought that if only *someone* had been brave enough *not* to wilt at the knees in front of my grandmother, and meekly submit to her outrageous behaviour, she might not have taken 50 of our earth years after passing over to be brought out of the shadows.

I must have been about 12 when she died, and I began to breathe freely. And then only after the funeral, for while her body remained in the house I fled, white-faced, up the stairs past her landing as if the devil were after me, fearing that her apparition would emerge to scare me in death as she had scared me stiff in life. Grown-ups who make a sensitive child feel perpetually like a rabbit mesmerised by a snake often inhibit that child's entire later life. Unfortunately she made many adults feel very much the same!

It was Gretcha, Catherine's twin sister in spirit, who brought her to me, with the request that she (Gretcha) should apport me a scented rose on her behalf. She had been "free" for two months, but evidently came with some misgivings, saying she did not know whether I would be pleased to hear from her, or not!

I knew for certain who it was when she said, in her old abrupt way, "I haven't seen much of the Old Cuss. Had enough of him before . . ." for that was how she always used to refer to her husband — my step-grandfather, who was always kind to me. I hope our short conversation through Catherine eased her mind. I encouraged her to put the past away and to explore the wonders of her new life.

If we could but learn how to *live* we would not cause nearly so much trouble when we "die!" When one thinks of the myriads of progressed spirits on the Other Side of life who spend so much time and energy endeavouring to help the myriads in the darker realms to climb into the light — and encouraging them to have the *desire* to do so — reason totters indeed.

Time is different over there, you may say, and fifty years might pass like a day and a night, even hundreds of years perhaps. But my experience of rescue circles tells me that though this may sometimes be so (if the spirit is "sleeping the sleep of the dead" and only rousing from time to time to experience "unpleasant dreams," as they think) it can also be otherwise. In fact what may seem like an eternity might pass before a wilful spirit will learn his or her lessons, or make an effort to change a character which has increasingly deteriorated by small faults growing into bigger and bigger proportions during earth life.

127

So I do beg all those kind-hearted people who have allowed themselves to become slaves and victims of elderly tyrants — and not always elderly either — because they cannot bring themselves to say boo to a goose, to review their situation in a new light, a light that is *truly* spiritual, and not a sentimentally distorted reflection.

By so doing they will give not only themselves a chance to grow and develop their own potential and individuality, which is the purpose of incarnation, but also help to save those they profess to care about from their lower selves *before* they pass over into conditions far from pleasant. This is loving in God's way.

WOMEN'S SPIRITUAL LIB.

The other day I read somewhere that it was comparatively recently that men, in some parts of the world, admitted that women have souls. It is indeed true that for long periods of history women were classed as animals (who were not thought to have souls), as beasts of burden, as chattels or possessions to be bought and sold, and as sexual conveniences either for man's carnal pleasure or for the production of more men. If they failed in the latter use, they were discarded.

Even though the enlightened Greeks admitted goddesses to the Olympian heights, they appeared to play second fiddle to the gods. While cultures which adhered to a monotheist belief naturally conceived of their god as being strictly a male deity — not even androgynous! It was only the Ancient Wisdom of millenia past that referred to the "Father-Mother God."

From the thousands of letters I have received over the past few years it has struck me forcibly that the fact that women not only "possess" souls but *are* souls, individual spiritual beings, has been acknowledged somewhat grudgingly by quite a large portion of the male sex, even in our Western society. They are probably not even aware that this is so.

Politically, of course, women have finally achieved the right to vote, but even this right is referred to by the System as "one *man* one vote" rather than "one *person* one vote!"

Domestically, in the more modern home at least, the wife and mother may not be regarded *quite* so much as an unpaid servant who never has a day off, and for whom there is no let-up in her declining years while her husband puts his feet up in retirement.

Spiritually, however, it appears to be a sadder story in far too many instances. Four centuries have passed since Henry VIII very nearly imprisoned one of his wives in the Tower for reading a religious book which he considered too liberal. But in many homes today it seems that this intolerant and intolerable attitude of the male partner has only changed in a matter of degree.

It is quite incredible the large number of letters I receive from desperate women who are spiritually imprisoned by their husbands. One will write: "I have been keenly interested in Spiritualism for a long time, for to me it is the only philosophy that makes sense — but I have to hide my books on the subject for fear of my husband who is totally opposed to it."

Another will write: "How I *long* to go to the Spiritualist church, but I have no means of transport. It is rather a long way and my husband refuses to drive me there as he is so against it. He does not wish me to go."

Yet another will write: "I have had many psychic experiences and would dearly love to join a developing group, especially for healing, but my husband would never allow such a thing. He is an atheist." One poor soul who *insists* on going to her local church has endured physical violence inflicted by her husband in his efforts to prevent her leaving the house to listen "to all that nonsense."

I wonder what a man's reaction would be if his wife dared to tell him he could not or should not go to his Saturday football, or his golf, or to his Masonic meetings? The question is a purely academic one, for the answer is a foregone conclusion. How much *more* important, then, is freedom of belief, freedom of conscience, and freedom to follow one's own spiritual path.

It is most regrettable when the partners in a marriage are on such differing levels of consciousness, such different planes of awareness. Yet if there is any bond of love on other levels of the relationship, how is it possible, one may ask, that consideration and respect for the partner's individuality as a human being can be so lacking?

The answer is, I am afraid, that far too many men *still* regard their wives as an adjunct to their own life-style. Someone preferably decorative and amenable, who will keep the house and do the chores, bear and rear the children, go out to work when this is financially necessary, and think and behave along the same thought-patterns — his.

How often, in our work with distressed people especially, do we get the identical answer when we ask a woman what she thinks about this or that: "I'm afraid I couldn't really say — I'd have to ask my husband." Suggest that she should take the smallest action on her own, and she will reply: "Well, I don't know if my husband would like that." Or "agree to that." Or "let me."

That such a degree of conditioned, in-built fear is by no means uncommon reflects a totally wrong conception of marriage and partnership. But when it throttles in its iron grasp the natural flowering of the woman's spiritual inclinations and aspirations it is an evil thing.

No one has the right to deny the freedom of another soul to pursue the spiritual path to which it is drawn, whether we personally subscribe to it or not. If a man has the inalienable right to be an atheist or an agnostic or a Mason or whatever he may decide, then this inalienable right belongs also to his wife.

I can hear more fortunate readers exclaiming at this point: "But why are these women so timid in asserting themselves or their ideas? Why can't they talk it over with their husbands? Haven't they heard of Women's Lib.?" It is not quite as simple as that — even if their husbands would *allow* a discussion on such matters without walking out of the room, or taking up the newspaper, or switching on the telly. The problem is much more basic.

For thousands of years women have been ruled by men and have been materially dependant on men, and in general men have preferred it that way. Fortunately this is changing with the New Age generation. But many is the time I have heard a man of the older generation state (while acting as an effective firescreen on *his* hearth): "Women who are financially independant become impossible!" — meaning that they can literally afford to *be themselves* and *speak* for themselves without the psychological fear of being relegated, as it were, to the dog-house.

This attitude lingers still, for it has been ingrained for so long, together with the age-old double standard of behaviour. What is sauce for the gander is *not* so for the goose, and here I am not merely referring to infidelity but to much wider issues.

I hope, therefore — though not very hopefully — that certain men may perhaps read this and take the message to heart. For however willingly a wife may undertake to love, honour and obey, her *first* duty is to obey the stirrings and dictates of her own conscience and her own spiritual intuition. That is her "duty" to the Great Spirit and, indeed, *the purpose of her incarnation* in the last analysis.

This is where the conflict often starts for a woman, whereas it presents no such conflict for a man. Even if the direction he wishes to take involves the constant risk of being burnt alive on a race-track or going off to sail round the world never to be heard of again, no woman can (or would) prevent him. The same applies to matters intellectual and, usually, spiritual. He is "his own man." His soul is his own.

Then again, how many women are haunted by the recollection of their marriage vows, especially the words "for better for *worse*" and "whom God hath joined together let no man put asunder." These latter words were inserted in a rather unpleasantly concocted liturgy to give the impression that because the priest or parson has joined them by enunciating certain phrases the couple are automatically "joined by God."

When you think of some of the reasons why many people enter into what is called "the holy estate of matrimony" this is little short of blasphemy. As a great spirit teacher of the White Brotherhood has said: "When two people come together because they are *soul mates* and are thus "joined by the Great Spirit" because spiritually this is so, then no man *could* put them asunder."

But how comparatively rarely this felicitude occurs on the earth plane — the plane of individualisation and kindergarten experience. And even when it *may* be so, we are often too swaddled and constricted by our personality problems, conditioning and neuroses to recognise the soul-link until we have, perhaps, reached much higher planes of spirit in the next world.

Or people may be drawn together to work out karma; or perhaps as selected parents for the incarnation of an evolved soul; or to undergo a necessary initiation for one or the other or both. This is on the inner level.

But on the outer, physical level, marriages may be entered into for numerous reasons, including "getting away from the family," for security, or money, or professional advantage or status, because of loneliness, because the woman has become pregnant, or, far too often, because of "falling in love" on the physical or emotional level *only*.

None of these are valid reasons, and are bound to rock the boat sooner or later. And the thing that rocks it more, perhaps, than anything else, is when one partner is on, or has reached, an entirely different plane of consciousness to the other. This can become, quite literally, soul-destroying, and every effort should be made, with due consideration for everyone concerned (especially the children if not already grown up) for the partners to liberate one another. And in such cases the new divorce laws of England have taken a great step forward in women's financial favour — at the same time as protecting men from the "one year of marriage and a life-time of alimony" syndrome.

I take my hat off to a woman who first wrote to me from Australia to where her husband had emigrated. In her mid-fifties, she could no longer tolerate her husband's intolerance in matters spiritual, for she was a true sensitive. From the moment she plucked up courage to take the plunge, to leave him, and to spend her last penny on the fare to England, the spirit world "took over." She seemed to be guided and led in a most remarkable way to exactly the right places and people, and within a short space of time found herself supported in a congenial job, found congenial friends, joined an excellent circle wherein her gifts of the spirit are already blossoming in service to others, and is naturally happier than she has ever been in her life.

It took a lot of guts to "go out into the darkness and put her hand in the Hand of God," but she found that beautiful saying only too true, for that *was* "better than a light, and safer than a known way." And there is a nice corollary to this story: in due course her husband acknowledged the error of his ways, eventually followed her home to England, and they are happily re-united.

Lest it be thought that I am advocating a wholesale evacuation by wives of obstructive husbands, I hasten to add that I am merely hoisting my flag and striking a blow on behalf of Women's *Spiritual* Lib. in the hope of encouraging and inspiring the victims of intolerance and spiritual serfdom to stand up for themselves and their beliefs in the face of the "enemy." They might even be surprised at the speed with which a shrug of the shoulders for the sake of peace will denote capitulation — or even a change of heart!

And to those men who find it difficult, or are unwilling, to grant freedom of conscience to their wives, I would like to remind them of what another teacher from spirit has said: that the role of woman is to be "the ear of God" for her man. Her feminine intuition and sensitivity is more often linked to the inner, subjective planes, while the man (in general) is more active on the outer, objective planes. If both would acknowledge this, and co-operate in harmony, it would indeed be to their mutual satisfaction and advancement, not only for themselves but for the world.

NO "EQUALITY" IN THE HEREAFTER

The other day I was in our sub-Post Office and village store. The man who runs it was distressed. Owing to his phone being out of order without his knowledge several manufacturers had been unable to get through to obtain his orders, so some items were out of stock. "I was just too busy to realise the phone hadn't been ringing," he said. "I suppose I was so grateful for a little *peace*. There's never time to stop, to 'get off the bus' ".

"That's why our mental homes are as crammed as your shelves," I said. He looked round at his shelves, display counter and freezer, all laden with a multitude of goods and foods, "instant" and otherwise, and sighed as he remarked, "And yet none of all this seems to make anyone any *happier*." He could not have said a truer thing.

No amount of material goods makes anyone *happy*, for happiness derives from a quality of spirit, from the heart and mind, from emotional and occupational fulfilment, from purpose in life, from friendships, children, humour, service, from striving, from a simple appreciation of beauty and of Nature, from sharing troubles (our own and other people's), and most of all from *loving*. None of these depend on material things, and certainly not on so-called "equality."

On the contrary, it is usually the case that when material advantages predominate, or are suddenly acquired, *real* happiness is absent. One has only to follow up the private lives of many who have won vast sums on the pools. If they do not get killed in the first year careering about in a Jaguar, their marriages frequently end in divorce, the huge spending spree brings no lasting satisfaction, they are besieged by begging letters, lose their friends and workmates, and eventually their money, having neither invested it to insure a comfortable income for life, nor put it to any public or charitable uses. That is, unless the "lucky" winner has a sense of spiritual values.

There is also truth in the phrase "poor little rich girl." I was born one. The isolation, alienation and sense of rejection by parents during early childhood was acute. We only knew our nanny, an under-nurse and a series of French governesses. Frightened to approach the "grown-up" part of the house, we were also admonished never to go into the servants' wing without knocking. How I envied the under-housemaid her freedom — roars of laughter from the servants' hall, and meetings by moonlight up Lovers Lane with the second groom!

I did not want my grandfather's tenants to bob curtseys at their doors as we drove up the village in the carriage (I waved back vigorously). Nor be met at the London station on the way home from school by the Station Master in frock coat and silk top hat, with people staring. But my release came with the aftermath of the first war and two massive lots of death duties. I went to London and had the thrill of earning a precarious living, often on a diet of cheese and sardines. The contrast was a sharp one, but I was *living*, and found a comradeship I had never known, and came up against people and experiences I had never dreamt of.

I write this merely to state that I have been privileged to live both the life of the wealthy and the life of the most impecunious. My total assets, at one time, were £2.50 with the rent due, and in those days no Welfare State in its present form to turn to. In fact I have lived at least five different kinds of life telescoped into one incarnation. And my point is that the very material philosophy of left-wing Socialism, with its accent on material equality, does absolutely nothing to enhance either happiness or spirituality because it is not in conformity with spiritual law — about which the neo-Marxist, being purely a materialist, is entirely ignorant. In fact I maintain that it often impedes any spiritual progress, which is our reason for earth living. I have seen it too often.

W. Somerset Maugham saw it, and was deeply shocked and depressed. In his younger days he was so moved by the wonderful spirit of open-hearted and open-handed comradeship and "togetherness" in a very poor area of London that he started to write a novel about it. Several years later, after the war, he returned to the district to complete his book. He was unable to do so: the old houses had been demolished, and rightly so. But the spirit of the inhabitants had been demolished also. In their newly built homes they did not know their neighbours any more, were suspicious and withdrawn, only looking to see the size of the telly screen next door, "living up with the Jones's," isolated.

When Harold Macmillan, as Prime Minister, told the people of this country: "You've never had it so good!" I do not think he was doing them a service. He was merely whetting the material appetites and augmenting the envy of many millions whose forbears had unfortunately suffered in

133

the pernicious Industrial Revolution, with the gross injustices inflicted at that time by upstart exploiters — upstarts who became "the new rich" at their expense, and behaved like men suddenly upgraded from the ranks to the position of officers (nearly always the *bêtes noires* of their men), having no idea of *noblesse oblige* or the tradition that officers always make their men and horses their *first* concern.

Harold Wilson, our present Prime Minister, once wrote a letter to my husband which was remarkable for its total lack of perception that spiritual values made any contribution to people's happiness or well-being. He genuinely seemed to believe that the magic formula was merely more houses, more money and more "equality."

Let it not be thought for a moment that I underrate the necessities of life! I long for every family in the world to have a home of their own; sufficient and healthy food; adequate means; care in sickness and old age; opportunity to work rather than live on the taxpayers. I welcome equal opportunity in education — and Edward Heath is a living example that a son of a working-class family can become Prime Minister in this country. It also proves that people are *never* equal, nor ever will be, for where are his class-mates?

Of *course* I ardently desire a decent standard of living for every man, woman and child. But I equally consider it morally wrong that dockworkers claimed £60 for a 20-hour week when doctors were getting £30 for an 80-hour week. (April 1970.) One also loses sympathy when a good lady, doubtless living herself on a small and diminishing "fixed" income, hands out food parcels to striking miners, only to find that 40 of them have flown off to Spain with their wives on holiday.

I am often reminded of two cowmen who, at different periods in the past, helped us with our herd of pedigree Jersey cows. They demonstrated opposite extremes. Tom was a real countryman. He had a personal, loving relationship with each cow, loathed going on holiday, loved his vegetable garden, old friends, local darts, farm talk, and his old broody hen. He and his diligent, happy wife had never wanted any so-called labour-saving devices (the cottage shone with her "elbow grease") had never in their lives bought on hire purchase, and had saved for years to exchange their motor-bike for a little car (paid for in cash) for which, when the great moment came, we built them a garage. Tom's quiet, steady presence about the place was like a benediction. And the sight of his wife's beaming face as she insisted on carrying trays of tea and sandwiches across 3 fields when my husband and I were harvesting was a joy. When my husband once asked her if Tom wouldn't like to have a herd of his *own*, she replied: "Good heavens no! The worry and responsibility would put him in his grave!"

They were richly happy because they *accepted themselves as they were, and never wanted to be anyone else.* They were wedded to us, the place, and the animals, and when we are in Oxfordshire they welcome us with open arms and a sudden welling of tears in the eyes. We shall meet again in the spirit world without a doubt, and I cannot wait to see Tom's unexpected delight when he finds his special favourites again, "alive and well," in the animal spirit realms!

Bill was the exact opposite in everything, including, of course, his politics. He had a perpetual chip on his shoulder. He imagined he might have been "something better" — had he not consistently absconded from school because he disliked work of any sort. A dislike which never left him! He could not accept his own character, and had to find something or someone to blame. As wages rose higher and higher, so did his hire purchase commitments, until the giant frig. washing machine, spin-dryer, electric polisher, telly, radiogram, records, huge rugs, picnic hampers, and one car after another were millstones round his neck. The radio blared unceasingly. Every weekend the last penny went on gallons of petrol or entertaining friends who spilled over our yard and even into our private garden. The 15-year-old daughter's array of 12 lipsticks made my solitary one look rather silly — as silly as she herself looked tripping about the farm in high heels and "dressed to kill."

Bill's work with the cows was an impersonal, unavoidable necessity, (they never took to him), and he always managed to leave the dirty work like dunging out calf-pens, scrubbing mangers and unblocking drains to my husband and me. He was a natural shirker. His wife's medical needs, real or imaginary, had cost the Health Service hundreds of pounds, yet she was outraged at having to pay 3p. income tax every other week. They were not happy people because they were never satisfied, and Bill's political creed was based on hate, or rather self-hate.

How different to my English teacher at school. She came from what is called "a very good family" but was so hard up at one time that she had to furnish her rented room (very prettily) with covered packing cases and boxes from the grocer. She was quite unconcerned. But then she was a Spiritualist, and was responsible for introducing me to Spiritualist literature when I was 14, for which I owe her a great debt.

It is an absolute fallacy that more wealth has anything to do with happiness and joy in life. Another fallacy is the attitude of recent years that *service* is *servile*. One dare not use the word "servant" any more. Yet we are all servants in some form, one of another, including the monarch. Did not the Greatest Son of God demonstrate the privilege of service by kneeling down on the floor to wash his disciples' feet?

Equality is still another fallacy, for no one is the *equal* of anyone else. There is no equality in the spirit world. If there were, there would be no lower astral regions, no intermediate stages, no "summerland," no escalation of spheres into which it is not *possible* for anyone to enter from a lower sphere — until they have earned the right to do so. No one, in the next world, possesses their own "home" till they have *earned* it by qualities of the spirit. (It goes without saying that spirituality bears no relationship to any material or worldly status.)

But how much happier everyone would be if they could accept the Law of Rebirth, and *know* that whatever their situation or lot in life they are placed in it — or their Greater Soul has chosen it — as the *best* means of learning certain lessons necessary for their progress, and also for working out the laws of Karma, or Cause and Effect.

How much less envious, discontented, full of self-pity and "chips on the shoulder" everyone would be if we *accepted ourselves for what we are* and did not wish or try to be someone else, but on the contrary be more truly our Selves. For the wonderful thing about inequality is that we are all absolutely *unique!* We all possess something completely individual which no other human being possesses. Every one of us forms a separate, distinctive jewel (however encrusted and unpolished as yet) in the Creator's crown.

Although of equal *value* to the All-loving Father Who breathed out all His children from His own Essence, we are all at differing points of the great circle which eventually leads back to God-consciousness and atonement with Infinite Love. All will be gathered into the sheepfold, in the Heart of God, when the very blackest sheep has become white. We are on a long and exciting journey, involving many many lives on this Earth or some other planet — the schoolrooms of heaven — so let us not allow the negative, unspiritual values of rank Materialism to be our goal in life, impeding our progress with their "dead-sea fruit," but seek always those simpler, deeper, more lasting joys and satisfactions which come from striving to do our best with courage, and above all with love, in whatever circumstances and situations we find ourselves — richer or poorer, in sickness or in health, in success or failure. We are never alone, never overlooked, never unloved, never unwept-for, however much it might *seem* so to the meths-drinker sharing his bomb site and his last fag with his brother . . .

THE UNACCEPTABLE CREED OF COMMUNISM

I wonder how many times, over the years, some starry-eyed young person has said to me, "After all, Jesus was really a Communist, wasn't he?" And I have never ceased to wonder on what incredible misconception this extraordinary statement could be based.

To begin with, it is impossible that the Nazarene, whose kingdom is not of this world, could have any part in an ideology or creed which is totally materialistic and which denies the concept of a spiritual universe or the spiritual worth or destiny of the individual.

How easily some of the idealistic young, having understandably thrown over the worn-out and distorted orthodox religions, and seeing the apparent injustices and other evils of the world (having little knowledge of human nature and none of Karma) can find themselves, even if temporarily, ensnared by the clever surface claptrap of Communism — so long as they do not have to live under its iron heel.

The words Comrade and Brother doubtless appeal to their innate longing for the brotherhood of man on earth, for a state of affairs where no one is done down or exploited; where greed or corruption cannot flourish; where the goodly things of this life are common to all; a world in which wars are no more waged. This, I am sure, is the Utopian dream of youth — as indeed it should be. But these ideals can never, ever be achieved through Communism.

An old friend of mine liked to preach Dialectic Materialism at me whenever we met. He used to say in all earnestness: "Communism leads to the greatest free expression of the individual." At that time he really believed it! (Needless to say, he had never set foot in a Communist country.)

He was a vital, brilliant composer, and his agony of mind began when his freedom as an individual was annihilated by a typed directive from King Street, the Communist London Headquarters. In this directive he was told exactly what kind of music he could and could not compose in future.

I have never seen anyone become so ill so quickly. Ashen-faced and haggard, he walked up and down his room with the directive in his hand for days on end, interrupted at intervals by the necessity of going out to vomit. His integrity as an artist was at stake. His remarkable gift of individual expression which energised his whole being was shot down in full flight . . . Where now was "the greatest freedom of the individual?"

Soon after this dagger thrust came the information that a group of Jewish doctors in a Communist country had been subjected to bestial treatment and then executed — not only for endeavouring to express the freedom of the individual, but also for being Jews.

Now my friend, though born in London, came of a Polish-Jewish family. He had revolted against his parents' orthodoxy and chose to call himself an atheist. Mass murder of "deviationists" or "enemies of the State" had not appeared to register too deeply with him, but the fate of the Jewish doctors struck nearer home. The famous words of Voltaire suddenly came to life in his own heart: "I disagree with what you say, but I will defend with my life your right to say it." (How often, I wonder, in his eight years in a frozen Siberian labour-camp must Alexander Solzhenitsyn have thought of those words?)

When my friend, having experienced his dark night of the soul, finally resigned from the Communist Party, the venom of his Comrades was so poisonous that he took up residence in Switzerland, where he set out on a spiritual safari towards the light which was always hidden in his own soul.

Let no one say that this article is political and therefore not germane to this magazine. For I maintain that its import is purely spiritual, and of vital importance to our spiritual welfare and also to the future of our children.

Scientists have discovered that there is a substance, a "something" in the universe called anti-matter. It operates in a directly *opposite* manner to all we have come to know about matter. Where matter coheres, for example, anti-matter disperses. In whatever way matter is known to behave, anti-matter does the opposite.

In like manner, and using the word "anti" to mean not only "against" but "*opposite*," the creed of Communism is anti-Christ. (And by Christ I mean not only the teaching and example of Jesus, but the Cosmic Christ Spirit whose greatest Messenger and medium he was and has been to date, a Messenger of Light to *all* humanity.) For instead of being based on the concepts of light, love, and freedom, the true brotherhood of man within the fatherhood of God, and the immortality and evolution of individualised spirit beyond all worlds, it is based on the exact opposites of all these things.

The word love, or indeed any conception of it in any form such as compassion, is unknown in the real policies of the Party — in what is known as "the steel-hardened cadre." The words Comrade or Brotherhood are deliberate, farcical misnomers to deceive the ignorant and the naive.

The virtues of filial affection and loyalty to family or friends are regarded as vices disloyal to the God-State. Children in school are given awards of merit for reporting the conversations and attitudes of their parents; friends are interrogated by the Secret Police about one another's thoughts, words or activities. There is not a soul one can really trust, for this pernicious practice gives unrivalled opportunity for "getting one's own back" for private grievances or dislikes.

All those suspected of the crime of thinking for themselves are watched, followed, have their telephones tapped and their rooms bugged, until the inevitable knock on the door in the small hours. Every foreign visitor or foreigner working in the country is treated likewise. The handful of seven brave people who protested in a public square against the invasion of a "brother State" with tanks and guns were never heard of again.

Intellectuals and the intelligentsia are sent to labour-camps, or salt-mines, or imprisoned, or locked away in mental asylums by the thousand when too outspoken. No one is free to travel at will. Under this creed no human being is free to be his or her true self. The spark of individuality or of conscience must be stamped on quickly if one is to preserve the precious permit to live with one's family, the permit to have a roof over one's head, the permit to buy food, the permit to work.

The State recruits its members of the dreaded KGB, the Secret Police,

138

either by fear (for only the brave or foolhardy would risk refusing to serve) or by appealing to the baser desires in human nature for unlimited power, prestige and privilege. Over half a million snoopers are paid by the State — totally unproductive citizens except in the production of victims.

President Kennedy told the West Berliners so rightly that in the West we have our faults, but at least we do not have to build a wall to keep our people inside. But the Wall against freedom became a desperate, despicable and humiliating necessity for Communism, an emblem of defeat in full view of the world — the first wall in history erected to keep people *in* instead of keeping invaders *out!* For before it was built over 4 million people had escaped to freedom. Since its erection a mere quarter of a million desperate people have got through at the risk of their lives, while hundreds have been shot down in the attempt.

The aim of the Communist creed is the total domination of the world by a handful of men who cannot be elected by the people because no rival party is allowed in a totalitarian State. But the means employed to this end, and the means of keeping in subjection those countries which have fallen, unwilling victims into its tentacles, constitute a creed wholly directed against the spiritual evolution of mankind.

Because weapons are now so terrible, so totally destructive, domination of the world must proceed by calculated stealth, by infiltration, by everywhere adding fuel in whatever manner possible to whatever unrest or disturbance there may be for any reason, anywhere, to weaken every country and every government of whatever kind or colour.

It is known that a former head of the all-powerful KGB was made responsible for getting Communists into all the key positions of all British Unions, so that already it is said that some 75% of unions are Communist-led, motivated and inspired at the top level — not to improve their members' conditions so far as humanly and economically possible, but, *under this camouflage,* to undermine and ruin the country concerned whatever the cost might be to millions of their "Comrades." Unfortunately the frailties of human nature, added to both spiritual and political immaturity, make many willing and well-meaning dupes, when fed on a cleverly concocted diet for long enough.

Does it never occur, I wonder, to any of our extreme elements in a country where they are free to stage demonstrations and protests ad. lib. about anything and everything, with the *protection,* moreover, of the police, that if they ventured on so much as a single protest in a Communist State they would either be sent to labour-camps, imprisoned, possibly tortured (mentally if not always physically), incarcerated in mental asylums or just exterminated as enemies of the Almighty State — a State where the ant-hill is far more important than any individual ant?

At this season of resurrection, therefore, when Nature is springing into a renewed life cycle in all its manifold beauty, reflecting the refulgence of the resurrected Light of the World, let us see to it that that Light is also reflected in our hearts. Let us show in our lives and thoughts and actions that we are dedicated to light, not darkness, to love, not hate, to freedom of the divine spirit in man, not tyranny, and by our prayer and attunement with the highest so enable the White Brotherhood of the Christ Sphere to penetrate the darkness which seeks to dominate, and to transmute it in the embrace of Love.

HERALDS OF THE NEW DISPENSATION

At 9.40 p.m., alone in the house, I walked through the kitchen to fetch something, and a blazing light attracted my attention on my left. I looked out of the wide west window and held my breath. For there, completely stationary, and seemingly no further than a mile away over the woods, was a brilliant UFO or Flying Saucer. It was absolutely beautiful, suspended against a darkening sky in which the turquoise from the earlier sunset still lingered.

"Oh, you *beautiful* thing!" I said aloud, gazing at it enrapt. I had not seen one, physically, for several years, since my son, then only three years old, had drawn my attention to six of them in broad daylight. (My other experience had been when I found myself astrally projected, totally "awake" by the window while my body was asleep on the bed. A saucer hovered over the lawn, and communication had been by telepathy.)

I ran through the house and into the garden. I opened my arms to it, longing for it to come closer. But it remained where it was, like a great beacon in the sky. How long had it been there? Eventually, after some ten minutes or so, I heard my husband return home in the car. As he walked from the garage behind the long hedge I shouted to him to come and look. But just as he reached the end of the hedge the UFO expanded in size and then vanished, much to my disappointment.

There was a sequel, however, about a week later. We were both in the kitchen when I happened to move across the room — and there it was again. "*Now!*" I said, "It's here *again — quick!*" But my husband is slow-moving, and before he had got round to the window it just disappeared once more. Perhaps he was not meant to see it. Who knows? It seemed strange, as well as maddening, that he should just miss it twice.

Then, nine months later, on coming down the outside oak steps into the garden from our Sanctuary (I had gone back to tidy up after a group meeting), there was this enormous shining thing so low over the woods about a mile away that the tops of the trees were lit up by its radiance. It was the size of my thumb-nail when my arm was outstretched against the sky. I hastened into the house to fetch my son, and we looked out of the kitchen window — not realising that from the ground floor it would have been obscured by a high stone wall. Not till next day did I realise that we should have gone back up the flight of steps, as it was so low. I have no idea, therefore, how long it was there.

I recount these comparatively uninteresting sightings purely because they are personal. After all, hundreds of people in Britain witness sightings. National Opinion Polls confirm that two out of three people now acknowledge the reality of Saucers. Following one of Rex Dutta's radio broadcasts from Manchester, a 45-minute phone-in the surge of letters continued for 8 weeks; while his staff could not cope with the letters and callers after his *2-hour non-stop* phone-in with Adrian Love at London Broadcasting on August 16th, 1974.

It is difficult to understand, therefore, why (in the words of the editor of a world-renowned publication who had commissioned an article from him) "the British Government does not like Saucers and has D notices on them," that is, censorship.

How many people in Britain know that when a bevy of top scientists flew in the Concorde 001 from Las Palmas to Tchad to photograph the solar eclipse in June 1973 they also photographed in colour an enormous UFO which they said had a diameter in excess of 200 meters, and was above the Concorde, that is, above 58,000 feet? The astrophysicist Monsieur Koutchmy said the luminosity was extraordinary. It was literally "burning" and had a red "summit."

How many people are aware that more than 20 Saucers have been seen, and many filmed, by some 30 astronauts (including the Russian Vokshod 1 and Vokshod 2) on their space missions? That Armstrong, Aldrin and Collins in Apollo 11 were followed for 2 days by a UFO on their way to the moon? That Conrad, Bean and Gordon in Apollo 12 said a UFO accompanied them to within 132,000 miles of the moon, preceding them all the way? That Borman and Lovell photographed twin oval-shaped UFOs with glowing undersides? That back on February 20th, 1962 John Glenn in his Mercury capsule saw three objects following him and then overtaking him at varying speeds? No wonder Ed. Mitchell of Apollo 14 states briefly and categorically: "We all know UFOs are real."

But are we told that a vast radio interplanetary communication system is being developed, called "Cyclops," to communicate with extra-terrestrial beings, in a joint effort with NASA and Stanford University scientists? One of these scientists is Prof. Ronald Bracewell who says: "We have no reason to fear aliens from outer space; we should, in fact, prepare to communicate with them."

I have never liked the word "alien." They are our fellow beings in whatever guise and wherever they come from, for all life and all consciousness is part of the Whole, of the Universal Spirit, of God. Although in the last few thousand years their recorded visitations, though spectacular, have been fewer than at present, this is because they withdrew their initial contact in ages past. But since mankind's destructive use of atomic energy they have been *returning* to planet Earth in ever-increasing numbers, and making increasing landings and contacts. They are nothing new.

Roman, Greek and Egyptian writers wrote of them as existing since remotest antiquity. The theme of contact and even union between earthlings and superior beings from the sky is basic in *all* mythology the world over, and mythology is always *based* on fact. Books have been written on this subject.

In aeons past primitive man existed in a state of innocent nature, unable to imagine any possible change. (A little like the remnants of certain remote tribes like the Pygmies, today.) Suddenly, a great leap forward occurred in the cycle of human civilisation with the arrival of vastly more advanced extra-terrestrial beings in their "winged discs." They brought knowledge of a heretofore inconceivable kind. Their coming led to a revolutionary change in the pattern of human existence. Nothing was the same. There now stretched an apparently endless prospect of continual progress, with all its *responsibilities*. The apple had been eaten. The apple which has always symbolised the ambrosia of the gods, giving to men an expansion of consciousness, higher vision, and the seeds of individual immortality (as opposed to that of the group soul). Also the serpent has always symbolised wisdom and knowledge throughout the ages, however misunderstood and castigated by the writers of the Bible. The serpent became the symbol of the winged discs of the gods, as well.

Much later, men came to look back on former times of innocence and ignorance with a yearning for the golden age now irretrievably lost, for the minds which had been opened by the vision of the "gods" could never again be contracted. In Genesis VI the writers state that the sons of god mated with the daughters of men. Indian scriptures refer to these sons of god as "Lords of the Flame." They brought the knowledge of making fire, of agriculture, healing and medicine, the science of levitation and transportation of objects by sound, and technology. They are also said to have brought wheat and bees.

It is interesting to note the dramatic cases of healing performed by Flying Saucers or their occupants — cases tested and vouched for by witnesses and doctors. In one such case it was a doctor who was healed. This doctor, living in the French Alps with his wife and small son, had been a gifted pianist until he stepped on a mine during the Algerian War which rendered him partially paralysed in the right leg and right arm. His piano-playing was over. His wounds, and paralysis, remained unchanged for 10 years.

To make matters worse, he suffered an accident to his left leg, a painful gash, on October 28th, 1968. Though the wound was treated at once, he was still in pain and moving with extreme difficulty on the night of November 1st when, sometime after 3 a.m. he was awoken by his small son calling out, and perceived through closed shutters powerful flashes of light. At first he took this to be lightning, but there was no thunder.

Opening the French windows, he limped on to the terrace and saw, down the valley, two luminous disc-shaped objects with vertical and horizontal antennae from which the flashes of brilliant light emitted at one-second intervals. The two discs started to move towards him, at the same time drawing closer together. The amazed doctor saw the twin objects fuse into one, and this one approached to within 200 metres of him, then remained stationary.

The rotation of the disc's lower portion speeded up formidably, the disc tilted, and the doctor received a powerful light-beam some 35 feet thick which shone all over him. He instinctively covered his face as the light beam reached him. An instant later he heard a muffled "bang" and the object dematerialised, vanished.

Badly shaken, the doctor immediately made notes, including sketches of the disc. He then woke his wife and told her what had happened. In his excitement he did not realise *he was pacing up and down the room,* until his wife exclaimed. The Algerian wounds, the partial paralysis of arm and leg, and the recent leg wound were all completely healed, and he plays the piano as well as ever.

Lack of space forbids me to mention other documented cases of similar healings, in at least one of which two beings under 4 feet in height actually descended from their craft to effect the healing by contact, in the presence of seven stupefied witnesses. This occurred on the night of October 25th, 1957 when the daughter of a wealthy Brazilian at Petropolis, west of Rio, was in the final stages of dying of cancer of the stomach. In December her doctor was able to verify that she was indeed cured of the cancer. The full details of his particular case are fascinating.

The reader may ask: what have Saucers and extra-terrestrial beings to do with Christmas? It is my belief, confirmed by spirit communication, that mankind is due for another leap forward now we are entering the Aquarian Age. Our present culture and pattern of civilisation has reached a point where it can go no further on the same lines without eventual self-destruction. Nor can it retreat, for it has passed the point of no return.

It appears, too, that moral decline and mental anarchy must precede the start of a new phase in our history. This we have today. And so it was at the commencement of the Piscean Age which heralded the advent of the Great Messenger, inspired and overshadowed by the universal Christ, who brought a new vision, a new concept and a new Light — however much that Light was dimmed and nearly smothered by the misconceptions and brutish nature of earthlings.

Each new Age has its own new Dispensation, and this time it is not the task of *one* Messenger of Light in one small portion of the globe's surface, but a multiplicity of Messengers infiltrating the entire planet — yet carrying out the work of the One. It is they who are prepared to nurse us through chaos, conflict and even catastrophe, to teach us new concepts, new skills, provided we allow them to do so by raising up our own consciousness, expanding our hearts, and committing our wills to the Light. (Those who prefer darkness will not be allowed to hold back The Plan indefinitely. There are other spheres in the universe wherein such ones can continue either their progress or their decline, as they may desire.)

So whether we celebrate Christ Mass as Christians, or in the older sense of the winter solstice Saturnalia; whether we celebrate the birth of *the* Son of God or *a* Son of God, we should all celebrate the birth in our own hearts of that concept of universal love which casts out fear, and enables us to welcome the heralds of the New Dispensation for which all people of goodwill so ardently yearn.

VIEW FROM THE MOON

Although little or no information has been given to the general public, I believe the trips to the Moon have brought forth technical and scientific discoveries which are now being usefully developed in various fields of industry, technology and medicine.

However that may be, these material discoveries pale into insignificance, in my opinion, compared with the breakthrough that appears to have occurred to a number of people in the field of metaphysics — or, if you prefer, religion in its widest and most fundamental aspects.

It really does seem extraordinary that it needs someone to actually stand on the Moon and transmit back pictures of the planet Earth as it appears from a little way off, for people to begin to sense its place in the cosmos "in a new light!". The actual sight of the Earth, as seen from the Moon, appears to have done something to extend mental and spiritual horizons.

May all power, courage and inspiration be given, therefore, to the astronaut Edgar Mitchell who, following upon the "staggering" success (his own word) of his ESP tests on the Apollo 14 mission, has joined America's *Psychic* magazine as Research Editor at Large. He has also formed a Corporation called EDMA, short for Edgar D. Mitchell and Associates, having as its aim "to help direct the course of history away from its present catastrophic trend of ever-greater global crises."

No less a person than Dr. Wernher von Braun, who fathered the Moon programmes, is among the Corporation's advisers, and some 75 scientists, physicians, psychologists, psychiatrists, educators and business executives have committed themselves to supporting its activities.

Mitchell is researching into and carrying out experiments in every known form of psychic phenomena, it seems, with the co-operation of well-trained reliable psychic channels, sensitives and mediums, and he hopes these experiments will awaken scientists and the public "to the reality of psychic phenomena and their implications for mankind."

"We have done things," he says, "with a very powerful sensitive under totally controlled conditions — things which science says cannot be done." He adds: "We are aiming high, but when the future of the planet is at stake, I believe nothing less than what I propose will be sufficient."

This is the kind of man we need — an engineer, test pilot, management specialist, with experience in other technical professions, not to mention his training and performance as an astronaut; a man possessing mental and intellectual capabilities of a high order, and having spent years learning objective science methods.

"From my point of view," he says, "the meaning of death is transition for continued life." He believes a major breakthrough to understanding the consciousness of nature is upon us. (Perhaps one day he will read the Master D.K.'s book *The Consciousness of the Atom* given through Alice Bailey.)

Mitchell admits that seven years ago, when he first studied para-psychology, he was "sceptical — and ignorant — about the whole field," adding "To my surprise, disbelief about the validity of these occurrences began melting away." He has a long, arduous and adventurous journey of discovery before him — more exciting and more vital than any Apollo mission — but he is only in his forties. If he and his group can eventually succeed in convincing a significant number of eminent intellectuals who have until now ignored the painstaking and recorded life work of psychic investigators over the past century, *and* can spread the still more important *teaching* from the higher spheres, we shall indeed be grateful that Edgar Mitchell once walked on the Moon.

It is well that he speaks of "the consciousness of nature," for one of the most important things that has to be impressed on people's minds is that all phenomena and all life in whatever sphere and on whatever frequency or dimension is *natural*, and *not* "supernatural," for all is one Whole.

As a great spirit teacher puts it: all-pervading Spirit is everywhere, being the Source of all, but can only be apprehended through the senses when individualised or particularised into "things," even into things like atoms and sub-atoms. It is like putting one's hand into a huge tank of water. One cannot know what portion of water one is touching. But if the water is poured into separate buckets, then one knows bucket 7 or bucket 4, and can study the water in that *particular* bucket when separated from the vast tank. Though it is *all water,* or *all Spirit.*

Every spirit teacher tells us that the time will come when all will be able to converse with loved ones in the next phase of existence. This is what they are working towards — eventually. Though primitive man was psychic, and close to nature, this psychism was more like the psychic awareness of animals. Primitive man had far less mental thinking brain — thinking only of his animal needs — but we have now gone down to the *bottom* of the valley of the shadow, not of death, but of living, and have now *begun* to climb up. Even carrying the weight of our self-created burdens, there is greater self-awareness, greater consciousness, mentality, wisdom and knowledge, and we are more individualised. Man, our teachers tell us, *will* turn his burdens into glorious effect.

But the path, like any path which leads up higher, is a hard one. And one of the things that makes it harder, it seems to me, is the abysmal lack of imagination in the vast majority of human beings. We are blind to our spiritual heritage; blind to our original Parentage before worlds were born; blind to the fact that we are immortals!

We surround ourselves with self-erected boundaries beyond which we think we cannot venture. In fact we do not even try, for our imaginations are so limited that we do not realise that there is anything beyond. Like those mariners who thought they might topple off the edge of a flat Earth which some said was held up by colossal elephants — though what the elephants were standing on they never did say!

Not so long ago (1600 A.D.) the great metaphysical philosopher Giordano Bruno was burnt alive by the Church for such concepts as the plurality of worlds, and his assertion that amid all the varying phenomena of the universe there is something which gives coherence and intelligibility to them and this something is God, the universal, unifying substance, from which all things of necessity come. While the Pope of the day was too afraid to look through Galileo's telescope and tried to get him burnt as well for inventing such a devilish and "sacriligious" device. So far had the Dark Ages sunk into ignorance through deliberately shutting out the knowledge of the great so-called pagan philosophers and astronomers of a previous time.

We still cannot realise that we have the *potential* within us to exist and experience on all spheres of the spiritual universe, in whatever dimension. We are only limited by our level of consciousness. And our level of consciousness is inhibited by lack of imagination.

Anyone, by closing their eyes in a few moments of quiet repose, can find themselves standing on the mountains of the Moon, in that pristine cold clarity against a black sky, and look with wonder and awe at the blue and silver planet Earth. One does not have to go there physically.

And in the looking at that lovely, spherical space-ship, held on its appointed course by the Love and Thought of God the Great Spirit working through the vast Spiritual Heirarchy, be filled with the pathos and the anguish of it all.

For spread over the surface of this beautiful ball, which it seems one can almost hold in the hollow of one's hand, masses of arrogant, hate-filled, fear-filled little human beings, like rogue ants, are torturing and destroying each other, and teaching their children to do likewise.

Looking more closely, with the eyes of the spirit, one sees lurid patches of blood all over the globe, where war, violence and terrorism are the order of the day. And the terrible thing about war and violence and terrorism is not even so much what it does to its victims (though that is ghastly enough) but what it does to its perpetrators.

Every mother's son (who is not psychopathic) has in the first instance to steel himself to kill or maim for life some other mother's son — or daughter or child. (The Hitler Youth, when starting training in Jew-baiting, had to take time off to be sick, until they gradually became hardened enough to obey their evil masters.) But having embarked on a course of killing, whether by bayonet, bombing, sniping, machine-gunning, burning with napalm, commando tactics or by whatever abominable method, this same mother's son is in danger of not being able to stop. Fellow human beings become no more than nine-pins. For such as these the bell tolls . . .

Though one is grateful for a few hours of respite, when in various areas of the world the killing stops for Christmas Day, (only to resume with ferocity on the morrow), does this not seem the most sardonic and sceptical, the *ultimate* insult to the Prince of Peace?

I consider the policy laid down for our television newscasters an extremely doubtful one, to say the least. It is true that if some personage of note dies a perfectly natural "death" at the appointed time, they are allowed to announce the fact in slightly slower, more portentious tones. But reports of the most horrible barbarities, in warfare, tyranny and terrorism, blighting the lives of thousands of families apart from the victims, are rattled off as glibly as the football results — and certainly with *less* hint of emotion than the cricket scores.

Surely this policy of strict impartiality can be taken *too* far. For when the abnormal becomes the norm, it is dangerous. And when sins to make the angels weep are seemingly less surprising than snow on the hills, it is very near the brainwashing of Orwell's frightening novel *1984*. Or so it seems from *my* view from the Moon.

I would like NASA to present every politician and every national leader throughout the world with a large coloured photograph of the Earth, taken from the Moon. Perhaps this view of our miraculous temporary home would help to introduce some sense of perspective, some conviction of the folly and futility, the bestial brutality, the self-destruction of war — and the astronomical cost in terms of the world's wealth and the world's suffering.

Perhaps, too, it would help to quicken the imagination of mankind; help to bring about a breakthrough of spiritual concepts to pierce the shroud of materialistic thought and aims; help to bring about a slowing down of insanity; "help direct the course of history away from its present catastrophic trend . . ."

For those brave words from a brave man, I salute you, Edgar Mitchell. You will not be alone.

BREAKING THE THOUGHT BARRIER

U Thant, when Secretary General of the United Nations, is on record as saying that, after peace, Flying Saucers are the most important question now facing humanity. I agree, inasmuch that humanity has now come to the point when it *must* break "the thought barrier" if it is to progress into an enlightened New Age of eventual peace and true brotherhood, and not be sucked down into the evil bog of parochial, materialistic concepts.

Typical of this blinkered, parochial and materialistic attitude is a news item in a daily paper. It stated that a certain American businessman, after seeing a Flying Saucer, immediately resigned his executive position and locked himself in his house! From shock? It did not say.

All Governments have detailed files on this subject in their possession, but after the first seven years of open discussion and reporting (1947 to 1954) came a conspiracy of silence. There was an official clamp-down in the majority of countries. Yet the sightings continued as before, in the region of at least fifty to a hundred a week around the world.

By 1960 a group of 50 infuriated and frustrated pilots signed a round robin demanding to know why their reports had been passed over, why they had been made to look like fools or liars, and if they were considered to be so unreliable why were they still allowed to fly aeroplanes?

I mentioned "the first seven years," but of course Flying Saucers are nothing new. They have been visiting planet Earth for thousands, perhaps millions of years. There is ample evidence of this fact if anyone takes the trouble to study the subject in depth.

But it was after "civilised" humanity developed and dropped the deadly and destructive nuclear device of death that our brothers and sisters from outer space took a renewed and intensive interest in us and in our destiny — which also affects their own.

Since 1947 no less than 260 books have been written about them in the English language alone. Probably many more by now. (While certain books have been censored or withdrawn by "higher authority"). There have been thousands upon thousands of sightings in every country of the world. Numberless photographs and films have been taken of them. There have been more landings than most people know of. Close inspections have been made of them while on the ground. Contact with their occupants has been established. Flights in them have been taken, and a great deal of communication has been received from them by various methods.

It is said that there have been to date 3000 contactees. I suspect there may have been more, because there are many among us who have preferred to keep such an event a purely personal one. There are investigating Saucer Groups of highly intelligent and qualified people, including scientists, all over the globe.

Fourteen different types of UFOs have been classified (most of which have been photographed), ranging from the gigantic "mother ships" to 18″ survey discs, and the "balls of green light" which are employed in highly polluted areas to soak up both noxious radiations and poisonous thought concentrations. Help — without interference with our freewill — is being given consistently.

These visitors from Fourth Dimensional space, with far greater technical knowledge than we at present possess, and of a far higher spiritual evolution than our present Fifth Root Race has arrived at, are able to materialise or take on the necessary bodily form to stay on Earth for limited periods, usually not longer than 12 weeks at one time, owing to the strain of our dense atmosphere and conditions.

And at this time there are many Venusians (and others) who have willingly taken the missionary step of incarnating on Earth through Earth-parents. These people are naturally among the contactees — hence the oft-repeated phrase: "To the apples we have salted away, we return."

The creators of that popular television series, "Star Trek" must surely have been inspired, at least to some extent, by some of the facts I have mentioned. Notably the idea of "energising" the occupants of the "Enterprise" out of and into their spaceship. This is nothing more nor less than teleportation, or apporting the human body by raising the vibrations of its atoms.

Though this is done, in the story, by scientific means at the push of a button, some occupants of some Saucers are able to do just this by mental control. When not wishing to be disturbed about their business, three occupants of a Saucer, finding they were being observed while examining something (plant-life?) in a wood, immediately vanished from sight, and within seconds, their craft (previously hidden by some trees) was seen to rise swiftly and vertically — and silently — and make off.

Among Earthlings only a very rare and advanced adept, such as certain Tibetan masters, are able to apport themselves from one place to another. It has also been done in the seance room when, on at least one occasion to my knowledge, the entranced medium was apported from one room to another instantaneously, (though in this case it was done *for* him by spirit control from the Other Side.)

In spite of stories like "Star Trek" being limited by adherence to advanced *material* technology, the concept of an Interplanetary Brotherhood is a good one, and I am sure helps to enlarge people's imaginations. But it always amuses me that Earth men and women should be depicted as the "heroes" who settle troubles elsewhere in the galaxy, whereas the reverse would be more in keeping with the truth — though perhaps less acceptable to our pride!

Let us now look at a communication received in 1962 from an advanced member of The White Brotherhood in the world of spirit: "Visitors to Earth from other planets will make their presence known by group arrivals from what may be named The Planetary Organisation. These landings will make men accept the truth that beings inhabit other worlds. As yet the sighting of but few of the space craft constantly on reconnaissance above Earth makes little impact. For more important and impressive appearances special preparations must be made — in the minds of those on Earth with whom contact must be made on a more formal footing than the previous instances of contact with individuals warranted.

"These few prepared the many. In the hundreds of testing, probing flights organised to take place above Earth, there have been few Earth people able to connect, in thought and vision, well enough to state clearly what they have seen and, in several instances, photographed. The exceptions are some true corroborators, with books and articles to their credit. Their work was possible through close harmony with the space visitors. Now will be organised appearances on conference level with important officials and statesmen of Earth.

"The reason for these visits from other planets, the work behind them and an inkling of the organised planetary system, including a close guard kept on the lesser worlds in the galaxies, is to be explained to mankind in the future. For the close guard there are many reasons: here outlined is one of the important issues. The guardians in more mature worlds, (which are inhabited by entities wise and cultured in the balance of power required in any one world in a particular galaxy), control those worlds, as they wax in vigour of attraction to universal unity — albeit the control is quite invisible to many worlds that are outside the speed of thought and action operating among the inhabitants of those controlling worlds.

"When a space craft, or Flying Saucer, makes reconnaissance over Earth, the parts of different countries under surveillance are, to the watchers on patrol, noted as influences to be studied, after absorption: being atmospheric discharges of thought as well as being conservations of vital agencies put to work by man, to create centralised spots of activity explosive in content, for the disturbance of more than just the Earth world — for other related spheres might be adversely disturbed by any convulsive eruption, man-made with evil and power-lusting intent.

"The guardian scout-surveyors are able to dispel or to gather up for dispersal far from Earth, the most virulent of the explosive content, which they can extract during hover flights over specified points mapped for survey. A giant vacuum-cleaner could inadequately depict in imagery the taking up of atmospheric disturbances created over particular spots, at given times of conflict in thought, added to demonstrative experiment, on work using energy fuels common to the complete galaxy — not exclusive to Earth, as mistakenly supposed by mankind.

"This sketches very briefly the outline of operative duty undertaken by the guards in charge of some of the planets directly connected with Earth, by similitude of outlook, living conditions or other characteristic tendencies, including a world's condition regarding advancement, or regression, in the community of planets within one galaxy.

"The 'Flying Saucer Squads' are alerted to make their presence known in no small measure to those on Earth, and increasing sightings of the crafts, especially at low level, must make their reality accepted even by the sceptics. When that happens, contact through sound and voice will be possible. This will indicate the intentions of those who are serious investigators of the minds of common men and their leaders. Intentions are often more worthy than action; if action more befitting a mature world of individuals can be offered by those from outer space with more experience, then their endeavour will be of great import to mankind.

"Later contact with man will not be as a 'last minute warning,' but will be simple and a direct part of normal life, with intermingling and fraternising between men and those who land for consultation. The visitors could easily take men to their planets in the vastly better equipped craft than men could devise by themselves. The impact of those visits from Earth would reveal the wise use of laws governing universal life, and could bring real, lasting peace to men."*

I have given this particular communication in full because it sums up in general the content of innumerable communications from spirit sources on this subject.

Unlimited is the range of the individual consciousness if only it can pass "the thought barrier." When we broke "the sound barrier" we did what used to be thought of as an impossibility: to travel faster than sound. The time will come when we shall achieve another "impossibility:" to travel faster than light, (thereby becoming invisible.)

Yet we *can* be free of all such barriers when released from the physical body during sleep. During the writing of this article I experienced the privilege of attending (out of the body) a large conference in another sphere. There were seemingly many hundreds of people watching and learning, seated in tiers around a large inner circle of people who were standing. As a visitor from Earth I was allowed to join this circle quite unobtrusively. No one turned to look. Scarcely had I done so, when two other visitors arrived from other planets, and also joined the circle, opposite me. To my surprise, they greeted me with a slight bow and an elaborate symbolic gesture which included a crossing of the feet. Feeling a little shy, I had the presence of mind to respond to this greeting in a similar fashion, before the conference commenced . . .

When the Thought Barrier is crossed, *All* worlds are One.

---

*Received through Miss Madeline Dingley.   151

SAUCERS, SCIENTISTS AND ASTRONAUTS

Following my article entitled *Breaking the Thought Barrier* I received so many letters from readers wanting to know more about Flying Saucers, or UFOs, that I feel justified in returning to the subject, however briefly. One particular letter was especially intriguing, from my point of view, for it confirmed and enlarged upon a vivid experience I had had during the sleep state, and which I described at the end of the last chapter.

I wrote:... "I experienced the privilege of attending (out of the body) a large conference in another sphere. There were seemingly many hundreds of people watching and learning, seated in tiers around a large inner circle of people who were standing. As a visitor from Earth I was allowed to join the circle quite unobtrusively. No one turned to look. Scarcely had I done so when two other visitors arrived from other planets, and also joined the circle . . ."

Now here is a slightly condensed version of what my correspondent wrote about *her* experience which took place three years ago: "*I have also been in the large conference room!* Each circle of seats had their own particular colour. I asked about the colours and was told they corresponded to degrees of knowledge. No one turned to look as I entered. The person who was with me said they were waiting for a teacher. . . . He stood alone on a platform in the centre.

"I do not remember what he said — except the one word LOVE. It vibrated like music from one row up to the next; like an echo, over and over again, in musical tones. Then, as the vibration reached the top of the roofless hall it ascended into the blue atmosphere. It was not one musical note, but had variations. I remember being awe-struck, for the music touched deeper than the word, or the lone figure."

The fact that people quite unknown to one another, and at different times, are able to compare, corroborate and expand on similar experiences of this sort proves to my mind that such experiences are "real" — i.e. objective on a certain level of consciousness, as opposed to merely subjective. I am thinking, too, of the number of "out of the body" experiences I have *shared* with Catherine, when she was our home circle medium.

In thanking me for bringing back to her this beautiful memory, this reader went on to tell me of a contact she had had with a Flying Saucer and its occupants on two consecutive nights — and this again was *very similar to a contact of my own,* many years ago. In both her case and my own we were "woken" in the night by vibrations, a quiet throb. In both our cases we "found ourselves looking out of the window," to see a Flying

Saucer quite close, gleaming in the moonlight.

In my case the communication which took place was by unspoken mental telepathy, as clear as the spoken word. But my correspondent was even more fortunate, for on the second night she was greeted with smiling affection by a young woman in a green tunic, who talked to her of many things: thought-waves, radiations, cosmic energy (knowledge of which she said we would eventually gain, saving the world from pollution). She spoke of truth, beauty, and goodness, and how beautiful we could make this planet if we tried. And that they, also, work with the Spirit, for all is of God.

Many other things were told her, but she made the fatal mistake of omitting to write it all down afterwards! She was also shown the control panel of the craft, at which three other young women, also in green, were working. This was obviously, as in my own case, a very vivid and conscious out-of-the-body experience which the real YOU is fully aware of *at the time,* and not at all to be confused with remembering *after* waking from sleep. These two types of projection of the etheric body cannot be compared.

Catherine, before she retired as our medium, has also experienced the former type of contact with a Flying Saucer and communicated with two beings from it, while consciously projected. For these craft, being Fourth Dimensional, can be seen on various levels of consciousness. I, in company with many thousands of people all over the world, have seen them physically, in broad daylight (and they have registered on radar and been photographed enough times). But there is also contact on other levels.

Scientific attitudes have changed so greatly in recent times that it is indeed gratifying, and something of a relief, that all of us who for years have been obscure pioneers in the field, voices crying in the wilderness, are not now regarded as "the lunatic fringe!" I think it important, therefore, to back up this statement with a few of the many outstanding quotations from outstanding scientists and others.

For instance Physicist *Stanton Friedman,* of Arizona, says: "The Earth is being visited by intelligently controlled craft from off Earth . . . Photos taken in Oregon, France, Utah, California and Roumania show that several crafts are identical although taken in different parts of the world."

Russian scientist *Felix Ziegel*: "The hypothesis with the least objections is that UFOs are vehicles from extra-terrestrial civilisations. We have well-documented sightings from every corner of the USSR . . . Illusions don't register on photographic plates and radar."

Dr Robert F. Creegan, professor of philosophy at the State University of New York: "I'm convinced there is intelligent life in outer space. UFOs are not just illusions. Some reports show them to be controlled objects. To me the most acceptable and realistic theory is that UFOs are controlled by intelligent beings from outer space."

Scientist *Bernard M. Oliver* of California: "In all likelihood intelligent civilisations have existed in our galaxy for four or five billion years." Scientist *Wilbert Smith,* of Canada: "Our best theory to fit UFO sightings is that they are controlled by beings from outer space." *Dr. J. Allen Hyneck,* scientific consultant to the U.S. Air Force's UFO project, and director of Dearborn Observatory and Lindheimer Astronomical Centre, Evanston, Illinois: "UFO's are now a respectable subject for scientific study."

Dr. Emerson W. Shideler, retired chairman of the Department of Philosophy at Iowa State University of Science and Technology: "I believe the evidence is quite clear that UFOs exist. The most probable explanation is that they are controlled by intelligence from another planet. There is a very real possibility that they are completely unlike our accepted ideas of normal life. I do not believe they are any threat to us. But their impact on our notions of culture and religion would be tremendous . . ."

Dr. Vyacheslav Zaitsev, the Russian philologist, reminds us of ancient accounts of these visitors, when he says: "Biblical accounts could refer to cosmic visitors, gods from the sky. The holy Indian sages in *The Ramayana* tell of two-storied celestial chariots with many windows. They roar like lions, blaze with red flames, and race off into the sky until they appear like comets. *The Mahabharata* and various Sanskrit books describe at length these chariots, powered by winged lightning . . . 'it was a ship that soared into the air, flying to both the solar and stellar regions.' If we really were visited centuries ago, we may again be on the threshold of a second coming of intelligent beings from outer space."

Prof. Carl E. Sagan, director of Cornell University's Laboratory for Planetary Studies, says: "Man is at a unique evolutionary period in which the old secure sense of where we are in the universe has eroded. Contact with extra-terrestrial life could help man re-establish his relation to other human beings and give mankind a new sense of where it fits into the universe."

Anthropologist *Ashley Montagu* goes further! "Some other forms of life are probably more intelligent than we . . . They may regard us as we would some forms of rabies or cholera."

And I applaud the remarks of *Dr. Kristen Stendahl,* dean of the Harvard Divinity School: "Discovery of life elsewhere would teach man that God's Universe is larger and would give him a better idea of his place in it. Contacting other beings may help men to stop viewing God in his own image, with all its limitations." Hear, hear, Dr. Stendahl!

But perhaps the words of astronaut Edgar D. Mitchell, of the Apollo 14 crew, are even more relevant: "I believe that intelligent life exists away from Earth, and more than likely in our own galaxy . . . ESP would be the best means to contact intelligent life elsewhere in the universe . . . If the phenomenon of astral projection has any validity, it might be a perfectly

154

valid form of intergalactic travel and a lot safer than space flight."

I hope it will not be long before Mitchell can say that astral projection *is* valid, and that his organisations of *EDMA* and *The Institute of Noetic Sciences,* with its 75 scientists and teachers to study the psychic potential of man and other forms of life, will arrive at the answers to their own "scientific" satisfaction. More power to them.

I may have risked being tedious in giving these quotations (only a few out of so many) but I do feel it is a most important development when scientists follow in the footsteps of sensitives. For the time must come when the words *Psychic* and *Science* are joined together, omitting the "and," in universal recognition.

Before concluding, I would like to say the following. In *Tales of Two Worlds* I wrote about the race for the moon in a way which I feel bound to modify slightly, in view of the reactions of many of the astronauts who made this brave journey. In referring to the search for what man calls God I had not at that time realised fully the poverty of the finite mind and imagination, or how prevalent this was, or is. I had urged the finding of God *within ourselves,* God Immanent in each one of us, God made manifest on our own doorstep. And in view of the gigantic humanitarian tasks awaiting us on Earth I regarded the astronomically expensive and somewhat feverish urge to get to the moon in the terms of Francis Thompson's inspired poem:

> Does the fish soar to find the ocean?
> The eagle plunge to find the air?
> That we ask of the stars in motion
> If they have rumour of thee there?

Yet, believe it or not, it took a *physical* flight to the moon to widen the parochial and materialistic concepts of some of these brave and brilliant men into a slightly broader and more global awareness. And I am sure this also applied to many of the millions who watched events on their screens.

Listen to what astronauts have stated since returning from the moon — stated, I am sure, most earnestly, as if they had just discovered some momentous truth!

Tom Stafford, of Gemini 6 and 9, and Apollo 10: "You don't look down at the world as an American but as a human being." (!)

Bill Anders, Apollo 8: "Seeing the Earth from out there evoked feelings about humanity and human needs that I never had before." (!)

Russell Schweickart, Apollo 9: "I am not the same man. None of us are. I completely lost my identity as an American astronaut. I felt a part of everyone and everything sweeping past me below."

James B. Irwin, Apollo 15: "We went to the moon as technicians — nuts and bolts men — and we returned as humanitarians."

Charles Duke, of Apollo 16, admittedly had a wider vision. He said: "I was overwhelmed by the certainty that what I was witnessing was part of the universality of God." (But what else could it be?)

But we witness "the universality of God" all day and every day! For there *is* nothing but God or Spirit. However, if going to the moon has effectively opened previously closed eyes and hearts, awakened imagination and widened spiritual horizons so that ALL is perceived as ONE, then it has been an evolutionary step forward, *if* pursued with peaceful and harmless intent.

Meanwhile, let us open out minds and hearts to our space visitors, to enable them to approach us more nearly and more clearly in the dawn of this New Age of Aquarius.

Acknowledgement for quotes to MAIN, Mark-Age MetaCenter Inc. 327 NE 20 Terrace, Miama, FL 33137.

CHRISTMAS AND THE CHRIST SPIRIT

As I write this, Christmastide is almost upon us once again. So before we begin to worry ourselves unduly with lists of presents, cards, overseas mailing dates, arrangements, school holidays, outings, guests, nephews and nieces, charities, Christmas trees, decorations, rolls of wrapping paper, silver-cleaning and food-planning (to mention a few of the things we *do* worry ourselves with, however much we make up our minds not to!) let us stop to ponder a little on what it is all about.

We are told by spirit teachers that Festivals *originated* in the spirit spheres. In very early times, Man, or rather spirit manifesting in form, was much more closely associated with the spirit world and was able to partake of the Festivals in spirit in a semi-trance state. In due course, as the veil thickened between the two worlds, the spirit Festivals gradually became earth Festivals, adopted, and adapted for different purposes, often to suit the various cults and religions which emerged (or diverged) from the One religion — for there *is* only one religion.

Different cults held different forms of Festivals at different times, for calendars were for ever being re-arranged. So it is not really surprising that the Festival adopted to celebrate the incarnation of the Nazarene — He who came as the most perfect instrument of the Cosmic Christ Spirit yet to manifest on earth — was the existing Saturn Festival, "the Sower of Seeds," even though Jesus was born under the sign of Pisces.

Be that as it may, a great Festival is held in the spirit spheres at this time, at which our beloved Elder Brother, the Prince of Peace, the Great Healer, the Christed One, is present. The messengers of the Great Spirit conjoin with him — the guides, the teachers, the inspirers, the light-bringers, the servers.

These are they whose rightful abodes are the higher spheres, but willingly they turn their backs on the blessedness they have earned in order to descend the scale of vibrations into the murky atmosphere of our world.

"I wish you could see and hear the Nazarene," says Silver Birch, "and feel that great love as he encourages us in our missions, as he expresses his knowledge of all that has been done, and urges us to go forward with new strength, with new hope, with new vision and with new purpose."

And he says: "The splendour of the Nazarene does not belong only to the past, but to the present. Where do you think he is today . . . with your world of matter full of distress, trouble and bitterness? The power which operated through the Nazarene is operative again . . . We are urged, encouraged and enthused. We return to strive to perform our allotted missions."

The so-called Christian churches which insisted on deifying him and despatching him to "sit at the right hand of God," only succeeded in creating a great gulf in men's minds which removed him from humanity and relegated him to some high heaven beyond our ken — in spite of his assurance: "Lo, I am with you always, even to the consummation of the world."

And not only this world. It must not be thought that the White Brotherhood, which he leads, is concerned with only one planet (even if it *is* the darkest) in our sun's family of planets. Or alone with our solar system, or even our galaxy.

Listen to the words transmitted by a Venusian who calls himself Ashtar, on behalf of a mighty army of Space Men involved in the "mission to Earth." In many communications Ashtar refers to him as "Our Master and yours," "our revered and Beloved Jesus, the Christ," "our Beloved Commander-in-Chief," "our Supreme Commander" . . .

In one message Ashtar explains how, a long time ago, they too were favoured with wise and patient Teachers from "Outer Space." "What they did for us ages ago," he says, "we now offer to do for you . . . The Christ Spirit manifests in many guises on all planes and planets . . . The Spirit of Kindness, of Compassion, of Mercy, of Joy, of Beauty, of Love in all its multitudinous forms, all of these are reflections of the Christ Spirit which our Master so magnificently presented for our emulation during his sojourn on Shan (Earth).

"As we made *our* lives conform with that inspired vision, we reached a point in our understanding where we were able to "see Him," not only with our spiritual eyes but with the sensitised lenses of our physical eyes until now, I can tell you in all truthfulness, we enjoy the almost inconceivable privilege of entertaining Him on many occasions when He visits Venus."

Do not be confused by scientists or astronomers who say there can be "no life as we know it" on Venus or on other planets. In terms of "as we know it," that is, on our low vibrational form of Manifestation, they are doubtless correct. Our range of vibrations is extremely limited — though the heightening and lifting of those vibrations is now beginning to take place.

But the vibrational rate of Venus, owing to its spiritual evolution, is very high compared with Earth, which is why Venus shines forth her own (not reflected) magnificently bright light in the night sky. White Eagle tells us: "One day man will realise he is surrounded, not only by spirit worlds and beings, but by *finer physical or semi-physical* worlds inhabited by people similar to himself. Mingling with you sometimes are spirits not of this world but from other planets. It is not unknown for spirits from other planets to speak through a sensitive human instrument. Man is set in his ideas, and cannot get away from his one-track mind."

Again he tells us: "In the beginning, messengers came to this planet not only from the spirit world, but from other planets and from outer space — God-men they were called. They came to bring man the vision glorious; to give him knowledge of the universal and celestial life."*

Is it so strange that they are doing so again, in humanity's hour of need, when we are at the cross-roads, when we turn every discovery into the means of destruction, when puny, unstable and unprincipled men can press a button and destroy a world? Is it so strange that they remind us of the Asteroid Belt, which was once the planet Maldek until its men of science took their lethal experiments too far?

And is it so strange that Teachers both from the spirit world, *and* those from other planets corroborate each other's statements, messages, descriptions, teachings? Spirit life is not a state of being "after death," as we so often think of it. We are living in a world of spirit *now* — as the Venusians are, as the Great Ones on Saturn are, as those from Outer Space are, as our friends who have left this Earth are. For *all* is spirit. *Life* is spirit. There is nothing *but* spirit, clothed in a form harmonious to it — and therefore on a wide variety of vibrations or frequencies.

"When people from a higher grade or degree of spirituality descend to a lower sphere," White Eagle explains, "there must be a stepping-down of the power, of adjustment, or slowing of the vibration before they are able to contact the more lowly. In the soul world, if there is an expedition from a higher level to a lower, the higher ones clothe themselves as it were with a cloak so that they will not cause too great a shock or disturbance. *It is exactly the same with the Masters, and with visitors from space:* they have to lower their vibrations and adjust themselves when they come near to Earth, because it would be impossible for ordinary people to bear their radiations."*

We should not, and must not, rule out as impossible the idea that from time to time even the beloved Nazarene, the Master of Masters, can and

---

*Quotations from Silver Birch and White Eagle from The Teachings of Silver Birch and The Wisdom of White Eagle.

does transmit his powerful thoughts through rare and finely attuned human instruments — even though the result, as with all mediumship of whatever kind, may not be absolutely accurate.

I would like, therefore, to give part of a message which was received by automatic writing through the same instrument who received the many Ashtar scripts:

". . . Lo, ye do contradict thine own selves! One moment you pray for a visible demonstration of the reality of One sent into flesh nigh two thousand years agone, that thus thy faith may be justified. The next moment ye deride and scoff at anyone who tells thee of beings (*not* from highest heaven but from advanced planets more easily comprehensible to untutored, immature minds) sent of the Father to lead mankind to a partial understanding of the spiritual laws by which man may progress.

"My words of Truth and Life have been discarded by the multitude as 'impractical,' have been distorted, have been mouthed in 'vain repetitions' until they have well-nigh lost their power to reach men's souls, have been relegated to the realm of childish fondness for pleasing tales, oft cast aside as they grow to maturity. Think these be fitting preparations for My manifestation in mortal guise?

"Oh, my little children of earth, list not to those who prate of vast stores of knowledge to be acquired through years of arduous study of ponderous tomes designed to confuse thy minds and divert thee from the simple, direct pathway leading to true companionship with thy Master in thy daily thinking and living! *One Truth* lived each hour of every day in conscious attunement with thy Master and the Heavenly Father doth bring Me closer to thee than endless hours of reasoning *about* this or that theory concerning Life and its purpose."

"To see Me with thy physical eyes would be to thee a boon beyond price, and this shall not be denied thee . . . yet will ye hasten the time of its occurring if ye will but behold Me in My spirit manifestation walking by thy side wherever duty calleth thee, revealing unto thee through our close understanding in what wise ye may best fulfil the tasks allotted to thee ere ye embarked upon they present earth span.

"Many now reading My written words be here as "ambassadors" from far flung vistas of 'outer space,' having volunteered to endure the irritations of fleshly existence that they might in some wise aid in turning men's minds towards a Christly mode of living. Unto these consecrated ones I say, 'Lo, I shall give unto thee, mayhap in a way ye be not expecting, a true vision of thy Master and His boundless love for thee!'

"Wouldst thou choose to see Me clothed in radiance of glory so dazzling you could not approach Me in thine earthly habiliments? Or may I come unto thee in seamless robe of perfect understanding of thine own earthly circumstances and problems?

"Choose thee the latter, I pray thee, and in due season thy faithful service, performed in My Name and by My Power, shall lead thee to the hour appointed by our Heavenly Father when thou shalt see thy Master face-to-face! . . . Thine ever present Friend and Counsellor, Thy Prince of Peace."

I do not wish to add further words to the above, but as we keep the Festival commemorating his descent into flesh at the beginning of the Piscean Age, may we also determine to co-operate with him and his messengers *now*, in the new Age of Aquarius, by endeavouring to "Live his Truth," and to pass that Truth on by love and service to the best of our ability to others. This is what Christmas is about.

TO THE ABYSS — OR THE NEW AGE?

It is now May, and in our small patch of England the stream gurgles between banks of bluebells. Blossom everywhere meets the eye, and the dawn chorus of the birds lures one out of bed, on tiptoe at the wonder of it. The gold-brown fox pads its customary path across the garden, the badger comes each evening for titbits, and the magpie which adopted our home two years ago sits on my shoulder as I type.

Here is escape into sanity. So it pains me to write this, to step into the realm of *insanity*. Yet I am impelled to do so, for only by knowledge of the enemy can that enemy be disarmed and kept at bay by mass prayer, mass protest, mass awareness and mass invocation to the Light.

There appears to be no government on earth, democratic or otherwise, which ever seeks a mandate from the people to pursue, sanction or sponsor certain hushed-up programmes. These programmes would never appear in any election manifesto. But eventually we discover that the whole of mankind has, willynilly, become helplessly implicated. We find we have "consented" by default.

Suddenly one comes across information which makes the most startling science-fiction mere bedtime stories for children. Suddenly one re-discovers the colossal arrogance, the immorality, the lust to conquer at any cost, and the criminal *stupidity,* in spiritual terms, of brilliantly clever men — so intellectually brilliant in their own field of activity that they are almost a race apart from ordinary mortals. Indeed, in their one-pointed fanaticism they appear to have abandoned any claim to the higher spiritual values and ethical standards of thought and behaviour which are the goal of evolving humanity. I think many are almost certainly reincarnations from the baleful, disastrous latter-days of Atlantis.

We marvelled at the amazing technical achievement of the trips to the moon, and marvelled still more at the skill and courage of the men who journeyed there. We were told it was "a peaceful exploration" — even though to many of the millions of people who had no say in the matter it seemed an astronomically costly venture (in fact something of a rather frivolous indulgence) when we have so mismanaged the affairs of our planet that two-thirds of the population either have not enough to eat or are dying of starvation, while a formidable proportion are engaged in killing each other or planning to do so by ever more hideous methods, and while crime, violence and other evils have escalated from a number of causes which are left untackled and unresolved. In short, that a step into space was being taken prematurely, long before earthdwellers were spiritually ready to make it.

We were told that the next step was the peaceful exploration, first by unmanned spacecraft, of our nearest neighbours. To most people this had become a matter of rather academic interest, akin to watching Patrick Moore's television programme "The Sky at Night." Explorers would always explore. Yet many people who thought about it felt vaguely unhappy about soft-landings on these planets. But care had been taken not to contaminate the moon, which was reassuring. So we continued to concern ourselves with the price of sugar . . .

But what do we find is going on behind our backs? To what end is this systematic and increasingly costly (and cruel) space programme leading? For what purpose is a veritable army of international scientists of all kinds working, with implacable dedication? For nothing less than a long-term plan to *conquer Venus for mankind!*

Furthermore, to make this a viable proposition, Professors Carl Sagan of the USA and Dmitri Martinov of the USSR, plan to *alter* the climate and atmosphere of Venus in a manner which will eventually make it possible for a mass-immigration of earth-dwellers! (Not being content with making a hell of large areas of our own planet, it is seriously proposed to do so on someone else's.)

The incredible arrogance with which these projects are being pursued defies description. The Russian sondes and the American Mariner probes both reported a Venusian temperature varying between 400 and 530 degrees centigrade. The atmosphere apparently has a carbon-dioxide content of 93 to 97 degrees, nitrogen 2 to 5 degrees, and oxygen only 0.4 with a water content of only 4 to 11 milligrams per litre. Although this may suit the highly spiritual and high-vibrationary beings of Venus, it does not suit Earthlings, so what to do?

Carl Sagan thinks that in a few decades space-ships with big cargo holds will unload thousands of tons of blue algae into the Venusian atmosphere and "blow" them to the surface! Blue algae can stay alive even at high temperatures, but reduce the high proportion of carbon dioxide by their metabolism. Owing to this reduction, the surface temperature would gradually fall to below 100 degrees centigrade. Blue algae would then cause the same chemical reaction as once took place on our earth. With the help of light and water, carbon dioxide particles would be transformed into oxygen, and once the blue algae had lowered the temperature, a rain like the Flood would fall on Venus. Light, oxygen and water would then provide the prerequisites for *our* kind of primitive life.

In addition, since scientists have already thought of evacuating mankind to another planet, they have also planned protective measures (for *us*, of course.) In the second phase of their colonisation of Venus, *chemicals* would be sprayed to destroy micro-organisms that might be dangerous to man.

Although this would take a considerable time to achieve, and at present scientists talk of 1,000 years before the first evacuation spaceship can travel to Venus, the possibility of unloading tons of blue algae on our sister planet *"in a few decades"* is horrifying in the extreme. Who do we think we are? What would be the reactions of these scientists if the peaceful UFOs in our skies decided to spray the earth with alien and destructive chemicals? And raise our temperature to 400 degrees, preparatory to an "invasion?"

Listen to what the great spirit teacher White Eagle says (through Grace Cooke): "The planet Venus is made of a finer matter than this physical Earth. The Earth planet is dark and dense. Venus is of a much lighter substance, of a finer ether altogether; and the bodies of those who live on Venus are of the same finer substance. The Venusians have scientific knowledge, spiritually scientific, which has not yet reached Earth. When man becomes a truly spiritual being, he too will discover the secrets of spiritual science.

"The Venusians live in brotherhood; they worship and adore God and the Sun. We tell you most earnestly that many of the Ancient Ones have come to Earth from Venus, wearing a form similar to the human in order to make themselves acceptable to Earth people. Some day the visitors will come in Venusian bodies, bringing with them a great spiritual power as before. They will bring knowledge that the more advanced on Earth will be able to hear and understand, although the masses will be unaffected and untouched. These more advanced groups will be ready to receive their brethren from other planets. Every department of life on Venus expresses love, harmony and brotherhood . . . There are no different countries, all fighting for supremacy; there is perfect brotherhood of all life . . .

"Try to realise that you are not God's only creatures; there are other worlds beyond anything you can imagine . . . All beings on other planets are spirit, as you are spirit. All spirit is clothed in a form of matter which is harmonious with the planet on which it is living . . ."*

We can only pray most earnestly that our planetary brethren will return to us in time, *within the next few decades,* before their beautiful planet is bombarded with blue algae. I think they will — for it is against the Law of the Universe to interfere with another planet. It therefore behoves all spiritually-minded groups and people to attune themselves and open their *hearts* for what may come. For Earth's sake, for Venus's sake — for God's sake.

But what of the horribly, insanely misdirected research taking place meantime in space-biology? In contrast to the words of White Eagle, listen to the German physicist and cyberneticist Herbert W. Franke, as reported by Erich von Däniken in his book "Towards the Stars." Dr Franke "put forward the sensational idea that in the decades to come spaceships would journey to unknown planets without astronauts aboard and search the universe for extraterrestrial intelligences.

"Franke assumes that the electronic equipment would be operated *by a brain separated from a human body*. This 'solo' brain, kept in a liquid medium which would have to be *constantly replenished with fresh blood,* would be the control centre of the spaceship. Franke thinks that *the brain of an unborn child would be the most suitable for programming . . .*" (my italics). "The human solo brain," says the elated Dr Franke, "is promoted to ambassador of our planet!"

Is there an outraged protest from the Church? On the contrary! A *Jesuit priest,* Paul Overhage of Frankfurt, who is also a biologist, echoes: "Its realisation can scarcely be doubted, because the rapid progress of biotechnology is constantly making it easier to carry out *experiments* of this kind."

And what are these experiments? Dr Robert White, in the USA (a Roman Catholic) is busy *exchanging the heads of monkeys*. The latest "advance" at Cleveland Hospital, Ohio, is *transferring monkeys' brains into dogs*. It is useless to look to Governments to curb or ban these obscenities because they sponsor them. Research teams of the US Navy, the US Air Force, and such firms as General Electric and the Rand Corporation are *working full time* on the solution to the problem of keeping brain cells alive without oxygen, to which end the Western Reserve School of Medicine in Cleveland have separated the brains of five rhesus monkeys from their bodies and kept them functioning for 18 hours. These separated brains *reacted unhesitatingly to noises*.

"The first reports of success," we are told. But what are those poor monkeys' brains experiencing? For surely, while any part of the body remains alive, the etheric body is still attached. The silver cord has not been allowed to sever.

This horrible state of affairs also exists as far as the donor is concerned when a living heart is transplanted into another person's body. Admittedly it is not the thinking, experiencing brain, but the heart has to be *alive,* and beating, otherwise the transplant cannot be achieved, and spirit teachers inform us that it makes it difficult to release and receive the heart-donor into the next phase of life in the world of spirit. This is *one* of the reasons why all teachers uniformly condemn this pernicious and retrograde step in the medical field, even though it might be considered a "technical advance" by materialists and the spiritually ignorant. An

163

"advance," moreover, achieved by the indefensible suffering of millions of dogs which not only exchange their hearts, but endure their living heads (and sometimes lungs and forelegs too) transplanted on to their fellows.

In spite of von Däniken's great erudition and constant flights around the world to prove his thesis that in aeons past Earth and Humanity were visited by and received knowledge from "extraterrestrials" (a fact which studious Spiritualists and mystics have always known, and which is confirmed by spirit teachers), his limited spiritual awareness is revealed by the following sentence in his book: "Strangely enough, man, who enjoys living and is terrified of death, has not welcomed this advance of medical science with open arms."

Is it so strange? That heart-transplants have not been welcomed with open arms gives us some hope. Incidentally, has no one remarked that, of the few hundred heart-transplants performed to date, no *woman* (at least as far as I can ascertain) has asked for one? And not *all* mankind is "terrified of death," Mr von Däniken — though I can understand that those who have denied Schweitzer's principle of "reverence for all life" and expelled compassion from their hearts, may well be so.

I am sorry to have to write this, but thinking people *must* be made aware of what is going on behind our backs (and what I have mentioned is only the tip of the iceberg.) If this feverish research in biotechnology, cybernetic organisms, isolated and programmed brains, not to mention the "alteration" of man and animals by manipulating the genetic code in the DNA molecule — if this is the colossal and ghastly cost of solving over-population, then far better, simpler and quicker (since mankind, *un*like animals, appears incapable of not breeding in adverse conditions) to introduce global, compulsory visectomy of every male after the birth of the second child. (Visectomy, which takes 10 minutes, is not irreversible). What gigantic suffering this would save! But it is too simple. It would take away the "free will" of men and woman to bring millions more babies into the world to die of starvation and disease. Apparently the conquest of Venus is considered preferable!

But where *is* our free will? Have we got any, or not? And if we have, what are we going to do about it? How can the millions of ordinary decent people compel or persuade the governments which are supposed to represent them to curb the unholy latitude allowed (and encouraged) to spiritually sick scientists? How can we, *the people of this planet,* deflect this monstrous scientific and Frankensteinian "progress" towards the abyss? There *must* be a way. And it *must* be found — *soon,* before it is too late. A decade is only ten years . . .

The world is not sufficiently evolved for the power of prayer alone to be effective in transmuting evil, when the Forces of Darkness are waging so fierce and desperate a battle as the 20th Century draws towards its close. Teachers from spirit tell us we have the right, indeed a duty, to defend ourselves when attacked in a far-from-perfect world in which reason, mercy, tolerance, compassion and love are still spat upon by the unevolved, and are all too frequently as pearls cast before swine.

Every virtue can become a vice, certainly a weakness, when over-played. Tolerance is good, but too much tolerance becomes a flabby acceptance of lowered standards and a decline in true values. Thus it aids and abets that decline. Compassion for a psychopath does not diminish his intention to kill you. It is not possible to reason with one devoid of reason. By giving in to violence or blackmail or any insupportable human behaviour we make sure that such practises pay off. *It is only necessary for good men to do nothing for evil to triumph.*

Most certainly we must pray, by seeking attunement with a higher level of consciousness and sending forth light to penetrate the darkness. By this means added power is given to the Forces of Light. *But this is not enough.* The White Brotherhood need our active co-operation on the earth plane. So as we approach the 21st. Century, they need every man and woman of goodwill to *act* and to be seen to act. Let us have the courage and energy to rise up in defence of the spiritual and moral values which are being attacked in so many areas of society; let us make ourselves heard; let us not tolerate the intolerable, or accept the unacceptable, *wherever* we find it.

Let us demonstrate in our conduct, in our actions and *reactions* the determination to uphold and renew true spiritual standards, because it is a spiritually-orientated society which is the only civilised society, and therefore the only free society. Let us make up our minds, too, as the political affairs of the planet are being shaken up in the melting pot from which the New Age will eventually arise — as the phoenix from the ashes — to strengthen the will of the overwhelming *majority* so that they refuse to be trodden underfoot and reduced to spiritual serfdom by the tyranny of a materialistic, God-hating *minority* which seek to undermine our countries.

Let that great silent majority find their voice at last, and march with one accord in the service of the Great Spirit to fashion a whip to drive out evil from the precincts of the temple. Let us echo in our hearts the militant and inspiring words of Churchill, when he thundered: *"Not so easily shall the lights of freedom die!"*

165

Sursum corda

The water whispers languorous caresses,
And gently lifts the seaweed's waving tresses,
And wistful, woos with cool translucent hands
The shining undulation of the sands,
And laps about the little rocks that keep
Their lonely vigil while the world's asleep.

Here, here in this retreat from man-made pain
The spirit lifts and finds its wings again;
Sings with the stars, and opens blinded eyes
To see the smiling grandeur of the skies.
Great Spirit, Father of the Spheres, who taught
The sun to rise and birds to sing, and thought
To fashion in a moment of repose
The snowdrop and the violet and the rose —
Teach men to cease their misery and strife
And learn the purpose and the truth of life!
Teach men to LOVE, and realise, if they can,
The dignity and majesty of Man.

(First published in *The Spiritual Healer* magazine.)

TALES OF TWO WORLDS

A Bedside Book
for the
NEW AGE

(Published 1972 and now in its 7th impression)

"An enthralling book . . ." Julian Duguid, Editor of LIGHT
"The perfect bedside book which I heartily commend." TWO WORLDS
"A bedside *must* . . ." PSYCHIC NEWS
"Illuminating and pungent . . ." THE GREATER WORLD

Some quotes from readers' letters:

"This is one of the most inspiring, delightful and most educational books I have ever read. If only it could be placed in every home in the universe."
"Your book has opened a new world to me."
"I kept on wishing your book would never end."
"I was so enthralled I could hardly put it down."
"It is the most exciting and enlightening book I have ever read."
"Your wonderful book touches my soul . . ."
"Your very fine, I should say stupendous book . . ."
"Thank you for giving so much to so many people."
"I have enjoyed every word, every thought, and the wonderful way you have expressed it — so clearly, so profoundly, and yet with such a sense of humour."
"There are no words to thank you."
"I was so enthralled by your wonderful book."
"If even 10% of the people who read it are as affected by your writing as I was, you will have done a superb job. Your book has helped tremendously."
"It's a wonderful book . . ."
"You have given me wonderful help and understanding."

Obtainable from the Author, ~~Mrs. PEGGY MASON THE LODGE 10 BROADWATER DOWN TUNBRIDGE WELLS TN2 5NG Telephone: (0892) 21592~~ *unbridge Wells, Kent. £2.00 plus 20p. p & p.*

Copies of this book can be obtained from

Mrs. PEGGY MASON
THE LODGE
10 BROADWATER DOWN
TUNBRIDGE WELLS
TN2 5NG
Telephone: (0892) 21592